INFRASTRUCTURE OF TERRORISM

INFRASTRUCTURE OF TERRORISM

A.K. Dixit

CYBER TECH PUBLICATIONS
4264/3, Ansari Road, Daryaganj, New Delhi-110002 (India)
Ph.: 011-23244078, 011-43559448 Fax: 011-23280028
E-Mail: cyberpublicationsdelhi@yahoo.com
Website: www.cybertechpublications.com

INFRASTRUCTURE OF TERRORISM

A.K. Dixit

First Edition 2010

Published by :

G.S. Rawat for **Cyber Tech Publications**
4264/3, Ansari Road, Daryaganj, New Delhi-110002 (India)
Ph.: 011-23244078, 011-43559448 Fax: 011-23280028
E-Mail: cyberpublicationsdelhi@yahoo.com
Website: www.cybertechpublications.com

Printed at: Asian Offset Printers, Delhi-53

Preface

IThis book has been prepared for direct dissemination to the general public and is based on the most reliable hazard awareness and emergency education information available at the time of publication, including advances in scientiûc knowledge, more accurate technical language, and the latest physical research on what happens in disasters.

This publication is, however, too brief to cover every factor, situation, or difference in buildings, infrastructure, or other environmental features that might be of interest. To help you explore your interest further, additional sources of information have been included.

The book has been designed to help the citizens of this nation learn how to protect themselves and their families against all types of hazards. It can be used as a reference source or as a step-by-step manual. The focus of the content is on how to develop, practice, and maintain emergency plans that reûect what must be done before, during, and after a disaster to protect people and their property. Also included is information on how to assemble a disaster supplies kit that contains the food, water, and other supplies in sufûcient quantity for individuals and their families to survive following a disaster in the event they must rely on their own resources.

—Author

Preface

CONTENTS

1

Introduction

The products of the chemical industry are ubiquitous in modern life. Plastics, fibers, drugs—these are a few of the products we encounter everyday in our workplaces and homes that are direct products of the chemical industry. Many more of the products we use daily—paper, fabrics, cosmetics, and electronics—are produced using the products of the chemical industry. The chemical sector is a key part of the national economy: while its products represent only 2 percent of the U.S. gross domestic product, they underpin most other manufactured goods and enable our way of life.

The chemical sector is diverse and wide-ranging. It includes firms that manufacture huge volumes of chemicals intended for many uses—such as major refineries processing thousands of tons of petrochemical feedstocks daily—and firms that produce small quantities of materials with highly specific uses, such as small pharmaceutical companies producing products in gram or kilogram quantities after many days of processing and purifying. The facilities in which chemicals are produced are similarly varied—from refineries covering square miles of land with many high-volume chemicals on-site, to startup companies occupying thousands of square feet in light industrial parks. Products can be transported to their final place of use by truck, rail, pipeline, or other means in both large and small quantities.

To identify the vulnerabilities posed to the nation to terrorist attack on or other catastrophic loss in the nation's chemical infrastructure, it is necessary first to somehow succinctly characterize this large and varied sector. This is done below in two steps: (1) a scheme for categorizing the vast number of chemicals produced by the sector and defining these categories and (2) a general model describing the sector's supply chain.

CHEMICAL CATEGORIES

Virtually all chemical manufacturing, storage, and use in the United States fits into one of the following categories:

- Petrochemicals and fossil fuels
- Inorganic chemicals including fertilizers
- Industrial gases
- Specialty chemicals
- Pharmaceuticals
- Consumer products.

A description of each of these categories, including a generalized discussion of the manufacture, transport, and use of the chemicals within that category, is given below:

Petrochemicals and Fossil Fuels

This category entails chemicals produced from hydrocarbon feedstocks, such as crude oil products and natural gas. It includes such chemicals as hydrocarbons and industrial chemicals (e.g., alcohols, acrylates, acetates), aromatics (e.g., benzene, toluene, xylenes), and olefins (e.g., ethylene, propylene, butadiene, methanol).

Manufacture and Use. Most of these chemicals are produced and sold in large volumes—so-called commodity chemicals—and most can be produced through several different chemical routes or processes. They are used as building blocks in many manufactured products. Many of these chemicals can be replaced by another, with only minor modification required to the user's manufacturing process and with only minor changes in the performance of the final manufactured product.

Hazard. Most of the products, intermediates, and by-products in this category are highly flammable, and some are toxic (e.g., hydrogen cyanide, hydrogen sulfide, phosgene). Some can form explosive vapor clouds upon release.

Locations of Production. A large percentage of manufacturing facilities for petrochemicals and fossil fuels are located along the Texas and Louisiana Gulf Coast, but significant installations are also found in the industrial areas of the East Coast, Midwest, and California.

Location of Storage and Usage. Nationwide.

Distribution. Refinery products and a number of petrochemicals (e.g., ethylene, naphtha, ethylene oxide, benzene) are transported to other plants via pipeline, barge, rail, or truck for further processing.

Inorganic Chemicals and Fertilizers

This category includes acids (e.g., sulfuric, nitric) and alkalis (e.g., caustic soda, soda ash), chlorine, ammonia, and ammonia-derived fertilizers. It also includes fluorine derivatives (e.g., hydrogen fluoride), phosphates, potash, pigments (e.g., titanium dioxide), and certain metals such as mercury.

Manufacture and Use. Many of these chemicals, such as chlorine, ammonia, and ammonia-derived fertilizers, are produced and purchased in large volumes as commodity chemicals and may rely on natural gas or crude oil as a feedstock. They are used both as building blocks for other manufactured goods and as end products in themselves (e.g., chlorine, ammonia-derived fertilizers). The chemicals in this category can be substitutable, although not always readily; for example, substances other than chlorine gas can be used to purify drinking water, but at a cost of time and money to effect the substitution that may not be acceptable to all communities.

Hazards. While many of products in this category are nontoxic and relatively unreactive such as potash and pigments, hazards found in this category include corrosives such as acids and fluorine derivatives and toxics such as chlorine, alkalis, ammonias, and heavy metals.

Location of Production. Inorganic chemicals are produced in many parts of the United States, but largely in the South and Midwest.

Location of Storage and Use. Fertilizers are stored and used throughout agricultural areas. Other products tend to be stored and used near manufacturing sites. Chlorine is often found stored in or near petrochemical plants where it is produced and stored in large quantities. Chlorine can also be stored in or near water treatment facilities. Other inorganic chemicals are used in mining and many other industries throughout the country.

Distribution. Chemicals in this category are transported to other plants or to end users via pipeline, barge, rail, or truck. Some facilities are able to generate some of these chemicals on-site on an as-needed basis in order to avoid transport and storage.

Industrial Gases

This category encompasses two general classes: (1) gases used primarily in large quantities as auxiliaries in other manufacturing processes (e.g., refining, petrochemical or steel manufacture), including nitrogen, oxygen, hydrogen, and carbon monoxide, and (2) specialty gases that are produced in smaller quantities to serve the electronics, food, and other industries.

Hazards. Hazards are dependent on the chemical under consideration and the quantity in which it is being used. For instance, nitrogen is a chemical asphyxiant that displaces oxygen at high concentrations, oxygen promotes combustion, hydrogen is flammable, and carbon monoxide is a simple asphyxiant that binds more strongly than oxygen to hemoglobin and is also flammable. Hazards from specialty gases are due typically to toxic, irritant, or asphyxiant properties.

Manufacture and Use. These gases are produced by multiple firms in both large and small facilities.

Location of Production. The first class of industrial gases is produced in large plants, often adjacent to large users, such as refineries on the Gulf Coast. Specialty gas manufacture is more distributed and occurs in smaller facilities.

Location of Storage and Use. High-volume gases can be manufactured at or adjacent to the point of use and are usually stored as liquids in specially designed cryogenic tanks. Both classes are stored in smaller quantities in gas cylinders.

Distribution. High-volume chemicals can be distributed via pipeline or as cryogenic liquids in railcars or tank trucks. Cylinder-sized volumes are transported by rail or truck.

Specialty Chemicals

This category comprises a large number of chemicals that are used as aids to the manufacture of other major products (e.g., in paper milling, plastics production, water treatment, mining), are used as end products (e.g., pesticides in farming), or are components of consumer products (personal care products, paints and coatings, adhesives and sealants, photographic chemicals).

Manufacture and Use. Most chemicals in this category are produced and sold in relatively small quantities (grams to hundreds of kilograms). Unlike the categories discussed above, specialty chemicals often have a single manufacturer. Their use is highly specific, but if some deviation in final product performance can be tolerated, most are substitutable.

Hazards. Some specialty chemicals are toxic.

Location of Production. Diversified.

Location of Storage and Use. Diversified.

Distribution. Chemicals in this category are produced in either continuous or batch (smaller, noncontinuous) plants and are shipped to users in 55-gallon drums or smaller containers.

Pharmaceuticals

This category includes prescription and over-the-counter drugs, diagnostic substances, vaccines, vitamins, and preparations for both human and veterinary uses.

Manufacture and Use. The large majority of pharmaceuticals have multiple manufacturers; most have available substitutions. A notable exception, however, is vaccines, which tend to have one or two suppliers and may have no substitutions.

Hazards. The production processes used are similar to those in large chemical plants, but pharmaceuticals are produced in much smaller quantities and with much more stringent quality control.

The production of pharmaceuticals can entail the generation of combustible dust as well as use of toxic industrial chemicals in relatively small quantities.

Location of Production. Diversified.

Location of Storage and Use. Pharmaceuticals are warehoused in prepackaged units until distributed to end users.

Distribution. Pharmaceutical manufacturing includes the production of pills or other end-products that are then packaged and sent to distributors and pharmacies.

Consumer Products

This category entails formulated products, such as soaps, detergents, bleaches, paints, solvents, glues, toothpaste, shampoos, cosmetics, skin care products, perfumes, and colognes intended for direct consumer use.

Manufacture and Use. Although each product within this category is somewhat differentiated from its competitors, all are readily substitutable with products from multiple manufacturers.

Hazards. The contents of consumer products may be toxic, corrosive, or flammable; many have quick skin-bonding characteristics; or their packaging may be pressurized. Consumer products can be particularly vulnerable to tampering since their distribution is widespread and under relatively loose control at the retail level.

Location of Production. Nationwide.

Location of Storage and Use. These products are used widely and are commonly found in households and retail outlets nationwide.

Distribution. All of these items are available to the general public and are sold in packaged form in retail stores, by mail order, and on-line.

THE CHEMICAL SUPPLY CHAIN

The description of the chemical categories above includes some specific characteristics of feedstocks, manufacturing, storage, and use for each. From these specifics it is possible and instructive to draw some generalizations about the chemical supply chain.

Here that supply chain is presented as a network using a model described by the characteristics of the materials and infrastructure involved; the pathways, links, and nodes between manufacturers and users; and the ownership and control of the components. The model as described applies to most of the chemical industry. Exceptions to the model are noted where relevant. The main characteristics of the network follow.

Materials

The chemical industry is materials intensive. Most chemical products can be produced from a variety of starting materials, although many of

those starting materials are dependent upon crude oil or natural gas as a feedstock. The supply network for these starting materials tends to be diversified: in general, a single supplier does not provide all of the starting materials for a final manufactured chemical product. Suppliers of materials may be domestic or international.

Infrastructure

The chemical industry is highly capital intensive, requiring substantial facility and equipment investment. Many chemical facilities contain specialized equipment that, if destroyed, would be difficult to replace quickly (e.g., cracking facilities). Most chemical manufacture requires a small number of personnel per square foot of facility. For example, a large petrochemical refinery with a footprint of several square miles may have only a few hundred employees on-site under normal circumstances.

Pathways, Links, and Nodes

The supply chain for any chemical is characterized by multiple nodes, links, and pathways. A node is a facility at which the chemical is produced, stored, or consumed; a link is the means (road, rail, barge, or pipeline) by which the chemical is transported from one node to another; and a pathway is the sequence of nodes and links by which the chemical is produced, transported, and transformed from its initial source to its ultimate consumer.

Dominant nodes are geographic locations in which a substantial proportion of a chemical is concentrated—possibly because of a small number of facilities with large capacities or a large number of facilities with small capacities. Dominant links are similarly defined as links over which a substantial proportion of a chemical is concentrated during its passage through the supply chain. Pathways and links exist in the transfer of materials between facilities, companies, and sectors. Transfer of materials requires transport, usually via rail, road, ship, or pipeline between plants.

The chemical supply chain also has dominant nodes—small geographic areas where large concentrations of products or intermediaries exist, (e.g., the Gulf Coast) or connecting points (dominant links) where many diverse streams in the supply chain converge, (e.g., a pipeline, large natural gas or ethylene storage terminals). Although the industry as a whole is geographically dispersed, some sectors of the chemical industry are geographically clustered (e.g., petrochemicals in the Gulf Coast), thereby creating a dominant node.

A highly complex and distributed supply chain makes it difficult to shut down the entire system by interruption at a single point. However, determining if an attack at a dominant node or a dominant link of the supply chain of a critical chemical would bring production to a standstill is a high priority in determining overall vulnerability. In order to achieve a widespread interruption in production for an extended period, multiple, well-placed interruptions would have to occur at one or more dominant nodes or dominant links (or both)—in most cases, at multiple geographic locations.

Ownership and Control

Most of the chemical infrastructure is under private ownership with the exception of certain feedstocks (e.g., oil reserves). Although most chemical companies in the United States are domestically owned, a number of companies are based in other countries with sites in the United States. Most large chemical companies have multiple sites or locations domestically and globally, which allows for highly decentralized ownership and control of the supply chain. Removing a single node or link is not sufficient to disrupt the entire supply chain for a given chemical. However, lack of centralized control may hinder a timely response to a terrorist incident or to a series of terrorist incidents.

At the plant level, many control systems are automated. Because of safety concerns, manufacturers give high priority to ensuring that automation does not exacerbate an emergency. The supervisory control and data acquisition (SCADA) system software is designed to shut down a process when it exceeds safe operating parameters, but it is not the primary safety system in a well-designed chemical production facility. Good process design in the chemical industry also includes safety shutdowns that are independent of the SCADA system. Plants conforming to standards ISA 584.01, International Electrotechnical Commission (IEC) 61508, and IEC 61511 are less vulnerable to catastrophic release due to attack through the SCADA system than those that are not compliant, unless these independent safety shutdown systems—either hard-wired or independent automated systems with no remote access to the outside world—have also been altered. Thus, effecting a release or other disruption through the automated control system requires not only reprogramming the SCADA software, but also physically infiltrating the site and systematically disabling these other fail-safe mechanisms. However, sabotage of an automated process remains a possibility, and the controls in place to mitigate the effects of an accident may not be adequate when intentional disruption or destruction occurs if the standards cited above have not been conformed to or if fail-safe mechanisms have not been properly maintained.

Robustness of the Supply Chain

Since the products of the chemical sector play such an important, underpinning role in our modern life and the national economy, the economic effects of a disruption to this supply chain must be considered seriously.

Unlike many other sectors that are considered part of the nation's critical infrastructure, such as utilities, the chemical sector has more than 200 years of experience operating in the free market. Strong competition has ensured that manufacturers have contingency plans in place to meet customer demands in the event of a disruption to their manufacturing capacity. These include product stockpiles, plans to shift manufacturing to other locations, plans to assist customers in shifting their processes temporarily to similar but alternative products, and in the case of large-scale interruption of manufacturing capacity, cooperative agreements between competitors during emergencies to ensure that critical needs for a given chemical can be met. In many cases, customers can simply acquire supplies from domestic and international competitors of their suppliers to fill their need. In cases where a specialty chemical with one or a few suppliers is disrupted, customers can be shifted temporarily to alternative chemicals, which may come at the price of slightly higher production cost or slightly altered product characteristics, but are generally within acceptable standards. To have a catastrophic national economic impact or result in catastrophic casualties, the chemical or chemicals whose supply is disrupted would have to (1) be critical to a large portion of the economy or to public health; (2) have a production process that is not readily restarted in a short period of time; (3) be unsubstitutable; and (4) be intended for an end use for which there is no other substitute. In other words, both the chemical itself and the product in which it is ultimately used would have to be unsubstitutable by some other chemical, product, or method of achieving the final end within the period required to drain whatever stockpile of the chemical or product exists. The competitive marketplace in which the chemical sector exists works against such a possibility, at least in the case of civilian products and uses.

Examination of the historical record backs up these assertions. For example, in 1999 two of the three plants worldwide capable of producing hydroxylamine, a key component of specialty chemicals used in semiconductor fabrication, suffered catastrophic explosions and ceased production. In response, chemical firms doing significant business with electronics manufacturers directed their customers to hydroxylamine-free products and processes until hydroxylamine capacity was restored. Although the substitution raised costs for semiconductor manufacturers slightly, fabrication did not suffer a significant disruption. Hurricanes, most recently Hurricane Katrina, have shut down significant portions of the nation's petroleum and natural gas supply (key feedstocks to the chemical industry), with subsequent economic loss but without catastrophic economic consequences. By the end of 2005, some four months after Hurricane Katrina hit, approximately 25 percent of petroleum and 20 percent of natural gas capacity from the Gulf of Mexico remained "shut in," down from roughly 50 percent in the weeks after the storm. The full extent of economic consequences from the disruption to supply remains to be seen as of this writing and will require evaluation in the years to come; the nation has seen higher gasoline and heating costs, and costs of consumer goods are expected to reflect these increased energy prices. Even with this, however, economic consequences *from the disruption to the chemical infrastructure* (though not from the hurricane overall) have been notable but not catastrophic to date. Katrina provides other examples of how the chemical infrastructure responds to disruption. For example, cooperative agreements between liquid hydrogen producers were activated to ensure that strategic needs for this cryogenic material were met. Even the worst accidents on record (Bhopal, Toulouse, Texas City) did not result in a situation in which the supply of the chemical or fertilizer in question could not be made available in a short time.

Agricultural chemicals and pharmaceuticals are the areas most likely to be impacted by single suppliers of specialty chemicals. However, major herbicides and fungicides have alternatives that perform as well or almost as well, so that normal agricultural practice can continue should the supply of preferred product be disrupted. Likewise, pharmaceutical manufacturers typically stockpile two to three months' supply of their products as a contingency against disruption of their manufacturing capacity. Should a disruption occur that cannot be rectified in that period, doctors have two to three months to migrate their patients to alternative drugs and treatment, which exist for every major category of pharmaceutical on the market. The exception is organism-specific pharmaceuticals, such as vaccines, for which a substitute may not exist.

METHODOLOGICAL APPROACH TO DETERMINING VULNERABILITIES

Vulnerabilities associated with the chemical infrastructure arise from the properties of chemicals, the properties of the chemical supply chain, and the environment within which the infrastructure and supply chain exist. The consequences from a deliberate exploitation of one or more of these vulnerabilities can be further magnified or dampened by public or societal response to the event. The description of the chemical categories, the generalized model of the chemical supply chain, and a consideration of environmental and social factors lead to a series of questions that can be used to identify those vulnerabilities that are of potentially catastrophic consequences.

CHEMICAL PROPERTIES OF CONCERN

Casualties are most readily caused by exploiting the toxic, explosive, or flammable properties of chemicals. By far the largest number of casualties would be anticipated from situations involving toxic inhalation hazards, that is, large-scale release of toxic chemicals in a gaseous form. For example, hazard estimates by staff of the U.S. Environmental Protection Agency's (EPA's) Chemical Emergency Preparedness and Prevention Office for a worst-case accident involving a flammable substance give a median population within the vulnerable zone of 15, and for toxic inhalation risk give a median population within the vulnerable zone of 1,500. Damage to infrastructure and subsequent economic loss are more readily caused by the flammable and explosive properties of chemicals.

Some chemicals are significantly more hazardous than others. For example, it is possible to rank chemicals with toxic inhalation properties according to toxicity, by using, for example, the Department of Transportation Hazmat Tables, which list toxicities according to LD_{50}. A compound such as methyl isocyanate has a much lower LD_{50} (i.e. is significantly more toxic) than, for example, chlorine. Properties of the specific chemicals involved are important to first responders attempting to mitigate a specific incident to prevent a catastrophic result. However, this report is concerned with identifying research and development that will help prevent any incident from crossing the threshold of catastrophic impact. Depending on actual event circumstances, which include many factors other than toxicity, chlorine can be of equal or of more concern than methyl isocyanate. As a result, above a certain threshold, the relative toxicity (or flammability or explosivity) of two chemical species becomes less relevant.

Whatever the specific chemical involved, all releases progress through a similar series of stages (e.g., release, transport, diffusion, exposure). The release consequences will be affected by the source (e.g., release rate, release duration, and toxicity), meteorology (wind speed, wind direction, atmospheric stability, precipitation), and population (e.g., population distribution and structural protection; response action) factors. Similar opportunities for emergency response and similar consequences (casualties, property damage, and environmental insult) are possible. This provides the opportunity for investments in science and technology development that mitigate speed and direction. The exposed area is likely to be only 25 percent (one quadrant) of the total vulnerable zone at most, and probably less.

The number of people exposed in such an event depends on the size of the impact area and the size of the population remaining in that area. This might be only a small fraction of the total number of people living in the vulnerable zone, especially if they are able to take prompt protective action such as evacuation or sheltering in-place. against all risks in this hazard category. Continuing with the above example, highly toxic chemicals have the potential to cause thousands of casualties with a single release under the worst circumstances. DHS therefore could make investments in science and technology development that are specific to the methyl isocyanate risk, or it can make investments that mitigate the methyl isocyanate risk while also reducing risks from other highly toxic materials. In the absence of specific threat information, it will be most appropriate at this time for DHS to invest its research efforts, including technology development, for general classes of vulnerabilities.

In the case of either casualties or economic loss, catastrophic levels of consequences are expected only where large quantities of chemicals with these properties are involved. However, social response may amplify the effects of an incident involving even small quantity of chemicals to the point where its economic effects, not its casualties, become catastrophic or at least of national concern.

SUPPLY CHAIN CHARACTERISTICS OF CONCERN

The model of the chemical supply chain considers materials, infrastructure, pathways, links and nodes, and ownership and control of the network—leads to characteristics that, if present in any given case, could pose vulnerabilities. These characteristics include the following:

- Key materials without obvious substitutions;

- Single suppliers of key materials with no potential alternative source;
- A plant or production process that uses high volumes of toxic, flammable, or explosive materials;
- Dominant nodes or dominant paths between nodes;
- Vulnerable points of control where theft of or tampering with a chemical can occur; and
- Interdependencies in the supply chain.

SITING CONCERNS

The consequences of an event at a chemical plant or storage facility can be greater or lesser depending upon the local environment in which the facility exists. If a facility is located within a major population center, the number of potential casualties increases. If the facility is near a major transportation corridor, disruption of that corridor and subsequent economic loss become possible. If the facility is near important public infrastructure, such as a water supply, potential consequences increase.

SOCIETAL RESPONSE

Societal response has the potential to transform the consequences of an event by either diminishing or amplifying them. For example, in the event of a hazardous material release, a community whose residents know how to shelter in-place and do so when instructed may suffer many fewer casualties than another community whose residents are not so prepared. Conversely, negative reaction can amplify the consequences of an event. One example of magnification is the loss of business faced by airlines in the weeks and even months after the September 11, 2001, events—many people refused to fly even though, arguably, flying was safer after that date with the implementation of new security rules. Amplification is most likely to affect economic consequences rather than casualties since, contrary to popular belief, people rarely panic in the face of disasters.

PRIMARY ANALYSIS OF VULNERABILITIES

The supply chain characteristics and chemical properties of concern, it is possible to construct a matrix representing the primary vulnerabilities posed within each category. This matrix is not meant to be exhaustive; rather it is meant to represent those combinations of supply chain characteristics and chemical properties that could lead to catastrophic consequences. The number of boxes checked does not necessarily indicate that any one class of chemicals is inherently more or less vulnerable. The checked boxes identify the highest areas of priority in each chemical category that can be utilized to guide investment intended to mitigate vulnerability.

A red teaming type exercise determined situations in which their exploitation could lead to catastrophic consequences.

These figures make it clear that the primary cases of concern can be narrowed to three general cases with potential catastrophic consequences:

1. Key materials (shortage)
2. High-volume toxic, flammable, and explosive chemicals
3. Vulnerable points of control (theft or tampering)

The aspects of nodes and interdependencies as vulnerabilities of the chemical infrastructure are depicted in the vulnerable points of control flowchart. These are the only vulnerabilities in the flowcharts that are not discussed as a scenario in the next chapter. No single vulnerable node within the chemical supply chain was identified that if disrupted, would lead to catastrophic consequences. Targeting of multiple nodes is required to have catastrophic consequences. Similarly, the interdependencies that were identified were not of a high level of concern. Previous analysis based on records of terrorist attacks against the chemical infrastructure reached a similar conclusion:

To do significant damage that truly impacts the U.S. critical infrastructure—rather than inflicting symbolic damage or causing large numbers of casualties—would require the large-scale targeting of select facilities, especially those that are key manufacturers of critical chemicals or single producers of raw chemicals. Most potentially catastrophic for the U.S. chemical critical infrastructure would be a coordinated attack on a number of facilities responsible for key precursors, the disruption of which would cause a bottleneck blockage. Fortunately, the selection of such facilities would require sophisticated knowledge of chemical manufacturers, industrial processes, distribution, and warehousing. It would also require a substantial effort by a relatively large, well-financed terrorist group with access to individuals with specific scientific or technical knowledge.

Although there are other vulnerabilities, only the three cases identified above clearly have the potential for catastrophic consequences. The scenarios are used to test and illustrate the conclusions and observations derived from the analysis.

REALISTIC CHEMICAL INCIDENT SCENARIOS

Open-source information about the chemical industry, information provided through briefings during the course of this study, and the knowledge and experience of the members of the authoring committee were analyzed using the methodology to envision potential scenarios with catastrophic consequences.

Scenarios that would not lead to levels of consequence considered "catastrophic" were discarded. All possible scenarios envisioned that resulted in catastrophic consequences were versions of one of three basic scenarios: high-volume release (fixed site or transport), shortage, and misuse (i.e., theft or tampering).

Because the charge for this study calls for identification of federal science and technology (S&T) investments that could prevent or mitigate these consequences, for each scenario the following questions were also considered:

- Would investment in S&T help mitigate or reduce the consequences of this scenario? In particular, can S&T solutions be proposed that can help prevent the event from rising to the level of catastrophic?
- Is there a federal role in the investments?

THE FEDERAL ROLE

Homeland Security Presidential Directive (HSPD)-7 establishes a national policy for federal departments to identify and prioritize the critical infrastructure and key resources of the United States, and to protect them from terrorist attacks. It directs federal agencies to enhance the protection of our Nation's critical infrastructure and key resources against terrorist acts that could:

a. Cause catastrophic health effects or mass casualties comparable to those from the use of a weapon of mass destruction;
b. Impair federal departments' and agencies' abilities to perform essential missions, or to ensure the public's health and safety;
c. Undermine state and local government capacities to maintain order and to deliver minimum essential public services;
d. Damage the private sector's capability to ensure the orderly functioning of the economy and delivery of essential services;
e. Have a negative effect on the economy through the cascading disruption of other critical infrastructure and key resources; or
f. Undermine the public's morale and confidence in our national economic and political institutions.

Based on HSPD-7, the following impacts are relevant when discussing the chemical sector:

- Impact on life and health (item a)
- Impact on government function (items b and c)
- Impact on the economy and/or the private sector (items d and e).

Societal response (item f) helps shape an incident and can either mitigate or exacerbate its effects. It is taken into account here as a source of possible amplification of the three areas of impact listed above. The statement of task for this study calls for a focus on potential *catastrophic* events. As mentioned previously, the U.S. Department of Homeland Security (DHS) *National Response Plan* defines a catastrophic incident as one that "results in large numbers of casualties and/or displaced persons, possibly in the tens of thousands." Similarly, an economic impact on the order of tens to hundreds of billions of dollars would be considered catastrophic. A catastrophic event is one whose consequences are so extensive that they overwhelm the ability of emergency responders, local, state, and federal government officials, and/or the general public to adequately and/or fully respond in a timely fashion.

Incident Scenarios

Using its knowledge of and information about the chemical sector, and applying the methodology, particularly the supply chain characteristics presented, the study committee set out to envision attack scenarios involving the chemical infrastructure that would be significant enough to require a federal response. It found that all plausible scenarios generated in this red teaming type exercise that had the potential to reach a catastrophic level of impact fell into one of three basic categories:

1. High-volume release (either fixed site or transport),
2. Shortage, or
3. Misuse.

Each of these three scenarios is illustrated below with an example that:

addition, such signals can have more public consequences, for example when a public protest arises about some proposed new development. These developments also ripple outwards to other people, to new areas and to new groups. The opposite effect is social attenuation, when media and other key influencers decide not to stress a specific subject and interest in it becomes reduced.

"Social amplification can lead to decisions that are politically unavoidable and are perhaps socially understandable, but which produce less than optimum results if the problem is regarded as being one of resource allocation."

discusses the vulnerabilities, gives estimates of their consequences if exploited, and discusses recommendations that result. The intention is not to review specific attack tactics and weapons for carrying out the scenario.

Estimates of the casualties resulting from a deliberate attack on the chemical infrastructure vary widely and have been controversial. A recent Congressional Research Service report details many of those estimates and discusses the differences in the analyses and assumptions that lead to them. To preclude the possibility that the conclusions of this study could be dismissed because they are perceived as being based on flawed modeling of casualties, this report uses consequences from the historical accident record to provide existence proof for the consequences postulated in its scenario exercise.

Accident records are used, rather than a record of terrorist attacks, because there have been an extremely low number of terrorist attacks against the chemical infrastructure to date, and even fewer of these have had significant consequences. The Critical Infrastructure Terrorist Incident Catalog, a database of attacks against critical infrastructure with information on incidents going back as far as 1933, lists only 10 possible attacks against the chemical infrastructure, two of which are probable accidents; only one of the incidents definitively determined to be an attack is identified as having had significant consequences (i.e., property damage).

Note that the casualty figures postulated here on the basis of the accident record cannot be taken as either minimum or maximum estimates. Casualties could be much lower if the correct convergence of factors does not occur. (Indeed, there are numerous historical examples available of similar accidents with much lower casualty figures.) It is also possible that casualties from a deliberate attack could be higher—one assumes that, unlike an accident, a deliberate attack will include efforts to control as many variables as possible in order to maximize casualties. However, in a deliberate attack, actual casualties will still depend on factors that are not entirely under the attacker's control, such as meteorological conditions, the ability of the populace to shelter in-place, and the status of emergency preparedness and response. With these caveats, major accidents, although few in number relative to the size and long history of the chemical sector, can be used to provide a realistic estimate of the impact of an intentional attack. Lessons learned from these accidents can be used to better mitigate, prepare, and respond to future terrorist incidents, whatever the cause.

HIGH-VOLUME STORAGE

The chemical industry stores many chemicals at its facilities in the form of raw materials, intermediates, products, and by-products. These products and by-products are then sold to customers who store them on their sites for direct use or for the manufacture of other products. The products of interest to a terrorist are chemicals that are toxic, flammable, or explosive, or a combination thereof. This scenario has particular relevance to storage of inorganic chemicals, industrial gases, and petrochemicals and fossil fuels. Examples of inorganic chemicals that are toxic and stored in large volumes include chlorine, ammonia, and hydrogen fluoride. Industrial gases that are toxic include carbon monoxide; nitrogen and argon are asphyxiants; oxygen and hydrogen are flammable. Most petrochemical and fossil fuel products, intermediates, and by-products are flammable, while a few such as hydrogen cyanide, hydrogen sulfide, and phosgene are toxic.

Scenario

Location. The fictional River City is located on a major transportation corridor, serves as an inland port, and is a centralized hub of industrial production. The city abuts a major fresh waterway that serves as a source of drinking water for millions of people in the city and downstream from it. River City's terrain is moderately hilly and a majority of the population resides in low-lying areas, increasing the potential for a persistent toxic cloud to develop over a large residential area at a concentration hazardous to life and health. Limited evacuation routes are available to the community. River City has a population density greater than 8,000 people per square mile.

Time of Incident. The incident occurs during summer at or around mid-night on a Saturday, Sunday, or holiday, when lower numbers and junior levels of permanent employees staff industrial facilities.

Ambient Conditions. The night is clear with a temperature of approximately 80° F. Wind speed is low (<4 miles per hour), and the wind is blowing from the chemical sources toward areas of high population density. The atmosphere is relatively stable.

Other Special Circumstances. Facility A is undergoing major maintenance and construction, so a large number of temporary contract staff is on-site, working around the clock.

Initiating Event (Stage One). Terrorists attack Facility A, triggering one or more explosions involving large storage containers of inorganic chemicals, petrochemicals, or fuels and specialty chemicals. (Examples might be potentially explosive fertilizers, light hydrocarbons capable of generating a large vapor cloud explosion, or high-energy reactive chemicals.) Multiple initiating pathways could be proposed that would generate significant pressure waves and projectile materials from the exploded storage vessels. The pressure waves and projectiles could further impact not only Facility A, but also facilities beyond its boundaries. Perpetrators provide plausible evidence to the media to demonstrate that the incident is due to terrorism.

Immediate Consequences (Stage One). The initial explosion results in 250 fatalities on-site, most of whom are contract employees; 100 people are killed off-site. 1,000 people are injured on-site; and 2,000 are injured off-site. The number of fatalities and injuries on-site severely compromises the ability of the facility to implement any emergency response activities. Most windows in the nearby vicinity are broken, destroying the capability for many to shelter in-place.

Cascading Events (Stage Two). In the proposed scenario, the potential exists for additional consequences resulting from the initial attack. These consequences can be described as "cascading event" consequences—for example, the initial explosion caused by the attack damages other equipment and causes further explosions or toxic releases that may be significantly more severe than the initial event. These events may not be anticipated or planned by the attacker, and in fact, the attacker may not even be aware of the potential for cascading events. The consequences described here would also obtain if disruption of the second facility was the result of a direct attack.

Pressure waves and projectiles from the explosion at Facility A strike large storage containers or rail cars at a separate plant (Facility B). The result is a loss of containment from the storage containers at Facility B, releasing highly toxic industrial chemicals (e.g., hydrofluoric acid, chlorine, ammonia, phosgene, hydrogen sulfide, sulfur dioxide, sulfur trioxide, hydrogen cyanide, selenium hydride). These chemicals will readily evaporate to form highly concentrated vapor clouds at the temperature postulated for the incident. The resultant vapor clouds will not dissipate or mix rapidly with the surrounding atmosphere because of the low wind speed and stable atmosphere that prevails at the time of the incident. The toxic gas cloud remains relatively concentrated and close to the ground, giving maximum potential exposure to the surrounding population.

Toxic chemical exposures of residents in the community are increased because of broken windows and other structural damage to nearby property caused by the initial explosion, because of the timing of the event (people are at home), and because of limited evacuation routes.

Another potential cascading event is a release of toxic liquid from a storage tank into the river. Materials with a boiling point near normal atmospheric temperature—for example, monomethylamine (boiling point "6° C)—could form a toxic vapor cloud, yet remain partially liquid and flow into the river. The pressure wave and projectiles from the initiating explosion could impact storage vessels at a third facility, Facility C, releasing high volumes of liquid chemicals (e.g., petroleum fuels; chemicals that are persistent and bioaccumulative) that flow into the river, the source of public drinking water and industrial water for River City and many downstream communities.

Immediate Consequences (Stage Two). On-site, 15 people are killed at Facility B; 1,000 are killed off-site; 20,000 people are exposed off-site, incurring injuries with a wide range of severity; business interruption occurs throughout River City. The consequence of Facility C's release grows subsequently in River City and the downstream communities as liquid chemical contamination of water supplies occurs.

Assessment of Impact

This assessment was made based on the historical analogies presented in Appendix A.

Impact on Life and Health. Release of a cloud of a hazardous toxic chemical would be expected to have a large, possibly catastrophic number of casualties. This fictional incident resulted in more than 1,000 deaths and 22,000 injuries. If a cascading spill of hazardous chemicals affects the water supply, a major impact would also be expected on downstream populations.

Impact on the Economy and the Private Sector. If Facility A is a petroleum refinery, immediate price hikes of refined products could occur due to anticipated shortages, even though no immediate inventory and distribution problems would be plausible because of large numbers of similar regional facilities and maintenance of transportation routes. U.S. petroleum refining capacity has remained relatively constant for the last two decades despite expanded demand. It is not anticipated that there would be larger regional or national impacts on distribution and transportation of chemicals. However, river transportation might be impacted for a short period of time as damage, contamination, and the possibility of a second attack are assessed.

Although the economic impact for the company affected in this scenario and its suppliers and customers could be enormous, the scenario as defined would not be considered catastrophic to the regional and national economy because of redundancies in operations at other facilities. Given that the event resulted from terrorism, social amplification could occur with further impact on the national economy.

Impact on Government Function. While this scenario would clearly be a major event and as an act of terrorism would invoke a federal investigation, because it is relatively localized it normally would not overwhelm the federal government's capacity to respond. Local governments, and perhaps the state government, might be overwhelmed in their initial ability to respond to the demands of the disaster. The number of casualties would overwhelm all but the largest metropolitan medical systems and thereby necessitate significant regional and national coordination of emergency medical transport and care.

Possible government regulatory response, such as mandating specific security measures to protect facilities, may occur as a result, with a subsequent impact on the economic function of these companies and, in the aggregate, on the economy as a whole.

Societal Response. The societal response to any act of terror will presumably be greater than if the same consequences occurred through a nonterrorist event. In addition to the immediate reactions of the affected population, populations living near similar facilities would probably express concern that their locations are also targets. Terrorists might exacerbate such fears by announcing or attacking additional targets. Possible effects resulting from social amplification could include demands that chemical facilities nationwide be temporarily shut down, comparable to the cessation of air traffic after 9/11. If such a shutdown were to occur, the economic impact would be large. If large numbers of deaths occur as a result of water contamination (which has not occurred in previous cases of contamination), there may be a generalized fear of poisoning of the water supply. Demands on the government to deploy forces to protect chemical facilities may draw troops away from other priorities.

Discussion

The initial event, under an adverse convergence of circumstances, could have catastrophic levels of casualties but not catastrophic economic consequences. The potential for such a cascading event occurring is low, but not zero. The potential for a cascading event is also very site dependent. However, terrorists could achieve similar or greater impact by attacking multiple, either closely located or geographically dispersed, sites.

Although a coordinated event (multiple attacks at multiple sites occurring simultaneously or in a series) and a cascading event may have the same physical outcome, they could have different impacts. A cascading event involves successive events that are physically close to the initial event, but coordinated attacks can occur in geographically dispersed locations, possibly increasing public concern and straining the response capacity. Note that both coordinated attacks and cascading events could take place over some period of time—hours or even days. It may be difficult to recognize that coordinated attacks are occurring since terrorists benefit by disguising the relationships among events until their objectives are realized. However, early recognition of coordinated attacks is key to preventing further consequences and managing the potential for social amplification.

Release of toxic materials has greater potential to lead to a catastrophic number of casualties than release of flammable or explosive materials, since the impact distance of a toxic release can be much greater under adverse conditions. A toxic cloud low to the ground could cause large casualties among the general population, particularly if the public is not alerted in an effective or timely manner or trained to respond appropriately to the emergency.

The properties of the chemicals involved (flammable, toxic, etc.), rather than the category of chemicals (pharmaceuticals, petrochemical, etc.), determine the outcomes of this scenario. The impact of this scenario depends on the volume of chemical released, the release rate of the chemical, the properties of the chemical, the number of people living or working near the affected site, and the geographic and meteorological conditions. Fires and explosions are less conceivable to cause an event to reach a "catastrophic" level of casualties without a cascading event to increase their impact. Toxic events can result in catastrophic levels of casualties without cascading events.

It should be noted that toxic, flammable, and explosive chemicals of concern include intermediate products in addition to starting materials and end products. For example, the methyl isocyanate released in Bhopal, India, in 1984 was an intermediate product, manufactured at the site, stored in large quantities, and consumed to produce a final product.

Because this scenario involves fixed facilities, pre-planning with the emergency response community and public is more readily achieved. However, experience with prior accidents has shown that planning and response capability has been weak and poorly exercised in many communities. Mutual aid agreements between communities might prove inadequate if multiple facilities are impacted simultaneously. Incident command structures would be similarly challenged. Also, the large number of casualties may reduce the effectiveness of emergency response, especially if emergency responders are directly impacted by the cascade of events.

Surveillance is feasible, but expensive. Terrorists are challenged by the increased security enhancements in the aftermath of 9/11, but there have been multiple media reports about the ineffectiveness and incomplete implementation of this security as well as significant security breaches. Frequent nonterrorist incidents, as observed on the Chemical Safety Board's Incident News Reports provide indications of potential vulnerabilities and attractiveness of chemical sector targets.

This scenario is set in an urban area. Storage of hazardous materials is necessary near urban centers—where gasoline is consumed, chlorine is used for water treatment, and factories are located near workers and consumers. Large storage tanks are present in urban centers; particularly those centers characterized as inland ports and centralized hubs of industrial production. Urban population centers have also grown to surround older factories. Increasing urban real estate valuation poses the additional vulnerability of nearby residential populations on former brownfield sites abutting active industrial facilities. Communication and analysis of information become complicated when incidents involve several facilities. Accessing the accuracy of information becomes more difficult, as is distributing that information to all involved in emergency response. The high human consequences of the initiating and cascading events will greatly constrain the flow of relevant information. Many companies already recognize the difficulties in communicating across facilities with different corporate control. Even with complete disclosure of accurate information, the audience—first responders and the general public—may have difficulty absorbing all of the relevant information regarding each event. The media will also play a key role here, and its reporting can diminish or amplify the perceived consequences and risk associated with the release. Paradoxically, the media has become much more diverse and fractionated in marketing to the public even as corporate ownership has become concentrated, thereby posing additional challenges to a coherent understanding of the event and appropriate response. The situation becomes more constrained as restrictive protocols (different levels of security clearances for emergency responders—police chiefs, fire chiefs, rank and file, volunteers) for information access are exercised in such complex scenarios.

Mitigating the Consequences of the High-Volume Toxic or Flammable Scenario

There are three possible approaches to mitigating the consequences identified in this scenario:

1. Reduce vulnerability by increased security.
2. Reduce consequence through detection and response.
3. Reduce vulnerability and consequence through inherently safer technologies.

Possible Science and Technology Investment

- Better fundamental understanding of material toxicity by inhalation. This will enhance our capacity to predict and model casualties. This includes the development of more Acute Exposure Guideline Levels (AEGLs), toxicity dose-response relationships for all important chemicals, and predictive toxicology.
- Improved scientific models that utilize the chemical properties discussed above and more accurately predict the consequences for a toxic or flammable release. Currently the government sanctions the use of the ALOHA (Area Locations of Hazardous Atmospheres) model for emergency responders, although some emergency responders use the manual method in the EPA's *Technical Guidance for Hazards Analysis* or the Table of Protective Action Distances in the DOT *Emergency Response Guidebook,* while much of industry uses proprietary modeling software such as the PHAST (Process Hazard Analysis Software Tool) model. The ALOHA model is very basic in its approach, and the results vary greatly from those obtained with the more sophisticated PHAST proprietary models. A more accurate model that can be used by everyone would greatly improve emergency response planning efforts and actual response.
- Enhanced real-time monitoring. This could contribute to early detection of and response to a chemical event. Investments could be made in the development of low-cost, accurate, and reliable sensors for toxic and flammable chemicals that could be placed strategically throughout a facility would provide early detection of chemical releases and aid emergency responders in monitoring the effects of the release.
- Improved equipment design, especially for chemical storage. For example, current methods used for storing

materials in adsorbents at the cylinder scale—as is done at computer chip manufacturing facilities—might be scalable for use in large containers (i.e., rail cars or storage tanks). Other examples would include improved metallurgy to make storage tanks more resistant to terrorist weapons and fire suppression systems or water curtains for critical flammable and toxic storage tanks.

- Research to develop inherently safer alternatives and apply them to current processes that require high volumes of toxic or flammable materials. Previous reports have noted that changes adopted in the chemical industry to reduce costs, reduce environmental impact, or improve safety have also enhanced security by reducing the availability of hazardous materials for use in an attack. These changes include the introduction of just-in-time manufacturing and delivery of starting materials or key intermediates, development of inherently safer processes that involve less toxic materials or smaller volumes of material, design of resilient engineered systems and process control systems, and introduction of "over-the-fence" or
- on-site manufacturing to reduce transportation and storage. It must be noted, however, that some strategies to improve safety simply shift the risk—for example, nitrogen trifluoride (NF_3) is currently the most environmentally friendly way to deliver the fluorine molecule, which is needed for efficient chamber cleaning of chemical vapor deposition equipment in the electronics industry. A new on-site fluorine generator has been developed that eliminates the need to transport and store NF_3. However, the on-site generator relies on the dissociation of hydrofluoric acid (HF) to produce fluorine and therefore requires transportation, on-site storage, and handling of the more hazardous HF. Other strategies to improve safety can in fact present new security challenges; proliferation risks from microreactors, which are inherently safer because they reduce the volume of chemical required to carry out a process, have been noted. Pre-competitive research to develop new means or more cost-effective means to minimize the chemical

inventory, develop new syntheses that utilize less hazardous material or less hazardous reaction conditions, and simplify existing chemical processes to eliminate unnecessary complexity will contribute to hazard mitigation in the chemical infrastructure.

High-Volume Transport

- This is similar to the previous scenario but differs in two important respects. First, the hazardous chemical shipment is in transit, rather than at a fixed site. Second, the quantity of hazardous chemicals in any one truck or rail shipment is usually far less than the amount of hazardous materials stored at a fixed facility—large truck shipments are typically on the order of 40,000 pounds, while rail shipments can be four times higher than this.

The key questions and supply chain characteristics to be considered during the decision-making process (i.e., high volume of materials, proximity of routes to population centers, robustness of containers) that can potentially lead to a catastrophic event in a scenario involving high volumes of chemicals in transport. The categories of chemicals that are of particular concern in this scenario include inorganic chemicals, industrial gases, and petrochemicals and fossil fuels.

Scenario

Hazardous chemicals are shipped by truck, rail, marine vessel, pipeline, and sometimes air (in much more limited quantities). These shipments often travel near or through urban areas. If a terrorist event were to cause a release to occur, its location will play a large role in any consequences as well as the potential for a cascading event. Although the amount of hazardous chemical involved may be significantly less than at a fixed facility, an explosion or release could lead to significant casualties if it occurs near a population center. According to the 2004 U.S. Fire Administration survey, fewer than 16 percent of fire departments in this country have hazmat units.

Assessment of Impact

This assessment was made based on the historical analogies presented in Appendix A for events involving high-volume chemical transport.

Impact on Life and Health. Depending on the chemical involved, the number of casualties could be significant—for example, hundreds to thousands of people in cases where there are large explosions or toxic materials are released in highly populated areas.

Because of the quantity of chemical involved, multiple attacks at multiple sites would be required to produce numbers of casualties that would be considered catastrophic by the standards indicated in U.S. Department of Homeland Security (DHS) National Response Plan. (The values given in certain widely publicized planning scenarios reflect all those who are in a vulnerable zone, not the actual number of fatalities expected for a given set of meteorological conditions and wind directions.)

- *Impact on the Economy and the Private Sector.* Impacts will depend heavily on the location of the incident and the hazardous chemicals involved. Economic impacts from most incidents would be localized. Greater impacts could occur as a result of cascading events, such as a tanker explosion that destroys a major terminal or other elements of the transportation infrastructure (e.g., bridges). Even so, these impacts will probably remain localized. Multiple events would be required to raise the level of economic impact to catastrophic levels.
- *Impact on Government Function.* The federal government regularly investigates transportation safety incidents involving toxic materials. Any terrorist act would almost certainly invoke a federal response. Government function would be more seriously impacted only if a targeted attack using chemicals on a major government facility was successful at a time that many key members of government were present.
- *Societal Response.* Social amplification will depend on the specific circumstances of an event. An event in an urban area may lead to calls for permanent bans on shipping of hazardous materials through urban areas, with subsequent economic impacts.

Discussion

- Transportation introduces significant variability of location into the scenario discussed for facilities. This variability may work to either the advantage or the disadvantage of terrorists. Because the shipment is in motion, security precautions that are in place at fixed facilities do not exist, and modes of surveillance are quite different and can be difficult to sustain. The aggregation of hazmat rail cars in major transfer locations may be less secure than at fixed industrial facilities, and they may be located in or near urban environments. At the same time, because the location of the target is variable, additional planning is required to carry out an attack at the right place and time. There are also differences for the different modes of transport—trucks can deviate from typical routes, but the movement of rail cars is much more constrained.
- Emergency response preparedness may be inadequate because preparations for a response in the exact location of the event may not be in place. Depending on the location of the incident, emergency response personnel may or may not be adequately trained and equipped for the hazardous chemicals involved in the incident, and the local population may or may not be prepared to take protective action. However, more densely populated areas are more likely to have significant hazardous materials response capabilities. Depending on the nature of the attack, there may or may not be time to take protective actions, at least in the immediate vicinity of the release.

Information may be a key factor in this scenario. Regulations require that shipments of dangerous goods display the nature of the hazards, usually on the transport container, and in general this information is easy to understand.

While this information is essential to effective response and aids in enhanced safety in general, some are concerned that the information may assist terrorists in identifying specific targets.

Mitigating the Consequences of the High-Volume Toxic or Flammable Transport Scenario

Response to a scenario involving high-volume chemicals in transit is similar in all but a few ways to the response for a high-volume storage scenario at a fixed site.

Key differences are that volumes tend to be smaller and the location is variable. In particular, transportation may pass through localities that are not prepared for hazmat response, do not have appropriate emergency planning, and are not prepared for hazmat incidents.

In addition, local jurisdictions' ability to coordinate their emergency preparedness and response action with hazmat carriers is inherently more limited than with fixed-site facility operators.

Possible Science and Technology Investment

Science and technology investments in areas described in the high-volume storage scenario will also help mitigate the high-volume transport scenario. The transport scenario leads to this additional potential science and technology solution:

- Rapid systems analysis and improved communication for emergency response.

Chemical Shortage

Single supplier, long replacement time, and lack of substitution are supply chain characteristics that lead to a shortage scenario. Figure 3.1 indicates that this is of particular concern in the chemical categories of pharmaceuticals, inorganic chemicals, specialty chemicals, and petrochemicals and fossil fuels. Obviously the chemical in question must serve a critical need for a shortage to be of concern.

[*Note*: While this report was in review, DHS released an avian flu scenario that mirrors many of the consequences discussed below. The significant difference between that scenario and this is that in this case, terrorist action negates the government's preparation to deal with a pandemic. This is a key element of the shortage scenario—it is by exacerbating an existing critical but perhaps manageable situation that terrorist action can cause a chemical shortage that is catastrophic in its consequences.]

Scenario

Location. United States.

Hypothetical Event.

The United States is preparing for what it is anticipating will be a "normal" flu season. Approximately 60 million flu vaccine doses are ready to be distributed. Unfortunately, the strain that actually emerges proves to be resistant to the vaccine and is unusually virulent—mortality is predicted at 5/1,000, only slightly less than the Spanish flu of 1918 (the mortality rate for those exposed to the Spanish Flu is estimated to have been slightly less than 1 percent with a case fatality of 2.5 percent). Fortunately, one of the existing antivirals has shown to be effective in greatly moderating the flu's adverse health effects. Although only 1 million 7-day courses of treatment are available, the sole manufacturer implements its emergency plan and promises 20 million 42-day treatments within 30 days at the bargain price of $200 per treatment course, or $4 billion. The Secretary of the U.S. Department of Health and Human Services (DHHS) publicly acknowledges the problem and states that with careful allocation of the limited supply of drugs and with new medication to be distributed "shortly," only a limited impact, comparable to the Asian flu, is expected. Information focusing on the high-risk population and instructions and recommendations on who should get the existing supplies and where they will be available are provided.

Terrorists attack the only production facility for the antiviral and disrupt the production and supply of the drug in the United States. Another manufacturer states that it can start a new production line in 90 days, with the first antivirals to be delivered in 120 days, after the peak of the flu season. The government and the original manufacturer begin negotiations with the second manufacturer over licensing, liability and price.

The U.S. government attempts to purchase medication from other countries that have their own stockpiles. However, there is concern that a worldwide flu pandemic, similar to the one in 1918, may emerge and foreign governments decide that they want to maintain their current stock rather than sell to the United States.

Several countries with weaker patent protection and drug regulation choose to manufacture their own version of the antiviral, both for their own population and for export. This "gray market" generates and distributes some effective, some ineffective, and even some dangerous medications, which exacerbate the impact of the pandemic—the death toll, illnesses, and numbers requiring hospitalization. The media highlights the role of the counterfeit drug market and its potential deadly outcomes,

thus increasing the population's psychological stress. Reports of senior government officials hoarding the drug for their own protection surface in some newspapers, leading the general public to believe that the government is underplaying the severity of the situation. "As the credibility of public authorities crumbled, so did social order." Major corporations shift production overseas and are rumored to allow critical employees to travel overseas to take advantage of foreign drug treatments. Apparently U.S. multinationals have been stockpiling antivirals in anticipation of a pandemic. The government considers confiscation of private stock to optimize distribution. Critical workers are using their personal allocation to protect their families instead of themselves, wreaking havoc with the government's allocation plans. Customs and Border Protection reports large numbers of U.S. citizens are traveling to Canada and Mexico to gain access to available medication. Our neighbors voice concern to the State Department and consider severely restricting cross-border traffic.

Assessment of Impact

By the time the pandemic has run its course and antivirals become widely available the United States has suffered several hundred thousand causalities and economic losses in excess of $150 billion.

This assessment was made based on historical analogies (the 1918 pandemic and recent influenza outbreaks) and available attempts to predict potential consequences of an avian flu pandemic.

Impact on Government Function. State and local governments in heavily affected areas may be overwhelmed in their attempts to respond adequately. During the 1918-1919

Spanish flu epidemic, hospitals in Washington, D.C., were overwhelmed with patients and those infected were placed in houses, apartments, and rooming houses, either with or without medical care. The pandemic may well affect enough localities that the federal government's capacity to respond is overwhelmed. National security considerations may lead to difficult allocation decisions and trade-offs regarding protection of the armed services, both at home and abroad.

Societal Reaction. Social amplification or attenuation can result as a consequence of the availability or lack of effective mitigation and preparedness initiatives; effective or ineffective leadership; and the ability or inability to provide accurate, up-to-date, and continuous information. The media plays an instrumental role in either amplifying or clarifying and explaining the impacts of shortages, as illustrated by coverage of the 2004 shortage of flu vaccine. Sensationalistic, biased, and inaccurate information contributes to the social amplification of these events. For example, the media may project and disseminate information indicating that without effective medical treatment about 1 million to 2 million people will die, leading to a widespread sense of vulnerability and helplessness that might cause a significant increase in hospital visits from individuals concerned that the symptoms they are experiencing are indication of a life-threatening disease. Accurate, clear, and understandable information, promptly provided by both the press and government officials, can make the government's response more manageable and the public's response helpful in managing the situation: "It is worth noting that this terror, at least in paralyzing form, did not seem to materialize in the few places where authorities told the truth."

Discussion

Our market economy works to prevent shortages through competition. As discussed in Chapter 2, the chemical sector has redundant supply chains, moderate stockpiles of raw ingredients, and collaborative agreements to provide redundant manufacturing in an emergency or crisis situation, such as a shortage. The federal government also monitors the supply of some key pharmaceuticals and stockpiles them in order to ensure that there is no unexpected critical pharmaceutical shortage. This scenario relies on particular characteristics of the market that could permit terrorists to capitalize on an existing situation and create a catastrophic event. The characteristic that makes the shortage scenario viable is the uniqueness of the chemical compounds involved. In this scenario there is a targeted demand for a drug, and the drug itself has limited market applications—that is, it has no use other than to treat a limited number of flu strains. Under normal conditions there would be a very limited demand for the drug, resulting in only a single supplier and moderate stockpiles. If the sole supplier's capacity to manufacture the drug were eliminated, it is unlikely that an alternative means of production could readily be found. This is particularly true for compounds with a long manufacturing lead-time from raw material to finished product—in other words, drugs with a complex manufacturing process. It is important to note that the federal government already has some safeguards in place to address pharmaceutical shortages. The Center for Drug Evaluation and Research (CDER) of the U.S. Food and Drug Administration maintains a list of drugs critical to national well-being. CDER also assists the Centers for Disease Control and Prevention (CDC) to maintain the CDC's Strategic National Stockpile (SNS), which has large quantities of medicine and medical supplies to protect the American public if there is a public health emergency severe enough to drain local supplies.

Once federal and local authorities agree that the stockpile is needed, medicines can be delivered to any state in the United States within 12 hours. Each state has plans to receive and distribute SNS medicine and medical supplies to local communities as quickly as possible. However, if an event were to reach a "catastrophic" level, the SNS may not have an adequate amount of medications in stock to provide the appropriate doses to all who are impacted. The Department of Defense (DOD) also maintains a list of critical material and their suppliers deemed important to national security.

Social amplification plays a key role in this scenario. The impact—economic impact, strain on limited medical resources, and possible social disruption—depends, in part, on how the event is portrayed by the media and how well the government responds and communicates with the public.

POSSIBLE SCIENCE AND TECHNOLOGY INVESTMENT

Several steps can be taken to reduce the nation's vulnerability to chemical shortages. Some are outside the realm of science and technology: for example, extra security measures at suddenly critical manufacturing facilities or plans to permit confiscation of private stocks of a critical chemical in times of dire national need. Possible science and technology investments for this scenario include the following:

- Real-time national inventory tracking of certain chemicals, and the ability to predict how extra normal but nonterrorist events might create the opportunity for terrorist-induced catastrophic shortages. This would greatly aid planning and protective measures.
- Flexible or swing manufacturing contingency plans (perhaps including trial manufacturing runs for the most critical chemicals).
- Collection of data and the development of models to enable rapid, high-confidence determination of how a limited supply of a chemical should be distributed to minimize consequences. Building and executing an effective simulation with all the appropriate feed data might not be feasible on an emergency time line.
- Social science to improve response and communication. This includes implementing current knowledge about disaster response from the social science community, as well as additional studies to determine the types of information, best communication channels, and most effective delivery of information required to reach all populations affected by such an event. Ensuring that credible, well-informed technical spokespeople, either government employees or private individuals, are available to communicate information about the event and actions being taken to mitigate the shortage should enhance a positive public response to the event.

The analysis used here did not identify any obvious key chemicals for which a shortage with catastrophic national consequences could readily be induced. Further economic analysis of the chemical industry would be appropriate to either verify this conclusion or identify chemicals that could, with exacerbating natural events, result in catastrophic shortages.

Misuse of Materials

Lack of control is the characteristic that makes the misuse scenario possible. As Figure 3.1 indicates, inorganic chemicals, industrial gases, specialty chemicals, consumer products, and petrochemicals or fossil fuels should be of particular concern in this scenario. Because of the ubiquitous nature of consumer products in the U.S. economy, they have significant potential for widespread social amplification.

Scenario

Small quantities of chemicals can produce only small, direct impacts over small or large impact areas, but specific locations or situations might be targeted specifically to cause social concern and amplify the physical impact, or repeated incidents could cause indirect impacts that exceed the direct impacts.

Location. Sunnytown, is a fictional midsized city located relatively close to major population centers, none of which have been subjected to terrorist incidents in the past. The local population, although concerned about terrorism, has no special concern that its city would be a potential target.

Initiating Event (Stage One). Terrorists contaminate a popular over-the-counter consumer product in the greater Sunnytown area with a highly toxic chemical. Depending on their objectives, these toxins can be either relatively common poisons that would cause death quickly, and would be relatively easy to identify, or more esoteric toxins that might be difficult to identify or track, and/or whose mode of action is slower, allowing multiple acts to occur before local public health and safety authorities recognize the threat.

Immediate Consequences. Depending on the extent of the tampering, the mode of action of the toxin, and the time required for authorities to realize and take actions to mitigate the incident, casualties could range from fewer than ten up to many dozens or possibly hundreds.

Cascading Events (Stage Two). Social amplification would be expected no matter what the extent of the actual deaths involved. If the poisonings have the appearance of being widely dispersed (e.g., multiple toxins are used, a wide variety of products are targeted—including food, pharmaceuticals, health and beauty products), social amplification would be more extreme, possibly leading to difficulties as people locally, regionally, or nationwide stop buying products they suspect might be contaminated and use up their own personal inventories of these products.

Supply Chain Consequences. Producers of the affected consumer product may experience significant economic downturns as affected and unaffected populations stop buying their goods.

Assessment of Impact

This assessment was made based on historical analogies presented in Appendix A for events resulting from misuse of a small or targeted amount of material.

Impact on Life and Health. It is difficult to conceive of a tampering scenario using a chemical toxin that would lead to massive casualties. The number of individual products compromised would have to be enormous, enhancing the chances of detection, and the source of the poisoning would probably be identified quickly, especially if the same toxin and same product were involved in all cases.

Impact on the Economy and the Private Sector. Because these incidents are so site and method specific, it is difficult to make generalities regarding economic impact. A single tampering incident that leads to a single illness would not be expected to have a major impact. However, multiple incidents could have significant economic impact on the targeted company. If a series of cases affecting a key pharmaceutical leads the population to believe that the entire supply is tainted, this could have a significant national impact if a replacement is not readily available or public concerns about tampering cannot be allayed quickly.

Impact on Government Function. The government response to such an incident would be significant, possibly very large in comparison with the small number of lives lost. The anthrax attacks in the fall of 2001—although not completely analogous to this scenario—are instructive in illustrating that a massive federal response can occur in the event of a comparatively small loss of life. If tampering is widespread and not immediately contained, a large federal effort would occur to stabilize the situation. However, such an incident would not overwhelm the ability to respond effectively at the federal level.

Societal Reaction. A scenario involving tampering will meet the definition of catastrophic only by invoking significant social amplification. This type of scenario, where the characteristics include poisoning of common items and multiple attacks that may be widely dispersed geographically, may lead to the perception that the attacker is anywhere and everywhere. Large portions of the population may shun buying or using the targeted consumer products in response to this tampering, whether or not they are actually at risk.

Discussion

While it is difficult to conceive of a tampering case that would lead to catastrophic numbers of casualties, the fact that this type of attack is relatively easy to accomplish, and involves small quantities of toxic materials, makes this scenario more amenable to multiple coordinated incidents and makes any attempt difficult to detect and intercept prior to its implementation. Perhaps the greatest vulnerability posed by this scenario is the potential for large social amplification. It appears that the anthrax attacks in 2001 were timed to take advantage of the uncertainty and insecurity felt by the American public after the September 11th attacks a month earlier. A tampering attack may likewise attempt to maximize the public's reaction to a prior event in an effort to create as much disruption as possible.

Manufacturers of consumer products and pharmaceuticals expend a great deal of effort to prevent product tampering. Because the consequences can be devastating for the company targeted, industry has significant interest in quality control of its products. In addition to criminal investigation, the role of the federal government can be significant, particularly in scenarios where multiple unrelated products are targeted simultaneously. In general, quick, effective action to respond to a tampering case, combined with effective and open communication to the general population, provide the best opportunities to attenuate the social amplification that will almost certainly occur in response to such an incident.

It may be all but impossible to prevent a determined attacker from successfully tampering with a product. However, the response by Johnson & Johnson to the Tylenol poisonings in 1982 illustrates the benefits of outreach to the public. Although the company lost approximately $1 billion in market value as an immediate result of these incidents, its quick actions in response to the poisonings (including recall and destruction of existing inventory and development of tamper-proof packaging), performed in an open and transparent manner, allowed the company to recover 70 percent of its market share for Tylenol. When a similar incident occurred in 1986, Johnson & Johnson again acted quickly and recalled inventory from all outlets, not just those in affected areas. These actions helped to lessen the overall impact of these events on the company and preserved Tylenol as a viable brand. In cases of widespread tampering involving multiple products, the affected companies will play a significant role in addressing public concerns, but coordinating bodies from the private sector (e.g., trade associations) and public sector agencies must play a role in relaying clear, accurate, and concise information to the public. The government's response to the anthrax attacks in 2001 is useful in illustrating both the positive and the negative aspects of crisis management and effective communication to the public in an ambiguous environment.

Mitigating the Consequences of the Misuse Scenario

The misuse scenario reaches a catastrophic level of impact only through social amplification. Therefore, consequences are best mitigated through effective communication and emergency response.

Possible Science and Technology Investment

- Increase the speed and accuracy of the population protection process: detect, classify, notify, warn, and respond.
- Improve response and communication. This includes social science research to determine the types of information, best communication channels, and most effective delivery of information required to reach all populations affected by such an event.

2

Managing the Terrorism Risk

As seen from the discussion in the previous chapter, and as demonstrated in the scenarios, social factors can be as important as technical factors in determining the preparedness for and consequences of a deliberate disruption of the chemical infrastructure. This chapter presents a model of disaster impacts and discusses risk perception, interdependent security, and consequent decision making from the individual chemical plant to broader societal impacts.

These concepts are useful to develop strategies for managing the vulnerabilities presented by the chemical infrastructure in a cost-effective manner. They point to management of emergency planning and response, and communication and social response, as important factors in reducing the likelihood that the consequences of an event will reach catastrophic proportions.

SOCIETAL IMPACTS OF HAZARDOUS INCIDENTS

Research conducted over the past 50 years has yielded a broad understanding of the process by which hazardous incidents affect local communities and the larger social units of which they are a part.

Hazardous inci- dents are events that are perceived by some segments of society as producing unacceptable impacts or as indicating the danger that such impacts might occur in the future. These incidents do not necessarily produce large numbers of casualties or damage, but they can result in a societal response disproportionate to the risks involved, relative to that posed by natural disasters, such as earthquakes and hurricanes.

A Model of Disaster Impacts

There are many apparent contradictions in the societal management of risk that can be explained (although far from perfectly) by recent models of disaster impacts and the social amplification or attenuation of risk. The effects of hazardous incidents are determined in part by three pre-impact conditions: (a) hazard exposure, (b) physical vulnerability, and (c) social vulnerability. When a hazardous incident occurs, it is subject to event-specific (d) hazardous incident characteristics that combine with the pre-impact conditions to produce (e) physical impacts. In turn, these physical impacts cause (f) social impacts. However, the physical impacts can be reduced by (g) improvised emergency response, and the social impacts can be reduced by (h) improvised disaster recovery activities. In addition, the impacts of the incident can be further reduced by means of pre-impact hazard planning and management actions such as (i) hazard mitigation practices and (j) emergency preparedness practices that reduce the physical impacts and (k) recovery preparedness practices that reduce the social impacts.

Some shortcomings must be kept in mind when applying the DIM to the chemical sector:

- The effects and relationships displayed in the DIM are not linear or unidirectional as shown. There are interdependencies and interactions among and between these components. There are many complexities within the model and interaction may occur within components not depicted in the figure.
- The DIM, which was developed from findings of research on natural hazards, can best be applied to chemical incidents that have a well-defined geographic impact area, such as the release of hazardous materials from a fixed site or in transport. To date there has been no research to confirm that the DIM can be applied to incidents lacking a well-defined geographic impact area, such as chemical contamination of food or pharmaceuticals.
- The DIM lacks analytic methods for assessing remote downstream supply chain impacts of the destruction of a single facility or small group of facilities.

Nonetheless, some useful general conclusions can be drawn from the DIM. The following sections describe the components of the DIM in greater detail.

Pre-impact Conditions

Pre-impact conditions play a large role in determining the consequences of a hazardous event.

Hazard exposure refers to the geographical areas that could be affected by the impact of a hazardous incident. For example, the areas around chemical facilities and their transportation routes can be mapped to identify the locations, known as *vulnerable zones*, where dangerous levels of chemical exposures could occur if some or all of the contents of a chemical container were released. There are 9 categories of hazardous materials listed by the Department of Transportation, which include explosives, gases, flammable liquids, flammable solids, oxidizers and organic peroxides, toxic (poisonous) materials and infectious substances, radioactive materials, corrosive materials, and miscellaneous dangerous goods. Only a few of these are sufficiently dangerous, stored or shipped in large enough quantities, or located close enough to populated areas to produce direct damage or large numbers of casualties. Many of these chemicals have been identified as extremely hazardous substances (EHSs) in accordance with the requirements of Section 312 of the Emergency Planning and Community Right to Know Act of 1986 or Section 112(r) of the Clean Air Act Amendments of 1992. In most communities, vulnerable zones have been estimated using the U.S. Environmental Protection Agency's (EPA's) Risk Management Plan (RMP) estimates required by the Clean Air Act Amendments. Vulnerable zones are areas around a facility in which people could, but would not necessarily, be exposed to harm by a worst-case event. The portion of the vulnerable zone impacted in an actual event is dependent upon factors such as meteorological conditions, wind speed, wind direction, et cetera, and is expected to be some fraction of the total vulnerable zone. Therefore the number of people exposed in an actual event would be lower than the total number of people living in the vulnerable zone.

Physical vulnerability refers to the susceptibility of persons and structures to the impacts of a hazardous incident. In the case of hazards to per- sons, this means deaths, injuries, or illnesses from extreme temperatures, blast pressures, and toxic chemicals.

In the case of structures, physical vulnerability usually means susceptibility to damage from fire and blast, but structures can also be vulnerable to toxic chemicals if the materials from which they are constructed are reactive with the chemicals involved or are difficult to decontaminate.

Social vulnerability can be characterized as people's inability to anticipate, avoid, respond to, or recover from hazard impacts. Thus, social vulnerability addresses the degree to which people lack information about hazards; are located close to hazard sources; live or work in buildings having low hazard resistance; have little or no access to warnings, training on how to respond, evacuation transportation, and shelter locations; and have limited assets to support recovery from disaster impacts. Social vulnerability is determined in part by the state of a community's emergency preparedness. In many cases, households' social vulnerability is systematically related to demographic characteristics such as gender, age, education, income, and ethnicity.

Event-Specific Conditions

In addition to existing pre-impact conditions, the consequences of an actual event will depend upon event-specific conditions—those unique conditions that obtain at the time of the event.

Hazardous Incident Characteristics. These include the availability of environmental cues, speed of hazard onset, scope of hazard impact, and duration of hazard impact. When hazardous incidents occur infrequently, with rapid onset, no environmental cues, large scope of impact, and long duration, it is difficult for households and local governments to improvise a successful emergency response. Although these conditions apply most directly to the storage and transportation scenarios, they also seem quite relevant to the chemical shortage and chemical misuse scenarios, as well.

Improvised Emergency Response. When an incident occurs, the emergency response organization must perform four basic functions: emergency assessment, expedient hazard mitigation, population protection, and incident management. Emergency assessment consists of those diagnoses of past and present conditions and prognoses of future conditions that guide the emergency response. Expedient hazard mitigation refers to actions that emergency personnel take to limit the magnitude of the disaster's impact (e.g., sandbagging a flooding river, patching a leaking railroad tank car). Population protection refers to actions—such as sheltering-in-place, evacuation, and mass immunization—that protect people from hazardous agents. Incident management consists of the activities by which the human and physical resources used to respond to the emergency are mobilized and directed to accomplish the goals of the emergency response organization.

As discussed further below, emergency response personnel increasingly use emergency preparedness practices such as planning, training, equipping, and exercising to guide their emergency response. However, emergency response personnel may have to improvise emergency response actions for one of two reasons. First, they might implement *maladaptive* actions because they have inadequate plans, training, facilities, equipment, or materials. Second, they might implement *adaptive* actions because they recognize that specific characteristics of an incident require actions that differ from those prescribed by emergency operations plans and procedures.

Improvised Disaster Recovery. During disaster recovery, the recovery organization must perform five basic functions: disaster assessment, debris clearance, resource management, physical reconstruction, and business resumption. Disaster assessment involves evaluating damage and casualties, and debris clearance involves removing damaged infrastructure, structures, contents, and vehicles. Resource management involves controlling the flow of personnel, equipment, and materials into the impact area, and physical reconstruction involves rebuilding or replacing damaged infrastructure, structures, contents, and vehicles. Finally, business resumption involves re-establishing links to employees, suppliers, distributors, and customers. In scenarios lacking a specific incident scene—the chemical shortage and misuse scenarios—there is no physical damage, so debris clearance and physical reconstruction will not take place. However, disaster assessment, resource management, and business resumption will still be needed. As is the case with improvised emergency response, improvised disaster recovery can be necessary because of inadequate recovery preparedness or because recovery personnel recognize distinctive characteristics of an incident that indicate a need to deviate from the pre-impact recovery plan.

Pre-impact Hazard Management Actions

Communities are best able to protect themselves from low-probability, high-consequence incidents by engaging in three pre-impact hazard management interventions—hazard mitigation, emergency preparedness, and recovery preparedness—to reduce the physical and social impacts of hazardous incidents. Hazard mitigation practices provide passive protection to persons and property at the time an incident occurs, whereas emergency preparedness practices develop the resources needed to support an active emergency response. Recovery preparedness practices provide the financial and material resources needed to reestablish normal patterns of social and economic functioning after an incident has been stabilized.

More specifically, hazard mitigation practices include hazard source control activities to prevent chemical releases, land use practices to limit the number and types of structures and persons that are exposed to a hazard, and building construction practices to prevent damage and casualties. For chemicals, hazard source control includes process design, facility construction materials, and operation and maintenance practices that reduce the probability of an incident. Hazard source control also includes flare towers, water curtains, or other devices that would reduce the magnitude of the impacts if an incident occurred. Land use practices include siting hazardous chemical facilities away from densely populated areas or locations of special facilities such as schools, nursing homes, or hospitals. Appropriate land use practices also include limiting residential and commercial con- struction and the siting of special facilities within the vulnerable zones of hazardous chemical facilities. Finally, building construction practices ensure that residential and commercial structures located close to hazardous chemical facilities can withstand the forces of fires and explosions and can resist the infiltration of contaminated air from releases of toxic or flammable gases.

Emergency preparedness practices develop the resources needed to support an active emergency response. These involve the development of emergency response plans, procedures, and training programs, the acquisition of facilities, equipment, and materials likely to be needed to support an emergency response; and the performance of drills and exercises to test the emergency response organization. To support the emergency assessment function, facilities, carriers, and local jurisdictions must develop the capability to promptly and accurately detect a chemical threat and to project its potential impact area to identify areas that require population protection actions. Consumer product and pharmaceutical producers and public health departments must have a prompt detection capability and an ability to carry out a response such as product recall in the event of contamination. To support the expedient hazard mitigation function, there must be an ability to control leaks, spills, and fires, to stabilize containers; and to quickly repair damaged production systems. To support the population protection function, it is necessary to have a capability for protective action decision making, population warning, protective action implementation (e.g., evacuation traffic management and evacuation transportation support, sheltering-in-place, use of alternative products, recall and collection of possible contaminated product), search and rescue, and transportation and treatment of the injured. To support the incident management function, there must be a capability to activate emergency response organizations, coordinate and document their activities, acquire additional resources, and communicate with the public.

Recovery preparedness practices provide the financial and material resources necessary to reestablish normal patterns of social and economic functioning after an event has been stabilized. These involve establishing pre-impact recovery organizations comprising representatives of all organizations that would participate in an actual disaster recovery, as well as developing a recovery plan that establishes the structure of the disaster recovery organization. In addition, recovery preparedness also involves the development of procedures to guide damage assessment; debris clearance (contamination cleanup in the case of persistent chemicals); resource management; physical reconstruction of infrastructure and residential, commercial, and industrial buildings; and business resumption. Finally, recovery preparedness also includes procedures for integrating hazard mitigation into the recovery process. This latter step ensures that the affected community is less vulnerable to future incidents.

HAZARDOUS INCIDENT IMPACTS

The principal physical impacts of a hazardous incident are casualties and damage, each of which can be caused by a primary hazard (e.g., an explosion or toxic release) or a secondary hazard (e.g., a toxic chemical release caused by an explosion as described in the high-volume scenario in Chapter 4). In addition to the direct casualties and damage caused by the primary and secondary hazards, there can be indirect physical impacts. For example, the destruction of a chemical plant that is the sole producer of a nonsubstitutable commodity could have the indirect effect of suspending production of all downstream products.

The social impacts of a hazardous incident can be classified as psychological, demographic, economic, and political. Psychological impacts can be categorized as emotional, cognitive, and behavioral. Emotional impacts include such negative manifestations as depression and post traumatic stress disorder but can also include positive manifestations such as a sense of community identification from helping to save the lives and property of others. Cognitive impacts are most likely to be changes in people's perceptions of hazard exposure, hazard impact characteristics, personal consequences of hazard exposure, and characteristics of alternative protective actions. Behavioral impacts include changes in people's daily activities such as work, education, recreation, social interaction, and basic functions such as eating and sleeping.

A principal focus of the DIM is on the ways in which physical impacts such as casualties and damage cause social impacts through the *direct* experience of the impact area population. However, some of those in the impact area do not experience damage or casualties, and this is also true for the entire population outside the impact area. Unlike direct experience, which occurs when people are themselves casualties or experience damage to their own property, vicarious experience occurs when people learn about casualties or damage experienced by others. Direct experience has a very powerful effect on people's beliefs and behavior, but it generally happens to a relatively small proportion of the population. By contrast, vicarious experience has a weaker effect on people's beliefs and behavior than direct experience, but can affect a much larger proportion of the population.

Demographic impacts are defined by changes in the population of the impact area including births, deaths, and migration (e.g., in- and out-migration). Economic impacts are defined by the changes in employment for households or profitability for businesses. In many cases, "losers" are counterbalanced by "winners" at the local level. For example, one business's inability to supply its products to customers can mean additional revenues for its competitors; money that victims spend on rebuilding their damaged homes generates revenues for construction companies. Thus, some of what appear to be economic *losses* are in fact only economic *shifts*. Political impacts include the enactment of regulations and legislation.

OPPORTUNITIES TO IMPROVE HAZARD MANAGEMENT

The above discussion of the Disaster Impacts Model suggests a number of areas in which research investments can significantly improve the nation's ability to manage the vulnerabilities to and consequences of terrorist attack or other catastrophic disruption of the chemical infrastructure. Investments in *hazard or vulnerability analysis* for the storage and transportation scenarios can provide the information on pre-impact conditions that is needed to identify locations with the greatest hazard exposure, structures with the greatest physical vulnerability and population segments with the greatest social vulnerability. Investments in *pre-impact hazard management actions* can provide better ways to reduce vulnerability before an incident occurs (hazard mitigation), respond effectively when an incident does occur (emergency response preparedness), and recover rapidly after an incident has been terminated (recovery preparedness). The development and implementation of effective pre-impact hazard management actions can significantly reduce reliance on improvised emergency response and improvised disaster recovery actions.

Hazard or Vulnerability Analysis for the Storage and Transportation Scenarios

The Federal Emergency Management Agency recommends that community emergency operations plans (EOPs) be based on an explicit statement of *situation and assumptions* derived from hazard and vulnerability analyses and should also have hazard-specific appendixes that address any distinctive disaster demands imposed by specific hazard agents. However, no one has examined whether EOPs do contain appendixes for the appropriate hazards and whether the distinctive demands of these hazards are correctly identified. The available research on local assessments of chemical vulnerability indicates that a significant percentage of local jurisdictions have used the *Emergency Response Guidebook,* rather than the *Technical Guidance for Hazards Analysis* or computer programs such as *ALOHA,* to calculate the vulnerable zones around chemical facilities in their communities. Research is needed to determine if this situation has improved in recent years and, if not, what the impediments are to improving the quality of these analyses.

Research is also needed to develop simple methods of assessing the physical vulnerability of buildings, especially to air infiltration of toxic chemicals. Emergency managers need to be able to determine which areas of their communities have sufficiently low levels of air infiltration that sheltering-in-place is a feasible protective action during a toxic chemical release. There can be significant variability in the air infiltration rates among structures within a neighborhood, which requires extensive sampling of these structures. At present, however, the testing procedures are time consuming and expensive so local emergency managers cannot afford to conduct detailed analyses. Developing simple, reliable methods of assessing air infiltration would overcome this problem.

Research is also needed to better understand the concept of social vulnerability to identify those population segments whose limited resources impede their ability to adopt hazard mitigation measures or to prepare for, respond to, and recover from disasters. Moreover, there is a need to understand the driving forces that determine that level of vulnerability.

Hazard and Vulnerability Analysis for the Chemical Shortage and Misuse Scenarios

Hazard and vulnerability analysis procedures have been developed for situations in which a chemical is dispersed in the air or water from a point source. Such situations correspond closely to the storage and transportation scenarios. However, hazard or vulnerability analysis procedures are less well defined for situations corresponding to the chemical shortage and misuse scenarios. Thus, research is needed to develop hazard or vulnerability analysis procedures for these types of situations.

Hazard Mitigation

Storage and Transportation Scenarios. Hazard source control both for fixed sites and in transport is currently regulated by the federal government (EPA and U.S. Department of Transportation respectively). Changes to local land use practices and building construction practices can also reduce hazard vulnerability, but these practices are determined by local ordinances—although state mandates have a significant effect on local implementation. Anecdotal evidence suggests that local jurisdictions do little to regulate incompatibilities between chemical facilities and other land uses, especially special facilities such as schools, hospitals, nursing homes, and jails. The federal government could assist, however, by investing in research to assess the benefits (effectiveness in protecting persons and property, usefulness for other purposes) and resource requirements (cost, time and effort, specialized knowledge and skill, interagency cooperation) of alternative land use practices that local jurisdictions could implement to reduce their vulnerability to chemicals. Similar research could help promote the adoption of building construction practices that reduce infiltration of contaminated air into structures near chemical facilities or transport routes—for example, cheaper, more effective methods of weather stripping and other retrofitting of air infiltration barriers. Research should examine the joint efforts of regulations, incentives, and risk communication on households and businesses and their decision making with respect to such measures.

Chemical Shortage and Misuse Scenarios. Hazard mitigation for the chemical shortage scenario can be achieved by preventing the loss of the production facilities needed to provide critical levels of the required pharmaceuticals. Hazard mitigation for the misuse scenario can be achieved by preventing terrorists from contaminating food and consumer products without being detected. This is achieved by normal industrial security during production, quality assurance or quality control (QA/QC) before packaging, QA/QC during distribution, and redundant security packaging that allows retailers and consumers to recognize package tampering.

Emergency Preparedness

Storage and Transportation Scenarios. Research could improve emergency preparedness in four areas: planning processes; emergency response; training and equipment; and drills, exercises, and incident critiques.

Planning Processes. Improved planning processes can help local emergency planners and emergency responders make the most effective use of their limited time and energy. The Superfund Amendments and Reauthorization Act of 1986 (SARA Title III) prompted the development of a community-wide emergency planning process that was quite consistent with the findings of social science research on emergency planning. This research has begun to develop a comprehensive model of the preparedness planning process but much remains to be learned. One important goal for future research is to better understand the ways in which local emergency management, fire, and police personnel can build community support for chemical emergency preparedness. Another goal is to develop new ways to enhance the effectiveness of interdisciplinary teams in planning, training, and exercising for chemical emergencies.

Emergency Response Functions. Further research is needed on all four of the emergency response functions: emergency assessment, expedient hazard mitigation, population protection, and incident management.

Major disasters require emergency managers to rapidly detect dangerous conditions, assess the situation, and decide how to terminate it. Improved detection technology, especially for transportation incidents involving unknown hazard agents could assist in this aspect of emergency assessment. In addition to sensing a release and identifying the agent, detection systems should provide rapid notification of the location at which the release is occurring. Research is also needed to improve incident managers' ability to utilize this information effectively. An improved understanding of the ways in which incident managers assess emergencies might identify judgmental heuristics and biases that impair the accurateness and completeness of these assessments. Once identified, training programs and decision support systems could be designed to overcome these heuristics and biases.

Many, if not most, major emergencies require local officials to initiate protective actions for the population at risk. This requires protective action selection (usually between evacuation and sheltering-in-place), warning, protective action implementation, impact zone access control and security, reception and care of victims, search and rescue, emergency medical care and morgues, and hazard exposure control. However, there is virtually no research on *preparedness* for population protection, or on the extent to which practitioners use the findings of scientific research in developing community preparedness for population protection. For example, sheltering-in-place is sometimes the most appropriate protective action recommendation, but the criteria for choosing between evacuation and sheltering-in-place can be complex and there appears to be no research assessing the adequacy of emergency managers' decision criteria for choosing between these alternatives. Nor is there adequate research on vulnerable zone populations' likely compliance and timeliness in implementing protective action recommendations. Moreover, little research has been conducted on community warning systems since the EPA supported a series of studies after the Bhopal accident. In principle, communities can design the most appropriate warning systems based on the characteristics of the hazards to which they are exposed (especially speed of onset and scope of impact) and the characteristics of the jurisdiction (e.g., population density, wealth). However, no research to date has examined the process by which this takes place. Research on this topic could identify impediments to the development of effective community warning systems and, ideally, stimulate engineering research to overcome these impediments.

Population protection also includes the transmission of warning messages that describe the threat, an appropriate protective action, and sources of additional information. There is a considerable base of research on warnings and risk communication, but there appears to be little or no research on the extent to which practitioners use the findings of this research in developing community emergency preparedness. As previous chapters have noted, appropriate communications can be the key that prevents the consequences of an event from reaching catastrophic levels. Research on preparedness for warning should address the choice of warning sources, warning mechanisms, and warning content and the reasons for choosing them. In addition, research should examine the extent to which emergency managers systematically consider the time required to disseminate warnings and the role of informal warning networks in the dissemination process.

There is a small but important research literature on protective action implementation that includes some significant advances in modeling distributions of warning and preparation times required for the populace to take protective actions, but recent data are mostly limited to hurricanes. Quantitative data are needed for a variety of incidents to assess warning and preparation time distributions for chemical incidents. In addition, research is needed to assess the extent to which these preparation time distributions are predictable from households' demographic characteristics (e.g., size and age distribution, transit dependence) so that emergency managers can use census data to adjust generic distributions to local conditions.

Quantitative models for computing evacuation time estimates from traffic models are also now available. However, there have been few efforts to validate the models to determine if analysts' assumptions about evacuees' behavior are accurate. One major uncertainty concerns the rate of traffic flow when the demand on evacuation routes in a risk area exceeds its capacity—especially when queues take many hours to clear. It is important to accurately estimate the duration of the queues but it also is important to know where they are located because queues, inside risk areas are potentially life threatening. Finally, research on preparedness for protective action implementation should address the behavioral parameters that affect the time required to complete an evacuation (see Table 5.1). These variables can have a significant influence on evacuation time estimates, but evacuation analysts appear to be making unfounded assumptions about them in the absence of reliable data.

Research is needed to justify the choice between evacuation and sheltering-in-place during chemical emergencies. Such research will require social scientists to collaborate with transportation planners and engineers on evacuation modeling and with mechanical engineers on shelter-in-place modeling. There is a modest literature on the effectiveness of sheltering-in-place, but virtually no research on people's perceptions of its effectiveness and the logistics of implementation. Emergency managers need to know much more about people's willingness to comply with recommendations to shelter in-place during chemical releases.

There appears to have been no research on preparedness for impact zone access control and security, search and rescue, emergency medical care and morgues, or hazard exposure control. Moreover, there appears to be no research on the ways in which these topics are addressed by local emergency managers in their emergency operations plans, procedures, and training. However, there is some anecdotal information about the utilization of research on the reception and care of victims; Mileti, Sorensen and O'Brien's (1992) review of the research on this topic was used as the basis for planning hurricane emergency response in Texas, but primarily because hazards researchers drafted the planning documents for the emergency management agency.

Little or none of the research in incident management has been conducted on *preparedness* for incident management or on the *utilization* of disaster research findings in the development of community emergency operations plans, procedures, or training. Particularly needed is an assessment of the degree to which the adoption of the Incident Command System-Incident Management System (ICS/IMS) has successfully addressed intra- and interorganizational coordination. One of the potential limitations of the ICS/IMS is the lack of explicit attention to the population protection function, especially warning, sheltering-in-place, evacuation, and mass care. Such activities take place away from the incident scene where the operations section chief cannot readily supervise them. Moreover, addition of these functions could overload someone who is already responsible for fire, hazardous materials, rescue, transport, and medical branches. Thus, research is needed to determine when and how to assign the population protection function to the jurisdictional emergency operations center.

Training and Equipment Needs Assessment. A recent review of research on training has called attention to the unique challenges of training for emergency response—including retention of infrequently practiced skills over long periods of time. In addition, the research literature on team training has addressed the coordination of individual efforts, distribution of workload, and selection of task performance strategies. None of this research has addressed the Incident Command System as defined by the National Wildfire Coordinating Group (1994) or the Incident Management System. Federal development and dissemination of the National Incident Management System makes it essential to examine the ways in which training research can be adapted to the needs of chemical emergency response.

Drills, Exercises, and Incident Critiques. Federal agencies have provided guidance on drills, exercises, and incident critiques that appears to be derived from practitioner experience. However, there appears to be no scientific research on emergency response organizations' performance of these tasks. This is unfortunate because there is relevant research on individual and team training that is relevant to this problem. For example, Hackman and Wageman (2005) proposed a model of team coaching that contains relevant concepts. An assessment of the applicability of this model to emergency response organizations is needed.

Misuse Scenario. Emergency preparedness for the misuse scenario can be achieved by prompt epidemiological surveillance that detects and recognizes a common source for seemingly disparate illnesses or deaths. Hazard detection can be followed by prompt action to remove contaminated products from the marketplace and warn consumers to return items from potentially contaminated lots to official collection points.

Recovery Preparedness for the Storage and Transportation Scenarios

Pre-impact recovery planning has been advocated by a number of scholars, but research evaluating its effectiveness is quite limited. Available research indicates that pre-impact recovery planning was associated with faster housing recovery and better integration of hazard mitigation into the recovery process, but much more research is needed to test the generalizability of these results.

Need to Refine the DIM for Chemical Incident Management

There is a need to resolve the apparent conflict between the results of previous disaster research, which support an all-hazards approach, and the increased focus on specific hazards that has emerged in recent approaches to homeland security. Expedient hazard mitigation is arguably specific to a single hazard or group of hazards with similar effects, and emergency assessment arguably also has hazard-specific aspects. However, most aspects of population protection and incident management appear to apply to a wide variety of hazards. Research is needed to determine if this assumption is correct.

How human responses to intentional terrorist events differ from those in response to natural or technological events remains to be determined. There has been much speculation that we cannot use past history to understand and predict how people would respond to events not previously experienced in this country. However, the likely responses to events such as suicide bombings, releases of biological agents, attacks with radiological dispersion devices, or releases of chemical warfare agents can be studied using careful empirical research before such disasters occur. Preliminary findings from the large number of post-9/11 investigations and studies of the 1993 World Trade Center and Oklahoma City bombings suggest that some types of behavior are similar to those observed in other large-scale disasters. Thus, the absence of panic and the large amount of altruistic behavior in these incidents come as no surprise. Other types of behavior, such as changes in travel behavior and product purchases, have not been studied in connection with disasters but have been observed in connection with stigmatized products such as cyanide-contaminated bottles of Tylenol and Alar-tainted apples. It is critical that comparative research efforts be made to document and understand the variations in human response to a wide range of hazards and social conditions if inappropriate negative responses and their consequences are to be mitigated.

Research should be conducted to develop a realistic model of the effectiveness of pre-impact hazard management actions in reducing the physical and social impacts of a chemical incident. Conventional risk analyses typically calculate the area exposed to a specified chemical concentration, the number of people that would be exposed, and occasionally, the number of casualties that might be expected from a given release magnitude. Such analyses are useful for site-specific analyses, but rational priorities for S&T investments in pre-impact hazard management actions should be guided by a comprehensive model that can assess the expected reduction in physical (casualties and damage) and social (psychological, demographic, economic, and political) impacts of chemical incidents given one or more specific hazard mitigation, emergency response, or disaster recovery actions. For example, analysts should be able to specify the characteristics of a storage and transportation scenario (e.g., quantity of toxic chemical, meteorological conditions, population distribution) and estimate the physical and social impacts under existing conditions of hazard mitigation (i.e., building air infiltration rates), emergency response (e.g., warning, evacuation, medical transport and care), and recovery (debris removal or contamination cleanup, resource management, business resumption). Analysts could then test the effects of alternative levels (e.g., moderate investment, substantial investment) of the model parameters to identify the pre-impact hazard management actions that provide the greatest reduction in physical and social impacts. A well-developed model should be able to identify which policies provide the greatest reduction in disaster impacts. In addition, it should be able to determine how much improvement in hazard mitigation, emergency preparedness, and disaster recovery actions can be expected from a given level of S&T investment.

RISK PERCEPTION

Traditional risk assessment focuses on losses that are often measured in monetary units. Risk perception is concerned with the psychological and emotional factors that have been shown to have an enormous impact on behavior. In a set of path-breaking studies begun in the 1970s, Paul Slovic, Baruch Fischhoff, and other psychologists began measuring laypersons' concerns about different types of risks. These studies showed that those hazards of which the person had little knowledge, and were also highly dreaded, were perceived as being the most risky. The general finding that laypersons see the world differently from the scientific community also raised a set of questions as to the nature of the decision-making process for dealing with risks.

The problems associated with risk perception are compounded because of the difficulty individuals have in interpreting probabilities in making their decisions. In fact, there is evidence that people may not even want data on the likelihood of an event occurring. If people do not think probabilistically, how do they make their choices? There is now a large body of evidence that individuals' risk perceptions are affected by judgmental biases. The availability heuristic is one of the most relevant ones for dealing with extreme events. Here people estimate the likelihood of an event by the ease with which they can imagine or recall past instances. In cases where the information on an event is salient so that individuals fail to take into account the base rate, there will be a tendency by many to overestimate the probability of the event occurring. Following the terrorist activities of September 11th, many people refused to fly because they perceived the chances of being on a hijacked plane to be extraordinarily high even though it could be argued that the likelihood of such events occurring in the future was much lower given increased vigilance and added protection by the federal government.

Other factors besides probability and consequences influence choices under risk and uncertainty. There is a growing body of evidence that affect and emotions play an important role in people's decision processes. These factors play a particularly important role when individuals face a decision that involves a difficult trade-off between attributes or where there is ambiguity concerning what constitutes a "right" answer. In these cases, people often appear to resolve tasks by focusing on those cues that send the strongest affective signals. In other words, rather than basing one's choices simply on the likelihood and consequences of different events, individuals are also influenced in their choices by emotional factors such as fear, worry, and love. It is also important to note that risk perception varies by previous experiences (e.g., prior exposure to an event), gender, race or ethnicity, income, and education, among other variables.

IMPACT OF INTERDEPENDENCIES OF THE CHEMICAL SUPPLY CHAIN ON RISK-REDUCING MEASURES

Weak links in the safety and security of the chemical infrastructure and supply chain networks can compromise the entire system. Given the decentralized nature of many parts of the supply chain due to distributed ownership and control, it may be difficult to coordinate risk-reducing measures across the system. Appropriate cost-effective measures must be identified to reduce risks from terrorism when there are interdependencies in the system. Strategies involving private-public partnerships can be developed to encourage firms to adopt these measures. These strategies include a combination of such measures as economic incentives, third-party inspections, insurance, and well-enforced regulations and standards.

One reason that units in the supply chain are reluctant to incur the costs of investing in risk-reducing measures on their own is that even after doing so they may be adversely impacted by other firms in the system that fail to adopt similar measures. An effective investment by any firm or unit in the supply chain to reduce the likelihood and consequences of a disruption is often a costly investment. When there are interdependencies between units in the system there is less incentive for one unit to invest in protective measures if the other units have not taken similar action. Even if modifications of a single unit can reduce the chances of a disruption to the supply chain caused by its own operations, it can still be adversely affected by a second unit that did not undertake similar protective measures. In other words, in an interdependent system, investing in security buys a single unit less protection when there is the possibility of disruption from another unit. In fact, in an interdependent system, reducing vulnerabilities in one area might inadvertently increase vulnerability in another since the terrorists will conceivably turn to attacking weak links when choosing where to utilize their resources. There is a need to utilize existing institutional structures such as trade associations to promote coordination among units in the system. One could also utilize economic incentives such as subsidies to encourage certain activities and taxation to discourage others that will lead to win-win situations for everyone in the system.

The more units in the network that do not invest in security, the less incentive will any specific unit in the system have to invest in protection. In other words, if one wants to protect the entire supply chain it requires coordination between all units in the system through either the private sector or some type of public sector intervention. That is, weak links may lead to suboptimal behavior by everyone. By coordinating the actions of all units in the supply chain, each firm will be better off because its expected profits will increase and society will be better off because the risks of disruption will be lower.

Tipping and Cascading Behavior

There may be ways of inducing tipping and cascading so that the welfare of every component in the supply chain is improved. *Cascading* refers to a domino effect. If one unit invests in protection, then there is an incentive for a second unit to do the same, which leads a third unit to incur these costs and so on. The concept of *tipping* (from the tipping of a scale) refers to many others in the supply chain simultaneously investing in security measures because one or more units in the supply chain have done so. In taking these actions, those units reduce the possibility that the supply chain will be disrupted and hence provide an economic incentive for others to follow suit.

Units or firms in any supply chain are heterogeneous; having different risks and costs associated with their activities. In the case of the chemical supply chain some units may have a much higher risk than others of causing a failure in the entire system through an accident or other disruption of its activities.

These units are referred to as *weak links* in the supply chain. It has been shown that one unit in the supply chain may occupy such a strategic position that if it changes from not investing to investing in protection, all other units will find it in their interests to follow suit. In this case, this single unit will *tip* the entire system.

Even if no single unit can exert such leverage, a critical mass may have the ability to do so. To best effect protection of the entire supply chain, units that could have the greatest negative impact on others in the system should be encouraged to invest in protective behavior, not only to reduce the possibility of losses to themselves and others, but also to induce other units to follow suit. Tipping suggests that it is particularly important to identify and then persuade these key players to manage risks more carefully through economic incentives (e.g., subsidies or fines). Working with them may be a viable substitute for working with everyone in the supply chain.

Tipping and cascading behavior has been documented in many contexts where there is a sudden change from one equilibrium to another due to the movement of a few agents (e.g., the sudden change in the demographics of a neighborhood).

Strategies for Reducing Interdependent Risks

The economic incentive for any individual unit in the supply chain to invest in risk-reducing measures is dependent on others taking similar actions. This situation resembles the familiar dilemma of the commons where there is no economic incentive for any individual or firm to take steps to reduce a risk, but if everyone adopted these measures, all would be better off. In these situations some type of intervention is required to address this problem of interdependent security (IDS). This intervention could be by a coordinating unit in the private sector, such as a trade association, or through well-enforced regulations or standards coupled with insurance and third-party inspection.

Role of Trade Associations

A trade association can play a coordinating role by stipulating that any member has to follow certain rules and regulations, including the adoption of security measures. For example, the National Association of Chemical Distributors (NACD) has developed a code of responsible distribution, has mandated third-party auditing of code compliance, and has actually terminated membership for noncompliance. Other chemical industry associations such as the American Chemistry Council (ACC), Synthetic Organic Chemical Manufacturers Association (SOCMA), American Petroleum Institute (API), and National Petrochemical and Refiners Association (NPRA) have member codes of conduct and can also play key roles in this regard.

Role of Third-Party Inspections, Insurance, and Well-Enforced Regulations and Standards

Well-enforced regulations and standards that require all units in the supply chain to undertake risk-reducing measures can play a role similar to that of trade associations. One example of such a regulation is Section 112(r) of the Clean Air Act Amendments. The passage of Section 112(r) of the Clean Air Act Amendments (CAAA) of 1990 created two new federal regulatory programs aimed at preventing releases of hazardous chemicals—the Occupational Safety and Health Administration (OSHA) Process Safety Management Standard and the EPA Risk Management Program. The OSHA program, enacted in 1992, required facilities containing large quantities of highly hazardous chemicals to implement accident prevention and emergency response measures to protect workers. The EPA Risk Management Program regulation published in 1996 went beyond the OSHA program by requiring facilities to perform a hazard assessment and to submit a summary report to EPA by June 1999 called the Risk Management Plan.

The EPA and other regulatory agencies have been searching for other alternatives to their centralized procedures to implement regulatory obligations due to their limited personnel and funds. Third-party inspections coupled with insurance protection can encourage decentralized units in the supply chain to reduce their risks from accidents and disasters and lead to a high compliance level. Such a management-based regulatory strategy shifts the focus of decision making from the regulator to individual units who are now required to do their own planning to meet a set of standards or regulations.

The rationale behind using third parties and insurance to support regulations can be stated in the following way. As pointed out above, one of the biggest concerns of a regulatory agency is that it doesn't have enough resources to audit all firms in the industry. By coordinating with the private sector, the number of audits the agency must perform can be reduced.

Third-party inspection in conjunction with private insurance is a powerful combination of two market mechanisms that can convince many firms of the advantages of implementing security measures to make their operations safer. If insurance companies provide lower premiums to companies that have passed audit by a recognized third party, firms will have incentives to voluntarily adopt security measures. Federal regulatory agencies can then focus their audits on firms that have not applied or qualified for the discount. Those units taking action can encourage the remaining ones to comply with regulations to avoid being caught and fined. This is another form of tipping behavior.

Without some type of inspection, low-risk units who have adopted risk-reducing measures cannot credibly distinguish themselves from high- risk units for regulators. However, if regulators coordinated with the private sector to delegate part of the inspection process through insurance companies and certified third-party inspectors, a channel would exist through which the low-risk units can distinguish themselves and avoid government audit. If a unit chooses not to be inspected by certified third parties, it is more likely to be perceived as high-risk rather than low-risk and is more likely to be audited by regulators. In this way, the number of audits needed is reduced because units that have received seals of approval from private third-party inspectors are known.

As demonstrated in the work of the National Transportation Safety Board (NTSB), the U.S. Chemical Safety and Hazard Investigation Board (CSB), and the 9/11 Commission, an effective system will also independently and publicly investigate when catastrophic failures occur. Investigations examine the root and contributing causes, including the sufficiency of policies, practices, and oversight in the private and public domains. Future investigations should include efforts to gather data about interdependent security.

Opportunities to Better Address Interdependent Security

The model of interdependent security can be better tailored to the needs of the chemical infrastructure. The following open issues need to be addressed for a better understanding of the challenges associated with IDS issues and the management of risk in the chemical sector.

Deciding whether to invest in security normally involves considerations over a period of time since there is an investment cost that needs to be compared with the benefits over the life of the protective measure. This is not currently accounted for in the IDS model.

There is a growing literature in behavioral economics suggesting that individuals make choices in ways that differ from the rational model of choice. Many individuals are not willing to invest in security for a number of reasons that include myopia, high discount rates, and budget constraints. Others take action because of anxiety and worry. These issues need to be considered when developing more realistic models of choice. The possibility of an attack on any unit in the system is likely to be influenced by what protective measures it has taken. Hence, these probabilities should be treated as *endogenous*. In the case of the chemical supply chain, terrorists are more likely to focus on targets that are less protected. Future research should examine how changes in endogenous probabilities impact IDS solutions and the appropriate strategies for improving the performance of individual units as well as the operation of the entire chemical supply chain.

Economic studies to explore the interdependencies of the supply chain, determine how these impact decision making on security measures, and determine the least secure links in the chain is appropriate. DHS's National Assets Database and its ongoing Risk Analysis for Critical Assets Protection (RAMCAP) analysis should be useful in identifying units that represent weak links in the security of the chemical supply chain. threats to its safe operation. The actions outlined in this chapter are those most appropriate at this time. The framework and methodology to address vulnerabilities presented in the earlier chapters offer an ongoing means by which new actions can be identified and taken over time.

MAJOR FINDINGS

Toxic, flammable, and explosive materials present the greatest risk of catastrophic incident. In the absence of specific threat information, it will be most appropriate to invest in mitigation and preparedness for general classes of vulnerabilities.

Absent any specific intelligence information, among chemicals having toxic, explosive, or flammable properties, analysis indicated little benefit in differentiating one specific chemical from another for the purposes of determining research and development needs for securing the chemical infrastructure. Using the example of highly toxic chemicals, consequences of a release depend on so many event-specific variables that it is possible that a release of one toxic material could actually lead to more casualties than a similar-sized release of another more toxic material under different circumstances. Furthermore, measures can be taken to mitigate the potential for and consequences of *any* large volume toxic release. During the analysis of the chemical categories listed in Chapter 3, it was determined that by focusing on general classes of vulnerabilities (i.e., chemical properties) within chemical categories, instead of on specific chemicals, more appropriate guidance for science and technology investments could be given.

By analogy with past accidents involving the chemical industry, it is possible that a single terrorist incident involving the chemical infrastructure could result in catastrophic loss of life or injuries.

This report adopts the definition of catastrophic incident outlined in the Department of Homeland Security's *National Response Plan*—one that "results in large numbers of casualties and/or displaced persons, possibly in the tens of thousands." In part due to lack of access to the results of off-site consequence models, this report discusses scenarios based on historical chemical incidents that serve as existence proofs (but not necessarily upper bounds) for the possible consequences. Using this approach it is easy to determine that a single chemical event could cause catastrophic casualties. For example, approximately 4,000 people died in the immediate aftermath threats to its safe operation. The actions outlined in this chapter are those most appropriate at this time. The framework and methodology to address vulnerabilities presented in the earlier chapters offer an ongoing means by which new actions can be identified and taken over time.

MAJOR FINDINGS

Toxic, flammable, and explosive materials present the greatest risk of catastrophic incident. In the absence of specific threat information, it will be most appropriate to invest in mitigation and preparedness for general classes of vulnerabilities.

Absent any specific intelligence information, among chemicals having toxic, explosive, or flammable properties, analysis indicated little benefit in differentiating one specific chemical from another for the purposes of determining research and development needs for securing the chemical infrastructure. Using the example of highly toxic chemicals, consequences of a release depend on so many event-specific variables that it is possible that a release of one toxic material could actually lead to more casualties than a similar-sized release of another more toxic material under different circumstances. Furthermore, measures can be taken to mitigate the potential for and consequences of *any* large volume toxic release. During the analysis of the chemical categories listed in Chapter 3, it was determined that by focusing on general classes of vulnerabilities (i.e., chemical properties) within chemical categories, instead of on specific chemicals, more appropriate guidance for science and technology investments could be given.

By analogy with past accidents involving the chemical industry, it is possible that a single terrorist incident involving the chemical infrastructure could result in catastrophic loss of life or injuries.

This report adopts the definition of catastrophic incident outlined in the Department of Homeland Security's *National Response Plan*—one that "results in large numbers of casualties and/or displaced persons, possibly in the tens of thousands." In part due to lack of access to the results of off-site consequence models, this report discusses scenarios based on historical chemical incidents that serve as existence proofs (but not necessarily upper bounds) for the possible consequences. Using this approach it is easy to determine that a single chemical event could cause catastrophic casualties. For example, approximately 4,000 people died in the immediate aftermath of the methyl isocyanate gas leak from the Union Carbide India Limited Bhopal plant in December 1984. Injuries have been estimated to range from 200,000 to 500,000 and contributed to an accumulation of 15,000 to 20,000 disaster-related deaths in subsequent years, based upon elevated mortality rates among those hundreds of thousands of injured people. In this country, an explosion involving 2,300 tons of ammonium nitrate in a Liberty ship at a loading dock in Texas City, Texas, on April 16, 1947 cascaded into widespread destruction of nearby petroleum refineries, chemical production facilities, and another fertilizer Liberty ship ultimately claiming nearly 600 lives and causing approximately 3,500 injuries—America's worst chemical catastrophe. On September 21, 2001, a huge explosion tore through the AZF (Azote de France) fertilizer factory in Toulouse, France when nearly 400 tons of ammonium nitrate detonated causing extensive physical damage including a 50-meter-wide, 10-meter-deep crater; 500 uninhabitable homes; and more than 27,000 damaged buildings. Casualties from this incident include the loss of 30 lives and approximately 10,000 injuries, and resulted in the medical treatment of more than 14,000 persons for posttraumatic stress.

The economic effects of a single terrorist incident involving the chemical infrastructure could be significant, but multiple terrorist events would be required to achieve nationally catastrophic economic consequences.

The chemical industry is quite diverse, with redundancies that mitigate the effects of loss of production due to major shutdowns. Where stockpiles do not exist, market forces quickly compensate for loss of production by increased production at another facility of the same or a different company, or by temporary substitution in industrial processes of another chemical with similar properties.

Although a single incident might not result in a nationally catastrophic economic loss, such an incident could result in changes to business and manufacturing processes across the industry, either voluntarily or through regulation. The costs associated with such changes could be significant to individual companies and to local economies, but will not have a major impact on the national economy.

Multiple attacks on the chemical infrastructure may not be immediately recognized as such. Prompt recognition and communication that an incident is an actual case of terrorism and may be part of a series of attacks offers the best opportunity to take actions that may limit the consequences of such attacks.

Recognizing that an attack is part of a larger coordinated effort may be hampered if incidents are widely dispersed, involve different types of attacks, or otherwise present challenges to recognizing a larger pattern, particularly if communication between affected parties is significantly impeded. Therefore, rapid analysis and communication is needed so that heightened surveillance could prevent attacks at subsequent locations.

Public response is significant in determining the consequences of attack on the chemical infrastructure.

Public response to any act of terrorism in this country involving the chemical infrastructure will undoubtedly be significant and could invoke both positive and negative consequences. While the impact of a terrorist incident in itself may be linear (that is, the loss of life and injury will be related directly to the size of a chemical release within a given category of chemicals), there may be significant nonlinear social consequences of the incident. These consequences could significantly affect sectors of the economy, such as the negative impact on the travel and airline industries after September 11th. It may also impact public morale, affect the level of trust and confidence in the government's ability to protect its citizens, and exacerbate feelings of vulnerability leading to social (sociological) and psychological effects. Conversely, a well-informed general population that is adequately prepared for such events could decrease negative consequences and unnecessary casualties.

Accurate information analysis and communication before, during, and after an event between parties responsible for response and to the public may be the best short-term means to mitigate the possible consequences of an event.

The importance of communication in determining the outcomes from any disruption of the chemical infrastructure.

The importance of communication in both pre-impact hazard management and emergency response and recovery. Effective communication response consists of several components:

- Acquiring reliable data—In an emergency, this includes reducing data errors and ambiguity to the greatest extent possible;
- Converting the data into integrated information and conclusions;
- Deciding on and communicating appropriate actions; and
- Communicating promptly to the public in an accurate, comprehensible, and believable fashion.

The perception of disasters sometimes escalates as a consequence of a breakdown in the communication process. Conversely, a well-informed public can often take action to minimize the effects of a disaster. Information must reach the end users in a comprehensible and useful form; it must be perceived by them as relevant to their situation (e.g., individuals need to be made aware and recognize their hazard risk and potential outcomes); end users must have the capacity and the necessary resources to use this information to better prepare, respond to, and recover from a hazard or disaster situation.

Near-term benefits can be obtained from research efforts directed toward enhancing emergency preparedness, emergency response, and disaster recovery. This offers an immediate means to mitigate the effects of a terrorist attack on the chemical infrastructure.

MAJOR RECOMMENDATIONS

DHS should support research directed toward enhancing emergency preparedness, emergency response, and disaster recovery.

Through study of past events, social science research has derived significant understanding of the components required to prepare a community or a populace for hazardous events and to effectively respond to and recover from those events. Efforts to increase this knowledge and to expand its use in practice can rapidly enhance our capacity to mitigate the effects of a chemical event. This could, in turn, make the chemical infrastructure a less attractive target for terrorists. It has the further benefit that such efforts are "dual use"—of near or equal value in the case of a chemical accident. Areas that could be addressed include

- Means to promote community-level hazard mitigation practices, such as land use regulation (e.g., buffer zones and density limits), building construction practices, incentives, and risk communication;
- Factors that promote adoption of more effective emergency preparedness and recovery preparedness;
- The extent to which existing research findings are implemented in local emergency operations, plans, procedures, and training;
- Development of better models to guide protective action decision making in emergencies (i.e., choosing between evacuation and sheltering-in-place), and other aspects of incident management;
- Adequacy of training and exercises for disaster response;
- Understanding how appointed and elected officials and the populace interpret information about hazards and perceive risks; and
- Better understanding of social vulnerability (i.e., identifying those segments of the population whose resources or abilities impede their adoption of hazard mitigation measures or their capacity to prepare for, respond to, or recover from disaster).

DHS should explore ways to enable rapid analysis and communication of data for decision making and communication to the public during and after an emergency.

Effective emergency response depends on the rapid analysis of information received in a crisis to determine its relevance and accuracy. This information must also be communicated rapidly and accurately to all necessary parties involved in decision making, and then integrated into the decision making process to determine an effective response. This is especially true in a chemical attack because event-specific conditions such as the type of chemical, quantity of material, and release location will be critical to determining the appropriate course of action. Research to determine the most critical information to be communicated between responders and to the public, and the means to gather and disseminate that information, can result in a rapid improvement in emergency response capabilities. Such research would be universally applicable to all chemical emergencies—independent of the type of incident or chemical involved.

In investing in and utilizing behavioral and social science research, DHS should give particular attention to understanding and preparing for the societal response that will occur following a major chemical incident.

The American public has long been recognized to be apprehensive about chemicals. Public authorities will need an understanding of social amplification and attenuation if they wish to successfully manage the aftermath of a chemical attack. Research can support the development of specific guidelines for limiting, and even mitigating, consequences by stimulating a positive public response and preventing negative social amplification. Community members and end users should be actively engaged in identifying their vulnerabilities, disaster planning and management, development of technology, and the communication process. The combination of engaging the end users and gaining a better understanding of the forces that cause social amplification or attenuation can effectively enhance the response to an event.

DHS should support research to extend the applicability of current disaster impact models to chemical events.

The Disaster Impact Model (DIM) and similar models presented here have been generalized from research on storage and transportation scenarios to the conditions that would exist in the chemical misuse and chemical shortage scenarios. Despite the apparent applicability of the model to the latter two scenarios, further research is needed to confirm that the model's assumptions and relationships are valid in these situations. Previous disaster research supports an all-hazards approach, in contrast to the focus on specific hazards that has emerged in recent approaches to homeland security. Furthermore, there is speculation, but little research, on whether human responses to intentional terrorist events differ significantly from responses to natural disasters or accidents. Such incongruities between current disaster models and current security concerns need to be identified and examined to determine what, if any, changes are required to our current understanding of mitigation preparedness, response, and recovery.

DHS should support research to determine the combinations of incentives and disincentives that would best encourage the private sector to invest in safety and security. This will require research to identify the nature of the interdependencies and weak links in the supply chain and consideration of public-private partnerships to encourage voluntary adoption of protective measures by the weakest links in the chain.

Due to the decentralized nature of many parts of the chemical supply chain, coordinating risk reduction measures across the system may prove difficult. To adequately integrate these risk reduction methods into such a decentralized industry, effort should be expended to identify those places within the chemical infrastructure where interdependencies exists and to understand the need to incorporate risk reduction techniques in these areas.

DHS should develop new or enhance existing cooperative links and collaborative investment strategies with other appropriate government agencies and stakeholders in the community and in the private sector as it seeks to encourage security investments. This would help ensure that efforts to mitigate vulnerabilities are developed in a balanced manner. The coordination of regulation with a system of insurance and third-party inspection, as discussed in Chapter 5, is one such example. The effects of hazard insurance on both individual and corporate decision making could also be fruitfully examined.

DHS should support research and development to foster cost-effective, inherently safer chemistries and chemical processes. The most desirable solution to preventing chemical releases is to reduce or eliminate the hazard where possible, not to control it. This can be achieved by modifying processes where possible to minimize the amount of hazardous material used, lower the temperatures and pressures required, replace a hazardous substance with a less hazardous substitute, or minimize the complexity of a chemical process.

Many of the advances required to develop practical alternatives to today's chemicals and chemical processes are fundamental and pre-competitive. The economic incentives for industrial funding are frequently absent, which leads to the need for either a government investment in research or government-provided financial incentives for industrial investments. Inherently safer chemistry such as process intensification, "just-in-time" chemical manufacturing, and the use of smaller-scale processes offers the potential for improved safety at chemical facilities. While applications show promise and have found use within the chemical industry, these applications at present are still quite limited in scope.

As a central element of a longer-term research program, DHS should seek ways to improve the safety and security of chemical storage in both fixed facilities and transportation.

A container holding significant quantities of a hazardous chemical provides an obvious terrorist target. While efforts to strengthen existing containers against intentional rupture are ongoing, there may be opportunities to fundamentally change the means by which hazardous chemicals are stored. For example, methods to store chemicals in adsorbents are currently available but are generally limited to small quantities of chemicals. Research could seek to enable use of adsorbents at the cylinder scale and also to use such storage methods for larger volumes involved in truck or rail shipments or on-site storage. Other possibilities for fundamental change in storage include low-pressure storage (which would reduce the release rate given an unintended rupture) or underground storage technologies (which would reduce the storage tank profile presented to terrorists).

DHS should invest in S&T to enhance real-time monitoring of breaches in containment, the chemical infrastructure and any disruptions to it, and any resulting consequences of an event.

The near-term objective of enhancing emergency response effectiveness can be furthered through efforts to develop reliable detection techniques that can be widely distributed, are easy to use, and would give accurate results quickly and clearly. These can aid in "early warning" of chemical releases to catch them before they become catastrophic and would aid in decision making and response, prevention of catastrophic release, or more timely and effective emergency response if the information reaches Emergency Operations Centers (EOCs) in a timely manner.

In research and development for chemical sensors, DHS should focus on furthering technologies that are relatively inexpensive to deploy and easy to use.

As it pursues sophisticated technologies for security monitoring, DHS should not neglect lower-technology solutions, such as inventory audits and inspections.

Using inventory controls as a means to quickly identify theft of hazardous chemicals may provide a fundamental means to prevent a terrorist attack. This capability may prove difficult if not impossible to mimic with sensor technology. Investments aimed at improving compliance with such procedures would be appropriate.

DHS should support the development and application of robust models to predict off-site consequences of chemical events and ensure that the type of model used is appropriate to the situation.

As shown in Chapter 3 and 4, the presence and use of toxic chemicals create vulnerabilities and could cause catastrophic casualties. Effective predictive models could greatly reduce these vulnerabilities and improve emergency planning and response. Different levels of accuracy and precision are needed for different levels of emergency planning and emergency response. The accuracy and precision of situational models and consequence analysis currently in use must be better understood. While the physics of a hazardous plume release can be described using models, the effect on populations is not yet well characterized. Limitations in understanding of the toxic effects of many substances, and in the understanding of the dose-response relationship of hazardous chemicals over time, especially for vulnerable populations such as children, the elderly, and the poor, limit current capacity to model casualties. Further efforts will be needed to understand the dispersion and toxicity of chemical mixtures. Furthermore, the reliance of early security risk assessments on the outputs of emergency planning efforts such as the Risk Management Plans submitted to the U.S. Environmental Protection Agency (EPA) has led to misimpressions of the potential consequences of individual events. While such data may have been useful for initial screening, they have also led to significant confusion and alarm among various decision makers and the public. Better, more appropriate data should be used, and clear explanations of the change should be provided to different stakeholders.

When considering investments to prevent or mitigate vulnerabilities, DHS should complete an overall risk assessment that would consist of analyzing the combination of vulnerability, threat or likelihood, and consequence of an event.

While the consequences of a terrorist attack on the chemical infrastructure are of significance to the population affected, there is no reason to deviate from the principles and approach of good risk assessment and management decision making when prioritizing investments to mitigate these consequences. Each assessment should consider a realistic scenario and its vulnerabilities, likelihood of occurrence, and consequences if it were to occur. The scenario should be processed through a series of tests to assess if it can be significantly disruptive or catastrophic. These tests should consider loss of life, economic impact, and the ability of state and local government to respond to the event and should also consider the impact of social amplification. This should be followed by an analysis to assess the trade-off between expected benefit and cost of the proposed solution.

CONCLUSION

The findings and recommendations listed in this report emphasize the importance of the development of new technology and investment in current technology and also highlight the need to combine this technology with effective communication strategies, reliable and effective mitigation techniques, and preparedness and response strategies. This combination is needed to minimize the possibility of a terrorist attack and its effects or consequences.

When confronting the potential for terrorist attack, it is essential to constantly reassess both the progress being made and the possibility of unintended consequences when implementing a technology "solution." The threat from terrorism is not static, and it is not unreasonable to assume that terrorist tactics will evolve with emerging technologies designed to defeat their threat. Some strategies to address terrorism reduce the chance of a successful attack, some reduce the consequences of such an incident, and some relocate the vulnerability—that is, these strategies may reduce the chance of direct casualties, but still leave financial and cascading impacts. All of these factors must be taken into consideration when assessing vulnerabilities of the chemical infrastructure.

While new and more advanced technology can enhance mitigation, preparedness, response, and communications for events impacting the chemical sector, it is not the complete solution to the potentially devastating impacts of such incidents. Effective, continuous, and up-to-date information is crucial prior to, during, and after a disaster situation. Research has shown that one of the most significant problems with warnings and dissemination of risk or disaster information is how this information is communicated to the general public. Such communication must take into account the audience's cultural background, language preference, and other socioeconomic characteristics that may significantly influence the receipt of and response to the message. The historical accident record and recent events such as Hurricanes Katrina and Rita highlight the need for effective disaster mitigation, preparedness, response, and recovery initiatives; raising community awareness; increasing disaster training for emergency response personnel and decision makers; and enhancing intra- and interorganizational communication and coordination at all levels of government and with the general public.

3

Cyber Terrorism and its Complications

Cyber terrorism is the premeditated use of disruptive activities, or the threat thereof, against computers and/or networks, with the intention to cause harm or further social, ideological, religious, political or similar objectives, or to intimidate any person in furtherance of such objectives.

If your look at the projected eCommerce number for this year, the Internet being down for just one day could disrupt nearly $6.5 billion worth of transactions. More than just eCommerce transactions flow over the Internet. eMail, voice communications, some banking machines, credit card authorizations for physical stores and the list goes on and on. Information is the life blood of commerce, regulatory oversight and even social status. The importance of the information and the ability to access it, transfer it and act upon it has increased to the point that it is unfathomable for all but the smallest of businesses to operate without computers or networks. As the value of the computing infrastructure increases so to does the value of disruption. The financial implications are one thing, but the psychological impact of the Internet disruption could be even more damaging. How likely is this to happen? It is not, if it will happen, but when. The likelihood of a cyber terrorism attack disrupting the Internet increases every day. The increased reliance on the Internet by business, government and society has made it a prime target for terrorist intent on disrupting our economy and way of life.

Security professionals have expressed their increasing concern over not only the increase in frequency of attacks against the Internet, but also the increase in the level of sophistication of these attacks.While the complexity of the attacks is increasing, the skill level of the intruder that launched the attack is decreasing.This is a very troubling trend.As the terrorists learn from every attack what works and what doesn't, where the vulnerabilities are, how we respond, and the methods we use to detect these attacks, they gain the knowledge that will increase their odds for success.

Could the northeast black out in August have been the first cyber attack? A question that is in the back of many people's minds.

What is the Current State of Attack?

Despite significant investment in technology and infrastructure, cyber terrorism represents one of the greatest challenges in combating terrorism.Every day the Internet and countless other computer systems are under attack.In the 2002 research study conducted by the Computer Crime Research Center, 90% of respondents detected computer security breaches within the last twelve months. In another more recent study conducted by CIO Online, 92% of companies have experienced computer attacks and/or breaches in the last 12 months.If that is not shocking enough, security professionals are worried about the increased sophistication of threats against computer systems.

Here are some interesting statistics.

In the first half of 2002, there were more than 180,000 Internet based attacks on business.

- Attacks against the Internet increase at an annual rate above 60%.
- The average business will experience 32 break-in attempts this week.
- Reported systems vulnerabilities and security incidents are doubling each year.
- The reported number of vulnerabilities a :d security incidents represent an estimated 10% of the actual total.

Most studies to date have shown that critical information infrastructures are potentially vulnerable to a cyber terrorist attack.The increasing complexity of information systems creates new vulnerabilities and challenges for IT management.Even if the technology is armor plated, insiders acting alone or in concert with other terrorists may be able to exploit their access capabilities to wreak considerable harm.

What would the Impact be?

The intention of a cyber terrorism attack could range from economic disruption through the interruption of financial networks and systems or used in support of a physical attack to cause further confusion and possible delays in proper response.Although cyber attacks have caused billions of dollars in damage and affected the lives of millions, we have yet witness the implications of a truly catastrophic cyber terrorism attack.What would some of the implications be?

Direct Cost Implications

- Loss of sales during the disruption
- Staff time, network delays, intermittent access for business users
- Increased insurance costs due to litigation
- Loss of intellectual property - research, pricing, etc.
- Costs of forensics for recovery and litigation
- Loss of critical communications in time of emergency

Indirect Cost Implications

- Loss of confidence and credibility in our financial systems
- Tarnished relationships& public image globally
- Strained business partner relationships - domestic and internationally
- Loss of future customer revenues for an individual or group of companies
- Loss of trust in the government and computer industry

New legislation is requiring system breaches to be reported (SB1386 California). Other proposed legislation would allow damages to be sought by victims of attacks that are launched from hacked web systems.California's SB 1386 is a sweeping measure that mandates public disclosure of computer-security breaches in which confidential information of any California resident may have been compromised.The bili further goes on to define personal information as an individual's first name or initial and last name in combination with a SSN, a driver's license number, or any account numbers, credit card numbers, debit card numbers, and associated passwords or codes.Think of the liability an organization would incur if their systems were compromised and thousands of individuals personal information were exposed and even exploited for financial gain - (funding terrorism).

With the "LoveBug" virus costing nearly $10 billion, it is hard to fathom the financial implications of a much more serious and comprehensive attack.Each and every day corporations in the U.S.and abroad spend millions combating the threats of cyber attacks and cyber terrorism.Corporate efforts reach tens (if not hundreds) of billions of dollars annually and with the increased frequency of attacks, the cost will significantly increase in the coming years.As we face more and more complex attacks from professional cyber warriors, corporations will increasing seek help from the governments around the world to thwart these efforts and stem the financial bleeding.

When will it Happen?

As discussed earlier as the value of our information infrastructure further increases and the capabilities of the cyber terrorists' increase, the likelihood of a significant incident increases.As figure 1 depicted, my bet would be the fourth quarter of 2004.Factoring in the increased value of the Internet before, during, and after a Presidential election along with the psychological impact that type of an event would have, coupled with the ever increasing capabilities of the attackers - that would be "PRIME TIME" for such an incident.Would such an attack have a significant direct impact on the election - NO.But if a terrorist were planning to send a message, I can think of no better time.

Thwarting Cyber Terrorism

Corporate America must be forced to wage an all-out war against cyber terrorism. Securing the information infrastructures will require a substantial effort on everyone's part.Close collaboration between government and the private sector is critical. Even more critical is the close collaboration within the computer, networking and software industries.These industries must work closely and continue efforts to enhance technology security capabilities.Security is designed in, not added on.Until the weakest links in the network are protected we all are vulnerable and may be impacted.The government sector must institute tougher penalties for cyber crimes and increased funding for law enforcement efforts to fight it. Easier said than done.This must be accomplished with a high degree of collaboration globally.Getting countries to agree on anything these days seems to be an almost unachievable task.Is cyber terrorism the shape of future conflict? Is a digital underground developing right now? Will our scientists, software engineers, and technical resources be able to stay one step ahead of these faceless terrorists? Only time will tell!

Computer and information security, data protection, and privacy are all growing problems. No single technology or product will eliminate threats and risk.I do not believe we have even begun to think of the social and economic implications of a considerable cyber terrorism attack against our infrastructure.Securing our computers, information, and communications networks secure our economy and our country.A global strategy and policy for combating this type of terrorism is need now.

HISTORY OF INTERNATIONAL TERRORISM

Terrorism - defined as violent action against civilians to achieve political ends - is hardly a new phenomenon. According to legend, Greek warriors used the fabled "Trojan Horse" to enter Troy and kill its occupants, an early act of terrorism. The sacking of Rome by the Visigoths also qualifies as terrorism. Ever since then, belligerents have employed terrorism and guerilla warfare when necessary and expedient. Generally, such tactics have worked.

Modern terrorism emerged during World War II and its immediate aftermath. Allied and Axis powers alike used unconventional warfare to achieve military objectives; for instance, the Allies used partisans to harass German forces in occupied Yugoslavia. Many future revolutionaries - including Mao Zedong and Ho Chi Minh - learned their craft during World War II.

After the war, the use of violence to achieve political ends continued around the world, including in the Middle East. Israeli revolutionaries used bombings to achieve political ends; the 1946 bombing of the King David Hotel, where British troops had made their headquarters, is one example. After Israel won its independence, both sides continued the use of bombings, ambushes, and assassinations.

In the 1960s and 1970s, terrorists around the world shared a number of common characteristics - whether they lived in Europe, Asia or the Middle East. Groups like the Red Army Faction and Irish Republican Army operated within certain boundaries. They hit military and political targets when they had the opportunity to do so, and generally abstained from civilian casualties for political reasons, knowing such deaths would hurt the way they were perceived. These groups remained fairly localized, and though some tried, they never managed to create a transnational terrorist coalition of the sort we see today.

Recent History: The Advent of Al Qaeda

In the 1990s, however, that changed. A confluence of factors, from the end of the Cold War to deepening global interdependence, triggered a paradigm shift in the form terrorism took. Previously-local terrorist groups now spread their wings and acquired a global reach, taking advantage of lowered international barriers to communication, money-transfer, and human movement.

Foremost among these groups was a band of so-called "Afghan Arabs" known as Al Qaeda. The exact details of Al Qaeda's birth remain murky. We know it formed initially as a loose band of insurgents during the Soviet invasion of Afghanistan, and that it was jointly sponsored by the United States and Pakistan. Al Qaeda became known as the "Afghan Arabs" because they included fighters from many other countries - Saudi Arabia, Pakistan, Egypt, Chechnya, and more - and because they were united under a common leader: Osama Bin Laden.

Bin Laden brought more than charismatic leadership to the organization, though his valor in combat against the Soviets still remains lore among the fighters. He also brought organizational and financial talents from his time running the Bin Laden construction business in Saudi Arabia, as well as hundreds of millions of dollars. After beating the Soviets in 1988, Bin Laden decided to continue his war for Islam where he could.

Al Qaeda started as a small band of guerillas in the mountains of Afghanistan. It slowly grew, as Bin Laden established operations in various countries. Al Qaeda didn't just export terror cells (many of which were, for security reasons, insulated from one another). It also established charities, hospitals, schools, and "consulates" of sorts in various countries around the Middle East and Africa. Al Qaeda built strategic alliances with financial institutions, charities, and other organizations around the globe, from Bosnia to the Philippines.

Soon, Al Qaeda had a global network that resembled that of a modern multinational corporation. It had the capability to move money, material and men into nearly any country it desired, either for charitable or terroristic purposes (or for purposes of terrorism guised as charity). Some of this was clearly legitimate; Al Qaeda established schools and health clinics in places like Bosnia and Chechnya the way that Hamas did in the Palestinian territories. However, these ventures also masked Al Qaeda's illicit activity, sometimes to the point where the two were indistinguishable.

Starting in the mid-1990s, Al Qaeda used this capability to attack American and Western targets. In 1996, Al Qaeda bombed the Khobar Towers in Saudi Arabia, killing 19 servicemen. In August 1998, it bombed two U.S. embassies in Africa. All of these attacks shared some common features. They relied heavily on the presence of Al Qaeda sympathizers in the attacked country, who were needed to facilitate immigration, safe houses and logistics. They depended on the "hawala" financial system, which is an informal version of Western Union, in which merchants around the world act as intermediaries for money transfers. And these attacks utilized modern telecommunications - including cellular phones and Internet e-mail - for command and control.

This sophistication would eventually become Al Qaeda's signature. It would enable Al Qaeda to launch increasingly audacious attacks - up to and including the attacks of September 11, 2001.

Today's Al Qaeda - Still A Global Terror Network, Though a More Diffuse One

In 2001, Al Qaeda was plenty dangerous, as the attacks evidenced. Today, the organization has become more decentralized, more networked, and more global as a result of America's successful campaign in Afghanistan. Al Qaeda has responded to the loss of their Afghan sanctuary by becoming even more amorphous and difficult to track down.

That said, the organization still relies on some of the same financial, communications and logistical enablers. In military parlance, these are the organization's "centers of gravity." If the U.S. can successfully deny Al Qaeda the use of its global infrastructure, then it will be able to reduce the organization to a heavily armed - but local - band of insurgents.

One major facet of this global network is its emigration/immigration capability. Al Qaeda has developed an unprecedented ability to move people around the world. This is largely accomplished through Al Qaeda's networks of supporters in foreign countries, who arrange immigration, travel, housing, and other logistical details.

Key Al Qaeda Enablers: Global Internet Capacities, Global Money Movement

Once its operatives have successfully been placed abroad, Al Qaeda uses various types of electronic communications to maintain command and control over them. Here, the organization has benefited tremendously from the spread of the Internet and its relatively diffuse structure.

With easily available encryption and spoofing (electronic concealment of Internet addresses) techniques, Al Qaeda operatives can send encrypted e-mail from hidden locations on the Internet to and from their commanders in the Middle East. Even with sophisticated Internet surveillance systems such as Carnivore, U.S. authorities have little hope of sorting through the vast amounts of e-mail sent every day, to find the few notes sent by terrorists. Meanwhile, by far the most important part of Al Qaeda's infrastructure is its ability to move money around the world. This capability includes much more than the ancient hawala network.

Early in its history, Al Qaeda built strategic relationships with legitimate financial institutions in nations like Kuwait, Saudi Arabia and Sudan. Today, these banks have acted as the gateway for Al Qaeda to the world's financial system, enabling the group's members to transfer money around the world - money that goes towards purchasing weapons and supporting their global operations. Many of these financial channels have been shut down by aggressive enforcement after September 11, but some remain.

How Al Qaeda Hides Behind Legitimate Businesses and Charities

In addition to this financial-services network, Al Qaeda also retains a network of "legitimate" businesses and charities that it can use to move money, men and materiel around the world. For instance, as noted above, the federal government has targeted the Holy Land Foundation and Benevolence International Fund for allegedly "fronting" for Al Qaeda.

Mostly, these groups do charitable work as the benevolent arm of the Al Qaeda operation. They finance schools, public health efforts, and other things designed to boost Al Qaeda's political capital and create a recruiting base for the organization. That's only half the story, however.

Federal authorities allege that these charities also raise money and funnel it back to Al Qaeda, in much the same way that the Irish Republican Army used to raise money in Boston for its operations in Ireland.

Such charities also allegedly use their legitimate financial accounts and relationships to move Al Qaeda money, as well as personnel and equipment, around the world. One well-known example is the use of Muslim charities to move partisan fighters and weapons into Bosnia-Herzegovina to fight the Serbs between 1992-1995.

Why "Material Support" Prosecutions Are A Key Part of Anti-Al Qaeda Strategy

One of the most controversial aspects of the U.S.'s strategy to stop Al Qaeda has been the effort to take down its support network in the United States. The strategy is twofold: First, it seeks to designate appropriate organizations as "terrorist" and list them as such. Second, it aims to prosecute those who support such organizations - financially, logistically, or otherwise. There are three basic legal sources for such power: FTO designations, "terrorist financier" designations, and "material support" prosecutions.

For some time, the State Department has had the authority to designate "foreign terrorist organizations." An FTO designation means, among other things, that it is criminal to provide the designated organization with material support. An FTO designation must be based on three State Department findings:

First, the State Department must find that the group is foreign. Second, it must find that the organization engages in "terrorist activity" as defined in the Immigration and Nationality Act. (The USA PATRIOT Act both enlarged the definition of "terrorist activity" and provided more legal consequences for the FTO designation. Third, that it must find that the organization's activity threatens national security or the personal security of U.S. citizens.

The Immigration and Nationality Act provides for judicial review of the FTO designation by the U.S. Court of Appeals for the D.C. Circuit. Generally, the D.C. Circuit has upheld the designations. However, on at least one occasion - in the 2001 case of *National Council of Resistance of Iran v. Department of State* - the Circuit remanded the FTO designation back to the State Department so that additional procedures could occur.

Meanwhile, under Executive Order 13224, the State Department can additionally, or alternatively, designate organizations as "terrorist financiers." This enables the U.S. government to seize these groups' assets and criminally prosecute individuals associated with the groups. Most recently, this tool has been used to designate the Benevolence International Foundation, seize its assets, and imprison one of its key officials.

Finally, there is a pair of federal laws that prohibit providing "material support" to terrorists, and to foreign terrorist organizations, respectively. This pair of laws was originally enacted in the mid-1990s. In October 2001, it was amended by the USA PATRIOT Act in October 2001. To date, the Justice Department has brought charges under these laws in several high-profile cases, including those of Earnest James Ujaama and Sami Al-Arian.

Fighting An Amorphous Enemy Means Using Multiple Tactics

Some have argued that these prosecutions are a diversion and distraction from the real task of prosecuting terrorists. They could not be more wrong. Assuming the government's allegations against them are accurate, men like Ujaama, Arnaout and Al-Arian are as important to terror networks as the men who actually carry out terror attacks - perhaps even more so. Without such individuals raising money, arranging immigration, and providing other forms of support, the terrorists in Al Qaeda could not conduct the kind of operation we saw on September 11.

America faces a dangerously amorphous adversary in Al Qaeda. Defeating this enemy will require more than a head-on military strategy, or a crime-busting legal strategy. Instead, it requires a subtle combination of both - and it requires prosecutions not only of terrorists, but of those who fund them. We must analyze Al Qaeda to find its most vulnerable parts, and then attack those parts relentlessly using every tool at America's disposal - cutting each of the heads off the Hydra, and making sure it never re-grows.

To ultimately prevail, the United States must attack every part of the Al Qaeda organization - especially its global infrastructure that enables it to strike across borders and oceans. Those who knowingly support that infrastructure are more than merely innocent individuals who gave money to the wrong cause - "small fish" caught in a big net. They are as much the authors of terrorism as those who do the bombing and the killing, and they are rightfully prosecuted as such.

CRITICAL INFRASTRUCTURE PROTECTION IN THE FIGHT AGAINST TERRORISM

The potential for catastrophic terrorist attacks that affect critical infrastructures is increasing. The consequences of an attack on the industrial control systems of critical infrastructure could vary widely. It is commonly assumed that a successful cyber attack would cause few, if any, casualties, but might result in loss of vital infrastructure service. For example, a successful cyber-attack on the public telephone switching network might deprive customers of telephone service while technicians reset and repaired the switching network. An attack on a chemical or liquid natural gas facility's control systems might lead to more widespread loss of lives as well as significant physical damage.

Another type of catastrophic infrastructure failure might be when one part of the infrastructure leads to the failure of other parts, causing widespread cascade effect. Such failure might occur due to the synergistic effect of infrastructure industries on each other. A simple example might be an attack on electrical utilities where electricity distribution was disrupted; sewage treatment plants and waterworks could also fail, as the turbines and other electrical apparatuses in these facilities might shut down.

Cascade events can be very damaging too, causing widespread utility outages. The blackouts in North-America and Europe during the last two years have put in evidence the vulnerability of energy infrastructures and consequently the need to find effective measures to prevent/or to mitigate the consequences derived from a major supply disruption. This use of cyberterrorism could also result in an amplification of the physical attack's effects. An example of this might be a conventional bombing attack on a building combined with a temporary denial of electrical or telephone service. The resulting degradation of emergency response, until back-up electrical or communication systems can be brought into place and used, could increase the number of casualties and public panic.

SPECIAL ACTION PLAN ON COUNTERMEASURES TO CYBER-TERRORISM OF CRITICAL

Goals of the Special Action Plan

The goal of this action plan is to protect the critical infrastructure from attacks of cyber-terrorism, which have the potential for large impacts on people's lives and on the economic activities of business using telecommunications networks and information systems. The government, primarily the Cabinet Secretariat, in close cooperation with the private sector, is working hard to implement this plan. In addition, as an objective of this plan, there are efforts to enhance the voluntary, independent participation by the businesses and regional public organizations associated with the critical infrastructure areas in the private sector (hereafter, called private sector critical infrastructure operators). Furthermore, the government will provide the necessary cooperation when the private sector critical infrastructure operators implement the plan.

The Threat of Cyber Terrorism

Many businesses and government activities have come to depend on information systems. It is also expected that there will be an acceleration in the use of information technologies and networking. For the critical infrastructure, like power supply, transportation, and electronic control, information systems also have a crucial role in maintaining public safety and stable supplies of indispensable services for the economic activities of business and the daily lives of the people.

An electronic attack using telecommunications networks and information systems (called a "cyber attack") on these important information systems that are fundamental to the critical infrastructure, has the potential to disrupt people's lives and business activities, as well as to cause large amounts of damage, placing people's lives at risk. This kind of attack, unlike a physical attack, can be made from a single computer by a person with the ability to intrude the information system. There is also the fear that systematic, large-scale attacks could be made for the purpose of causing disruption and confusion to business activities and people's lives.

Overseas, there have been cases of damage to financial information systems, and individuals known as hackers intruding critical information systems, denial-of-service attacks (DoS attack), as well as instances of large amounts of damage caused by the spread of computer viruses; so it is clear that this threat is already becoming a reality. The United States is developing a congressional plan to handle the threat of financial damage, confusion, injury or death caused by attacks on critical networks by terrorist groups or criminal organizations having advanced technical skills. Connections via the Internet and other networks continue to develop, and interdependence increases. There is also increasing standardization and commonality in the specifications of information systems. These trends increase the threat of cyber attacks, even on information systems that currently face little danger from outside intrusion. In addition, there is always the possibility of such attacks being made by inside personnel. It must be recognized that even an information system that is not connected to any other networks is not immune to the danger of an outside attack.

Critical Infrastructure Fields

At the present time, the critical infrastructure fields that are considered likely to have the largest impact on financial activities and people's daily lives in the event of a cyber-terrorist attack are telecommunications, finance, aviation, railroads, electrical power, gas, and government/administrative services (including regional public organizations). The ministries and agencies with jurisdiction over each of these critical infrastructure areas are making efforts to appropriately implement this plan for each of the areas. In order to protect the critical infrastructure of Japan from the threat of cyber-terrorism it is also important for fields other than these critical infrastructure fields to refer to this special action plan and strengthen the countermeasures as needed.

Preventing Damage (Raising Security Level)

In order to prevent damage, risk analysis will be performed for the information systems of the target critical infrastructures, and measures will be implemented as needed according to the importance of the information system. It is also necessary to continually raise security level in each of the fields with critical infrastructure.

(1) Raising security level in private sector critical infrastructure fields

- Private sector critical infrastructure operators are working to raise security level by referring to "Guidelines for IT Security Policy" (issued July 18, 2000 by the IT Security Promotion Committee), the guidelines on information security from the various ministries and agencies, and the OECD security guidelines, and establishing risk analysis and information security policies.

- When private sector critical infrastructure fields as well as regional public organizations (hereafter called "private sector, etc.") use information system with a common standard specification, or are connected to other information systems, there shall be proper handling of the shared risk for that field. To achieve this, investigations shall be made to establish countermeasure guidelines for these private sector, etc. groups.
- In order for the government to contribute to improving security level for the private sector, etc., efforts are being made to provide information, advice, and instruction, and to support the efforts of the private sector etc. groups.

(2) Raising security level to establish electronic government

- The various ministries and agencies implementing the necessary measures to improve security level, starting by establishing an electronic government foundation by 2003, and following the policies established according to the "Guidelines for IT Security Policy".
- The special advisory team of the Cabinet Secretariat is providing technical surveys and advice on security countermeasures for information systems for the various ministries and agencies.

Establish and Enhance Communication and Coordination Systems between Government and the Private Sector

For the various critical infrastructure fields, it is necessary to establish and enhance systems for the government and private sector to coordinate prevention, response, and sharing of security data (data required to improve security) as well as warning information (information needed for emergency response and warnings, such as data on the occurrence of cyber attacks).

Particularly, as the threat of cyber terrorism grows, it is necessary to quickly establish a communication and coordination system between government and the private sector to handle cyber terrorism, and based on the situation in each field, it is necessary to develop the next level of systems, within one year of establishing this plan.

(1) Communication and coordination systems for private sector etc. critical infrastructure groups

Build a communication and coordination system between operators associated with cyber-terrorism countermeasures, while making use of existing communication mechanisms, to fulfill the following roles.

- Collect, distribute and share the common security information in the various fields, as well as the warning information.
- A communication system for when a cyber attack occurs, or when there is a danger of such an attack
- Implement unified, centralized communications for the government and related agencies

(2) Communication and coordination systems with other critical infrastructure operators

In cases of interconnection to other information systems and operators of important infrastructure in other fields through networks, develop, as needed, the communication and cooperation systems for cyber-terrorism countermeasures.

(3) Establishing a communication and cooperation system for government

The government, centering on the Cabinet Secretariat, will fill the following roles in developing the communication and cooperation systems

- Collecting, distributing and sharing security information and warning information
- Collecting information when a cyber-attack occurs, or when there is a danger of such an attack
- Within government departments, communication with related agencies and the private sector etc. critical infrastructure groups

(4) Handling of data

For the information collection and sharing, the appropriate data will be provided by the private sector etc. critical infrastructure groups. To achieve this, there must be efforts made to build a relationship of trust between all interested parties, such as obtaining a consensus on handling this data rigorously and correctly.

(5) Cooperation with private sector etc. critical infrastructure groups

The government will make efforts to cooperate with the private sector etc. critical infrastructure groups, including providing security and warning information.

Detection of Cyber Attacks and Emergency Response Through Government and Private Sector Cooperation

In addition to determining the measures to be taken for each of the critical infrastructure fields in the event of a cyber attack, or when there is a danger of such an attack, it is necessary to strengthen the response capabilities of the government and private sector overall.

(1) Detection of cyber attacks

- The government and private sector etc. critical infrastructure operators shall determine in advance the appropriate handling measures for the situation, including type and extent of the damage, and locations, in the event that damage occurs to a key information system, assuming that it is difficult to judge whether it is a cyber attack, based on adequate consideration of the potential scenarios.
- The government and private sector etc. critical infrastructure operators will collect security data and warning data from government agencies, organizations related to information security, and information system vendors, etc.

(2) Establishing an emergency response plan

- To establish countermeasures and an emergency response plan in the event of a cyber attack, or when there is a danger of such an attack on the private sector etc. critical infrastructure operators, investigate while making use of the communications systems established as described in section 5. (Expected issues for the emergency response plan)

Communication, containment of damage, verification of safety, recovery (temporary measures), prevention of recurrence, etc.

Furthermore, it is important that this plan outlines the procedures over time after a cyber attack is detected, so that it is possible to respond quickly.

- The actions during an emergency will sometimes require a high-level judgement, so procedures like the emergency response plan will be determined so that the appropriate persons, having the proper authority and responsibility, can make decisions quickly.

(3) Information and communication procedures during an emergency

- In the event of a cyber-attack, or when there is an information indicating a danger of such an attack, the emergency information communication procedure is as follows.

(a) Communication of information related to the cyber attack

1. The ministry, agency or private sector, etc. critical infrastructure operator that is subject to a cyber attack, or obtains information indicating the danger of such an attack, in addition to quickly taking the appropriate steps, will also provide the relevant information to the specified personnel in other key private sector infrastructure fields, local government offices, and related agencies.
2. The ministries and agencies that receive this information will provide guidance and advice to the private sector, etc. critical infrastructure operators subjected to the attack, as well as informing the Cabinet Secretariat of the relevant information.
3. The Cabinet Secretariat will coordinate the related ministries and agencies, and collect information.

(b) Communication of warning information

4. The Cabinet Secretariat notifies the various ministries and agencies of warning information when it is necessary

based on the contents of the information indicating an attack or the danger of an attack.

5. When the various ministries and agencies receive warnings from the Cabinet Secretariat, they will quickly notify the local private sector etc. critical infrastructure operators.
   - The government and private sector, etc. critical infrastructure operators will run drills of cyber terrorism countermeasures as necessary.
   - In the event that people's lives or business economic activities are affected due to damage from an attack, the government and private sector, etc. critical infrastructure operators will make every effort to quickly provide the relevant information to those involved.

(4) Strengthening the government's emergency response system

- In the event of a cyber attack, or when there is a danger of such an attack, the Cabinet Secretariat will collect information and coordinate the cooperation and efforts of the various ministries, as well as organizing the ministries and agencies for the action guidelines when it is necessary for the government to take action.
- The Cabinet Secretariat will establish the required communications systems with the cooperation of the various ministries and agencies. In addition, the information gathering system and the response systems for cyber terrorism will be enhanced by the various ministries and agencies.

Establish Foundations of Information Security

Training of personnel, research and development, widespread application, and appropriate laws and regulations on information security fundamentals is required in order to further develop countermeasures to cyber terrorism.

To provide protection from cyber attacks on critical infrastructure, the operators and users of general information systems, not just those of the key systems, must be aware of the threat of cyber attacks, deepen their understanding of the need for security measures, and take the necessary security countermeasures so that there is a widespread general awareness and effort to handle this issue.

(1) Promote development of human resources

- The government and private sector, etc. critical infrastructure operators will work to continuously train educate personnel, and to develop specialists in security technology.

(2) Promote research and development

- The government and private sector, etc. critical infrastructure operators will promote cooperation and communication between the government and the private sector on research of the technology, countermeasures, threat analysis, and development of the required technology to build a strong foundation against the threat of cyber terrorism.

(3) Promote widespread application

- The government will announce the occurrences of illegal access, publicize information on defense against illegal access, and raise general awareness on cyber terrorism threats both inside and outside Japan.
- The government will promote research and study of information security for the personnel of the private sector, etc. critical infrastructure operators.

(4) Add and revise legislation

- The government will consider changes to the law, such as the basic criminal law, from the perspective of maintaining safety for the telecommunications networks and international harmony.

International Cooperation

Cyber attacks can be made without regard for national boundaries, so international cooperation and coordination is required in order to handle such attacks.

- The government and private sector, etc. key infrastructure operators will work to accumulate information from information security organizations outside Japan.

- The government will promote cooperation with the international organizations related to cyber-terrorism of the OECD and G8.
- The government will work to strengthen international cooperation, information exchanges and shared training with the counterparts in other nations.

Action Plan Revisions

This action plan is the first version, focused on establishing a means of communication and coordination between the government and the private sector. The government will periodically review and revise this plan as required, according to future progress and developments.

4

Control Systems and the Terrorist Threat

Much of the U.S. critical infrastructure is potentially vulnerable to cyber-attack. Industrial control computer systems involved in this infrastructure are specific points of vulnerability, as cyber-security for these systems has not been previously perceived as a high priority. Industry sectors potentially affected by a cyber-attack on process control systems include the electrical, telephone, water, chemical, and energy sectors. The federal government has issued warnings regarding increases in terrorist interest in the cyber-security of industrial control systems, citing international terrorist organization interest in critical infrastructure and increases in cyber-attacks on critical infrastructure computer systems. The potential consequences of a successful cyber-attack on critical infrastructure industrial control systems range from a temporary loss of service to catastrophic infrastructure failure affecting multiple states for an extended duration.

The National Strategy for Securing Cyberspace, released in February 2003, contains a number of suggestions regarding security measures for control systems. A focus on the further integration of public/private partnerships and information sharing is described, along with suggestions that standards for securing control systems be developed and implemented.

The Homeland Security Act of 2002 (P.L. 107-296) transferred and integrated several federal entities that play a role in cyber-security of control systems into the Department of Homeland Security. These entities include the Critical Infrastructure Assurance Office, the National Infrastructure

Protection Center, the National Infrastructure Simulation and Analysis Center, and parts of the Department of Energy's Office of Energy Assurance. Additionally, the Homeland Security Act of 2002 created a new class of information, critical infrastructure information, which can be withheld from the public by the federal government.

Efforts in increasing the cyber-security of control systems occur both at federal government facilities and, in critical infrastructure sectors, through industry groups. The Department of Energy National Laboratories, the Department of Defense, and the National Institute of Standards and Technology all have programs to assess and ameliorate the cyber-vulnerabilities of control systems. Industry-based research into standards, best practices, and control system encryption is ongoing in the natural gas and electricity sector.

Possible policy options for congressional consideration include further development of uniform standards for infrastructure cyber-protection; growth in research into security methods for industrial control systems; assessing the effectiveness of the new exemptions to the Freedom of Information Act; and the integration of previous offices in the new Department of Homeland Security. This report will be updated as events warrant.

INTRODUCTION

This chapter addresses the cyber-vulnerability of critical infrastructure industries which regularly use industrial control systems. Industrial control systems may be vulnerable to infiltration by different routes, including wireless transmission, direct access to control system computers, exploitation of dial-up modems used for maintenance, or through the Internet. This report will specifically discuss the potential for access to industrial control systems through the Internet. The vulnerability of U.S. critical infrastructure to cyber-attack and catastrophic failure was brought to light in 1997 in the report of the President's Commission on Critical Infrastructure Protection. Among other concerns, the computer systems used to remotely control process equipment were highlighted as specific points of vulnerability. These systems were updated during the Y2K crisis, but their cybersecurity generally has not been a high priority. The events of September 11, 2001 have heightened the public awareness of the nation's vulnerability to terrorist attack, and a National Research Council report has identified "the potential for attack on control systems" as requiring "urgent attention."

Critical infrastructure is defined in the USA PATRIOT Act as those "systems and assets, whether physical or virtual, so vital to the United States that the incapacity or destruction of such systems and assets would have a debilitating impact on security, national economic security, national public health or safety, or any combination of those matters." Several industry sectors considered to be critical infrastructures use industrial control systems in their daily activities. These industries could be significantly affected by a cyber-attack targeting industrial control systems such as supervisory control and data acquisition (SCADA) systems, distributed control systems, and others. The President's Commission on Critical Infrastructure Protection report stated,

From the cyber perspective, SCADA systems offer some of the most attractive targets to disgruntled insiders and saboteurs intent on triggering a catastrophic event. With the exponential growth of information system networks that interconnect the business, administrative, and operational systems, significant disruption would result if an intruder were able to access a SCADA system and modify the data used for operational decisions, or modify programs that control critical industry equipment or the data reported to control centers.

CURRENT INDUSTRIAL CONTROL SYSTEM VULNERABILITY

The most commonly discussed industrial control systems include supervisory control and data acquisition (SCADA) systems and distributed control systems (DCS). SCADA systems are often used for remote monitoring over a large geographic area and to transmit commands to remote assets, such as valves and switches. For example, they can be found in water utilities and oil pipelines, where they monitor flow rates and pressures. Based on the data that these systems provide, computer programs or operators at a central control center balance the flow of material. Generally, SCADA systems process little data internally, instead performing analysis in a more central location, but are the primary conduits for raw data to and commands from a control center. They may be vulnerable to implantation of faulty data and to remote access through dial-up modems used for maintenance.

Distributed control systems are process control systems, commonly deployed in a single manufacturing or production complex, characterized by a network of computers. DCS generally provide processed information to, or a series of commands from, a central location. For example, at a chemical plant, a DCS might simultaneously monitor the temperature of a series of reactors and control the rate at which reactants are mixed together, while performing real time process optimization and reporting the progress of the reaction. An attack targeting a DCS might cause extensive damage at a single facility, but might not affect more than the single site. These process control systems can be interconnected within a single industry as well. This might be the case in an infrastructure which both transports and processes material. As an example, the oil and gas infrastructures contain both processing and refining sites, as well as holding facilities and distribution systems. Refining and processing sites may utilize DCS in discrete locations. The distribution and holding facilities might be managed by a SCADA system which collected data from and issued commands to different geographic sites from a single location. Industrial control system technologies are often employed in critical infrastructure industries to allow a single control center to manage multiple sites. Industrial control systems were originally implemented as isolated, separate networks. They were viewed as secure systems which protected remote locations from being physically broken into and mistreated. For example, the establishment of remote control systems in dams reportedly protected against unlawful release of the dammed water, as no hand-operable valves and switches were accessible. The networking of industrial control systems on a greater scale has led to increased synergy and efficiency, and, due to market needs (e.g. deregulated markets), real time information from these systems is increasingly important for commercial purposes. Consequently, industrial control systems are becoming linked to corporate computer systems, potentially making them vulnerable to cyber-attack through the Internet. Original control systems were designed to be free standing networks without Internet access. Therefore, it has been necessary to add network access capabilities to these legacy systems to integrate them into the corporate structure. This has created, in the worst cases, a labyrinth of connections which is perhaps not rigorously constructed for cyber-security or well documented. Many organizations, including the General Accounting Office, researchers at several Department of Energy National Laboratories, and private security and consulting companies, have identified systemic and specific security vulnerabilities in select process control systems. Among these vulnerabilities are poor cybersecurity practices, such as weak passwords, a lack of robust protocols, and communication in clear text. While some vulnerabilities arise from the manner by which the process control system is operated, others are believed to be integral to the control system configuration itself.

Some industrial control systems, including legacy systems, are proprietary, and contain non-standard architectures and command syntax. This can be considered both an advantage and a disadvantage. Proprietary systems with esoteric command structures are often non-intuitive, and could be difficult to operate by an untrained individual. Incorrect commands could cause no results, and may increase the probability that the intruder would be noticed and removed from the system. Additionally, different companies may have different command sets, even if they are both members of the same industry, as their proprietary systems may have significantly different structures. Thus, if a hacker or terrorist successfully attacks one company, that experience may not be valuable for use at the next company.

Others assert that many new control systems, as well as upgrades to legacy systems, are being assembled from commercial, off-the-shelf equipment and software, providing commonalities across different industry sectors. They point to the needs of system maintenance and new component integration as leading to similar control system architectures both within and between critical infrastructure sectors. By adopting such equipment and software, vulnerabilities that are identified impact all sectors. The degree of integration between control system networks and publicly accessible networks is difficult to judge from the open literature. This makes assessment of the vulnerability of critical infrastructure industries from Internet based attack difficult to know with certainty. Faced with an unclear risk, it may be difficult, from an industry perspective, to justify the additional costs of upgrading privately-held industrial control systems to higher security standards. Current offthe- shelf industrial control systems have been designed for operational speed and functionality, rather than for secure operation, and therefore may not have a high degree of operational security. Addition of security requirements may degrade the performance of these components below operating standards.

Events have shown that utility control system networks may be vulnerable to cyber-based incidents. Computers at an inactive nuclear power plant in Ohio were infected by the Slammer worm in January 2003. The infection disabled some computer functionality, including monitoring systems for portions of the power plant.

Also, it has been reported that other control system computers have been compromised by other viruses. Given the uncertain vulnerability level and the potential systemic weaknesses involved in current off-the-shelf technology, there appears to be little market incentive to directly increase industrial control systems security. Therefore the security systems for the corporate network, which block initial intrusion through the Internet, may be the sole planned protection for the industrial control systems. Such an approach has been criticized, as while it may provide initial barriers to intrusion, it would not reduce any inherent vulnerabilities in the control system network.

Security analysts also contend that industrial control systems are less obscure now than when they were initially developed. Foreign utility companies increasingly use current commercial off-the-shelf industrial control systems, increasing the international availability of systems and their documentation. Due to the similarity between these systems and systems installed domestically, potential terrorists need not break into an American utility to test their plans. Instead, preliminary testing might be performed outside of the United States on equipment held in other countries.

Some security analysts believe that the industrial control system vulnerability should be addressed before potentially catastrophic events occur, and that techniques for reducing the vulnerability are already known. They contend that the majority of attacks on industrial control systems will come through corporate networks, via the Internet. While standardized information technology protection methods have not yet been developed specifically for industrial control systems, these analysts contend that if general network benchmark standards were uniformly applied across corporate networks, corporate networks vulnerability to intrusion could be reduced by 80-88%. This would indirectly reduce the industrial control systems vulnerability to intrusion, as routes through the corporate network would no longer be available. These benchmark standards include disabling unneeded server functionality, patching known security flaws, and updating programs to the most recent version.

Other security analysts claim that in addition to general network security, specific protection for industrial control systems must also be established. Such protection might be addressed by successfully isolating the control system network from the corporate computer network or by implementing stronger security measures at known junctions of the two networks. Such an effort might significantly increase the difficulty of infiltrating the control system network from the Internet. In contrast, control systems may have vulnerabilities unrelated to those associated with corporate networks, and may require more specific protection, including against attacks not transiting the corporate network. Protecting corporate networks from intrusion may not address enough of the vulnerable access routes into industrial control systems. Joe Weiss, Executive Consultant with KEMA Consulting, asserts that firewalls, intrusion detection, encryption, and other technology need to be developed specifically for control systems. Some companies have taken aggressive steps to protect their industrial control systems, and are possible examples for how secure industrial control systems can be established. While most security experts agree that critical infrastructure industries which view secure industrial control systems as a priority can reduce vulnerabilities, some assert that most critical infrastructure industries are not willing to voluntarily commit resources, time and effort into reducing these vulnerabilities. Stuart McClure, President and Chief Technical Officer of the security company Foundstone, claims, "[Industries] have fallen into the regulation trap. Unless the government regulates it, they're not yet taking [security] seriously."

The Magnitude of the Terrorist Threat

Some critical infrastructure industry representatives are skeptical that a cyberterror attack would target industrial control systems. Since there are no reported terrorist cyber-attacks on domestic critical infrastructure industrial control systems which have caused significant, publicly reported damage, even in cases where hackers have successfully broken into these systems, industry representatives believe the cyber-threat to be low. Diane Van de Hei, executive director of the Association of Metropolitan Water Agencies and contact person for the water utility Information Sharing and Analysis Center (ISAC), was quoted as saying, "If we had so many dollars to spend on a water system, most of it would go to physical security." Analysts have also doubted that terrorist groups will use cyber-attacks to affect critical infrastructure.

They point to the lack of documented terrorism-related cyberattacks on critical infrastructure as indicative of low threat probability. "It suggests that, as so many commentators have noted, that cyberterror or cyberattacks on infrastructure are an unlikely threat to the security of the United States." Some critical infrastructure companies believe that the potential damage likely to be caused by a cyber-attack on control systems would be small and manageable through already existing procedures. Since fluctuations and equipment failure are part of expected, normal business, plans and procedures for these naturally occurring events are in place. They assert that the damage caused by cyber-attack would be similar to that already routinely seen. Some industry representatives emphasize that the unfamiliar and uncommon commands used in legacy industrial control systems will continue to provide as high a barrier to future destructive attempts as it has in the past.

While utility industry leaders agree that they have been the target of millions of cyber-security incidents, some do not analyze the origin or method of attack. Will Evans, vice president of IT services at People's Energy Corp., reportedly claimed, "[A large utility] could have a million [intrusion] events that need to be analyzed. I don't think anybody has the capability to do that in-house."

Utility industry representatives contend that the vast majority of computer intrusion events are searches for vulnerable computers in the corporate network by inexperienced hackers, and, of the dangerous minority actually performed by experienced crackers, many are focused on economic aspects of the corporate network rather than the industrial control systems network. From the perspective of critical infrastructure industries, discontented employees who possess inside information about industrial control systems are a greater security risk than external attempts to breach security.

There is evidence that al Qaeda is interested in the vulnerabilities of the U.S. public and private utilities. The discovery in Afghanistan of a computer containing structural analysis programs for dams, combined with an increase in Web traffic relating to SCADA systems, prompted the National Infrastructure Protection Center (NIPC) to issue a warning information bulletin. An analysis of cyber-attack data collected during the second half of 2001 showed that the corporate systems of energy industry companies are attacked twice as often as other industries, and that a large number of these attacks originate from the Middle East. Additionally, according to one expert, these statistics do not reflect intrusions directed at control systems which lack firewalls or intrusion detection systems, resulting in an under-reporting of the actual number of attacks. There have been examples of individuals specifically breaking into utility companies' control systems. The most notable event occurred in Maroochy Shire, Australia, where, in Spring, 2000, a discontented former employee was able to remotely access the controls of a sewage plant and discharge approximately 264,000 gallons of untreated sewage into the local environment. In 1994, a hacker successfully broke into the computer system of the Salt River Project in Arizona and was able to gain access to computers monitoring canals. Another example, from March, 1997, occurred when a teenager in Worcester, MA was able to remotely disable part of the public telephone switching network, disrupting telephone service for 600 residents, including the fire department, and causing a malfunction at the local regional airport. Reportedly, an intrusion into the SCADA systems of a global chemical company occurred where a former employee attempted to disable chemical operating systems at a production plant. Often, it is difficult to assess from public reports to what degree a critical infrastructure industry has been breached. For example, a cyber-break-in at the California Independent System Operator (Cal-ISO), California's primary electric power grid operator, went undetected for 17 days in April, 2001. Greg Fishman, a representative of Cal-ISO, reported the intruders "never really got close at all to our operational systems that run the grid." It is not clear what information was compromised during the intrusion, who the perpetrators were, or what their goal in gaining access was. To date, there has been no indication that the perpetrators of this attack were able to access any sensitive information or systems.

POTENTIAL CONSEQUENCES OF A TERRORIST ATTACK

The consequences of an attack on the industrial control systems of critical infrastructure could vary widely. It is commonly assumed that a successful cyber attack would cause few, if any, casualties, but might result in loss of infrastructure service while control was wrested from the attacker and damage repaired. For example, a successful cyber-attack on the public telephone switching network might deprive customers of telephone service while technicians reset and repaired the switching network. An attack on a chemical or liquid natural gas facility's control systems might lead to more widespread physical damage.

Lower probability events include catastrophic infrastructure failure, where the failure of one part of the infrastructure leads to the failure of other parts, causing widespread effect. Such failure might occur due to the synergistic effect of infrastructure industries on each other. A simple example might be an attack on electrical utilities where electricity distribution was disrupted; sewage treatment plants and waterworks could also fail, as perhaps the turbines and other electrical apparatuses in these facilities shut down. On August 5, 2002, the faulty closure of an emergency valve at one of Singapore's two natural gas suppliers blocked the flow of natural gas to seven electrical power plants. As an immediate result, power levels dropped 30%, and even after reserve power was employed, there was still a 8% shortfall. The power outage lasted up to 90 minutes. Several chemical production plants were forced to shutdown their facilities during the power outage, and required several days to restore full production.

Some experts warn of a cascade event, where a terrorist is able to manipulate control systems and cause catastrophic failure within an infrastructure. Cascade events can be very damaging, causing widespread utility outages. Twice in 1996, arcing between high voltage transmission lines and trees resulted in widespread power outages. On July 2, 1996, a cascade event left 2 million customers in 11 states and 2 Canadian provinces without power. Most service was restored within 30 minutes. On August 10, 1996, a similar event caused 7.5 million customers in seven western states and part of Canada to be without power for up to nine hours. The August 2003 blackout of the northeastern United States and parts of Canada, also a cascade event, has been invoked as indicative of the potential effects a successful terrorist cyber-attack on electrical utility control systems.

While it was quickly determined that the power outage was not caused by terrorism, there were questions whether control system failure, computer viruses or worms, or operatorerror played roles in the outage. It has been suggested by some that the Blaster worm, which had been contributing to congestion of the Internet, might have exacerbated the problems faced by utilities leading up to the blackout event. The scenario which causes the highest degree of concern among experts is the combined use of a cyber-attack on critical infrastructure in conjunction with a physical attack. This use of cyber-terrorism could result in an amplification of the physical attack's effects. An example of this might be a conventional bombing attack on a building combined with a temporary denial of electrical or telephone service. The resulting degradation of emergency response, until back-up electrical or communication systems can be brought into place and used, could increase the number of casualties and public panic.

Others believe that the consequences of a cyber-attack on critical infrastructure would be very limited, and that excessive focus has been given to an unsubstantiated terrorist threat. Cyber-security experts who doubt the effectiveness of such an attack range in opinion regarding an attack's impact. Some believe that a cyberattack on critical infrastructure control systems, while having some effect, would not be devastating, but rather only have minor impact. For example, security managers in some electric utilities reportedly believe that experience in dealing with natural disasters and power outages may translate well to recovering quickly from a cyberattack. Other believe that there could be significant impacts from a successful attack on control systems, but that such success would be very unlikely. Finally, some believe that while it is possible to use computers to generate high consequence attacks, it would be much more likely that a terrorist group would resort to a simpler conventional attack which would yield results of a similar magnitude.

CURRENT INITIATIVES DEPARTMENT OF HOMELAND SECURITY

The creation of the Department of Homeland Security has centralized within the Directorate of Information Analysis and Infrastructure Protection a number of offices related to critical infrastructure control system security: the Critical Infrastructure Assurance Office (CIAO), the National Infrastructure Protection Center, the National Infrastructure Simulation and Analysis Center (NISAC), and part of the Department of Energy's Office of Energy Assurance. CIAO and NIPC were created in response to Presidential Decision Directive No. 63, issued in 1998. CIAO coordinated the federal government's initiatives on critical infrastructure assurance and promotes national outreach and awareness campaigns about critical infrastructure protection. NIPC was a national critical infrastructure threat assessment, warning, vulnerability, and law enforcement investigation and response agency. Among other programs, NIPC developed the InfraGard program, which serves as a clearinghouse for information sharing and analysis for members of critical infrastructure industries. NISAC was created in 2001 through the passage of the USA PATRIOT Act. It is charged to "serve as a source of national competence to address critical infrastructure protection and continuity through support for activities related to counterterrorism, threat assessment, and risk mitigation." This center is to provide modeling and simulation capabilities for the analysis of critical infrastructures, including electricity, oil, and gas sectors. It is located at Sandia National Laboratories and Los Alamos National Laboratory. The Department of Homeland Security created a National Cyber Security Division, located in the Information Analysis and Infrastructure Protection Directorate, to identify, analyze, and reduce cyber-threats and vulnerabilities; disseminate threat warning information; coordinate incident response; and provide technical assistance in continuity of operations and recovery planning.

This division has the responsibility for implementing programs for research and development in cyber-security, using expertise from the Science and Technology Directorate to provide research and development functions and execution. The President's Critical Infrastructure Protection Board has released *The National Strategy to Secure Cyberspace*, in which a general strategic overview, specific recommendations and policies, and the rationale for these actions are presented. This document addresses concerns regarding digital control systems and SCADA networks, rates SCADA network security as a national priority, and recommends joint public/private efforts in discovering solutions to potential vulnerabilities. This strategy identifies the Department of Homeland Security, in coordination with other federal agencies, as the department responsible for developing best practices and new technologies to increase SCADA security. Some cyber-security experts have criticized this plan, claiming that vulnerabilities will remain because of its lack of enforcement regulations.

Department of Energy

The Department of Energy's Office of Energy Assurance has also been involved in developing techniques to secure energy production and availability. Part of this effort has been the development of "simple, common-sense approaches to improve the overall level of protection in SCADA and digital control networks." A document describing a general approach to improving cyber-security in SCADA systems has been released.

Department of Energy National Laboratories

The Department of Energy National Laboratories have developed a series of test bed facilities to test security measures developed for critical infrastructure. The Idaho National Engineering and Environmental Laboratory, in conjunction with Sandia National Laboratory, are developing a SCADA test bed to help identify vulnerabilities and improve the security and stability of SCADA systems. This test bed is part of an integrated Critical Infrastructure Test Range, which includes cyber security, wireless communications, power transmission, and physical security testbeds. The Pacific Northwest National Laboratory has developed a Critical Infrastructure Protection Analysis Laboratory where, among other things, the vulnerability of SCADA systems can be determined. Research into advanced technologies is currently underway at Department of Energy laboratories to address process control system security.

For example, Sandia National Laboratory under the Laboratory Directed Research and Development program has been developing secure control systems for the energy industry. Research includes new information architectures, cryptographic methods, and information system security assessments. Much of this work arises from needs discovered through partnerships with systems manufacturers. While a prototype system to demonstrate proof of principle has been implemented at the Sandia National Solar Thermal Test Facility, this system has not been widely implemented in the field. Similar security efforts, though less directly focused on industrial control systems, are being developed at both Lawrence Livermore National Laboratory and Los Alamos National Laboratory.

National Institute of Standards and Technology

The National Institute of Standards and Technology (NIST) has initiatives in industrial control system security. NIST, in conjunction with a number of industry groups, federal government agencies, and professional societies, have created the Process Control Security Requirements Forum to develop process control information security requirements. Through their Critical Infrastructure Protection program, the National Institute of Standards and Technology is developing information security requirements, best-practice guidelines, and test methods for the process control sector. Scientists at NIST are also actively involved in many industry-standards forums.

Department of Defense

The Department of Defense, through the Combating Terrorism Technology Support program, provides support for the protection of infrastructure elements. As part of this program, encryption algorithms for SCADA systems are being developed and tested with the end goal of providing recommendations to industry regarding their use.

FEDERAL ENERGY REGULATORY COMMISSION

The Federal Energy Regulatory Commission (FERC) is an independent regulatory agency within the Department of Energy that, among other duties, regulates interstate commerce in oil, natural gas, and electricity. FERC has published a final rule related to critical energy infrastructure information. In this rule, critical energy infrastructure information (CEII) is defined as:

> *... information about proposed or existing critical infrastructure that: (i) Relates to the production, generation, transportation, transmission, or distribution of energy; (ii) Could be useful to a person in planning an attack on critical infrastructure; (iii) Is exempt from mandatory disclosure under the Freedom of Information Act, 5 U.S.C. 552; and (iv) Does not simply give the location of the critical infrastructure. Whether or not information falls under the CEII categorization is initially determined by the companies submitting the information to FERC. Categorization of select information as CEII may lead to greater information sharing between industry and the federal government.*

The FERC has also published a notice of public rulemaking which includes cyber-security standards for the electric industry. This proposed regulation would require the electric industry to self-certify that they are meeting minimum cybersecurity standards. It has been reported that FERC will likely adopt standards developed by the North American Electric Reliability Council in the final version of this regulation. The final version of this regulation has not been issued.

Industry Initiatives

Some industry groups have taken steps towards addressing control system security, generally as part of an overall cyber-security initiative. Some groups have launched initiatives in developing infrastructure security programs. The North American Electric Reliability Council has developed a set of minimum cyber-security standards for the electricity industry, as well as guidelines for securing remote access to critical electric infrastructure. Another approach is to develop voluntary best-practices for process control system security. Several organizations are taking part in such initiatives. For example, the Instrument Society of America has formed a committee, ISA-SP99, to develop a series of reports on best-practices and procedural improvements which would enhance control system security. Similar efforts are underway in other technical societies, including the Institute of Electrical and Electronics Engineers and the International Electrotechnical Commission, where working groups on process control systems and their security are established.

Some industry groups have focused on developing near-term solutions to the legacy equipment security vulnerabilities. For example, the Gas Technology Institute has focused on developing cryptographic protection of SCADA communications and developing a mechanism for retrofitting legacy equipment to handle these encrypted signals. Other groups have increased outreach efforts to improve understanding of security issues relating to cybersecurity and process control systems.

Policy Options

The vulnerability of industrial control systems may be reduced through a range of federal actions. These include the development of standards, either voluntary or mandatory, for cybersecurity of control systems; identifying and addressing critical infrastructure interdependencies; developing encryption methods for control systems; identifying and establishing technologies to address existing vulnerabilities; funding long-term research into secure SCADA systems; providing for free exchange of risk information between the federal government, private industry, and other critical infrastructure sectors; and assessing federal activities in this area.

Developing Standards

The federal government could mandate and enforce a uniform security standard for cybersecurity of industrial control systems, or support the development of industry developed and based standards. Because of the national importance of critical infrastructure systems, a uniform standard might be developed, with the input of advocates, industries and the federal government, which would include the functionality necessary to protect industrial control systems, while providing for more secure operation. A voluntary, standards-based approach has been developed for server operating systems with some success, and a similar mechanism might be used to develop standards for commercial off-the-shelf control systems. Alternately, processes and specifications currently being developed through industry-led programs might be generalized across critical infrastructure industries and established as a voluntary standard. Critics of this approach cite the many different uses of industrial control systems in different industry sectors as making such a standard unwieldy. Some experts have expressed concerns that a mandated standard would be less effective than a voluntary standard, as solutions to new problems could not be implemented immediately, but would wait for changes to the standard, and that such a standard may not be uniformly applicable across industry sectors. Others have stated that there is a need for federal requirements to assure that appropriate attention is focused on process control system security.

IDENTIFYING SECTORAL INTERDEPENDENCIES

Identifying the dependencies between critical infrastructure sectors, the vulnerabilities that are present in information technologies in these sectors, and the possible cross-sectoral impacts of a control system attack may lead to a greater understanding of the scale of the control system threat. As shown by the August 2003 blackout, the loss of a single infrastructure sector, here the energy sector, may have serious effects in other critical infrastructures, such as public health and transportation. Both the Department of Homeland Security, in its role of protecting infrastructure, and the Department of Energy, in its role of ensuring a robust and reliable energy infrastructure, perform activities in determining sectoral dependencies and commonalities. Policymakers may wish to enhance current funding into SCADA security research, test bed modeling, or critical infrastructure vulnerability assessment to further clarify the current vulnerability.

Securing Control System Communications

Another option would involve supporting encryption research to protect industrial control system data transfer. Encrypting the information transmitted between remote units and their controllers would inhibit inclusion of false information to and from industrial control systems. Current encryption technology may not be compatible due to the time required to process the encrypted data and the level of technology built into control system components. Industrial control systems have stringent timing requirements and tend to be built out of less computationally robust components, which complicate the use of current encryption technologies. While a prototype encryption method for industrial control systems has been developed, it is still in the validation process and is only recently being evaluated for implementation in industry. Further research into encryption techniques for these processes could provide efficient, market-driven technology for securing industrial control systems information. Some experts highlight that securing data transfer does not assure the security of the control system itself. They assert that other routes of attack exist that do not rely on the security of the control system communications. Thus, securing those communications, while lowering system vulnerability, may not be addressing the most likely threat.

Securing Legacy Equipment

Further research and development into methods for retrofitting existing SCADA systems with more secure components or communications may be another method to reduce system vulnerability. This approach has been taken by researchers in both industry and federal government laboratories. While potentially addressing short term needs to reduce vulnerability, retrofit solutions are not likely to solve inherent shortfalls in SCADA security especially with respect to the inclusion of COTS equipment potentially vulnerable to cyber attack. Critics of retrofit solutions cite high costs and potential compatibility concerns as barriers to easy implementation of such solutions.

Increasing Research and Development Funding

A long term approach to limiting the vulnerability of SCADA systems is to provide further targeted investment into developing "next-generation" secure control systems. Development of a secure SCADA architecture may provide incentives to replace components in a secure manner during the normal replacement cycle, incrementally reducing the present vulnerability. While some argue such product research and development is a responsibility of private industry, others may assert that control system security is of national import, requiring enhanced federal investment.

Several National Laboratories have developed complementary testbed facilities to investigate potential vulnerabilities and solutions to SCADA systems. Such testbed facilities could be used to evaluate and validate the security of commercial SCADA systems, act as a proving ground for new technologies, or be dedicated to the development of federal efforts in secure process control systems.

Increasing Information Sharing

The new FOIA exemptions created in the Homeland Security Act of 2002 (P.L. 107-296) may provide a higher volume, freer exchange of information between the federal government and industry, as industry may become more forthcoming about potential vulnerabilities. The Critical Energy Infrastructure Information category for electrical infrastructure information may provide a model for how regulatory agencies might craft regulations protecting critical infrastructure information within a sector. Comments from various groups on the proposed implementation of the Homeland Security FOIA exemption have indicated that industry concern still remains over the potential release of information given to the federal government by private industry. Policymakers may wish to inquire into whether vulnerabilities transmitted to the federal government are eventually reduced, and how the information being provided to the federal government is used.

OVERSIGHT OF DEPARTMENT OF HOMELAND SECURITY COORDINATION

Policymakers may also wish to assess the effectiveness of the Department of Homeland Security in coordinating security enhancements to control systems, promoting government/industry partnerships, and performing risk and vulnerability assessments. With the concentration of previously existing agencies into the Directorate of Information Analysis and Infrastructure Protection, previous duplication of effort may be removed, but critics have suggested that difficulties in integrating these agencies may lead to a reduction in effectiveness. Some policymakers have expressed concern that the priorities DHS have placed on physical and cyber-security are not appropriate for the risks involved. Oversight of DHS's efforts to rectify this potential homeland security vulnerability may provide insight into successful models used within critical infrastructure sectors which might be used across multiple sectors.

5

Examining the Terrorist Threat

'Energy security is among the most serious security and economic challenges, both today and in the future. As the economies of the World grow and societies develop, so does the importance of energy. And so does the importance of the infrastructures that produce and supply this energy' (Dr Raphael F. Perl, Head of OSCE Action Against Terrorism Unit).

In the last decade, major terrorist attacks –such as the 9/11 attacks in the US and the Madrid train bombings– have catapulted international terrorism to the top of national security priorities around the globe and highlighted the massive devastation, civilian losses and fear that terrorism can cause. Moreover, images of civilian casualties in these dramatic attacks have influenced our perception of the targeting choices of today's terrorist groups, which are assumed to focus on civilian targets. This view, however, is not supported by the available data on terrorist attacks: according to the US National Counterterrorism Center's WITS terrorism database and the Global Terrorism Database (GTD), many violent non-state groups carry out attacks that usually avoid civilian targets. In fact, a significant and increasing number of attacks are on energy infrastructures, including oil, gas and electricity facilities as well as energy sector employees.

Examining this trend more closely it can be seen that in 2003 roughly 25% of terrorist attacks were aimed at the energy sector, having jumped to 30% and 35% between 2003 and 2007 –the long-term trend revealing more attacks aimed at energy infrastructure (EI) occurring annually–. With oil accounting for nearly '40% of the world's energy and 96% of its transportation', the protection of energy infrastructure has thus become a top priority for most industrialised nations. Efforts have been made to enhance the protection of these assets throughout North America and the EU but the main oil and gas exploration and production facilities are increasingly located in politically unstable countries that are marred by poor economic and social conditions. Additionally, the benefits derived from attacking the energy sector have risen considerably in the 21st century as they generate widespread media attention and can create broad economic turbulence –translated into higher global energy costs– due to the energy market's interconnected nature, the growth in demand and the short-term supply shortages caused by disruptions.

Africa, with respectively 10% and 12% of the world's proved oil and gas reserves, has 12 countries that are currently net oil exporters. Its leading producers are Nigeria, Algeria, Libya and Angola. A closer look, however, shows that Africa's web of oil and gas pipelines and critical facilities are frequently in areas subject to internecine strife and home to transnational terrorist groups. North Africa is an important source of energy –mainly gas– for Europe, particularly for Spain, Italy and France, who are dependent on North African gas supplies to meet much of their energy needs. However, resources in the region are threatened by ongoing conflict and violent politically-motivated groups –such as al-Qaeda of the Islamic Maghreb (AQIM)– that have begun to threaten and/or attack the energy sector. This paper examines the changing global energy security scenario and highlights the threat to energy infrastructure in North Africa and its implications for Europe.

A Changing Scenario

Since the 1980s, energy infrastructure has been used as a strategic weapon and symbolic economic target by various non-state armed groups operating in many largely fragile countries. But while targeting energy infrastructure is not an entirely new phenomenon, in the 21st century local events have global consequences, communications and information move rapidly through a variety of media, financial systems are intertwined and developing nations now compete for vital natural resources to feed their burgeoning economies. According to the US State Department, between 1996 and 2004 there were at least 80 terrorist attacks against oil companies worldwide, that resulted in kidnappings, casualties, damages and large monetary losses.

This trend shows that not only are energy resources being targeted both inside and outside conflict zones, but that the energy sector is increasingly sensitive to disruptions, whether perceived or real, due to a number of factors that relate to the 'peaking' of supplies. Such factors include increased demand from growing developing economies –as well as continued robust demand from developed countries–, short-term supply shortages, tight production characteristics (little spare capacity for oil production) and the lack of growth in OPEC production between 2005 and 2007, accelerated speculation, higher oil exploration and development cost (much of it in deep-water, offshore locations), a weaker US dollar and increased commodity prices. In short, higher energy costs have been the result of market fears that rising demand will eventually outgrow available supply. These concerns are reinforced by threats to energy supplies. The current climate, in which crude oil prices have dropped beneath US$40 per barrel –due to circumstances arising from the global credit crunch–, has led to a lower demand and hence a situation of oversupply, is only temporary. OPEC has already begun to cut its supply in an effort to keep oil prices at around US$40-50 per barrel during this downturn. Once the global economy recovers, however, and demand starts to grow again, oil prices will most likely rise to new heights. Hence, in the long-term, the markets will continue to be sensitive to disruptions.

While market-related factors, such as tighter supply chains and changes in demand, are the primary areas that dictate global energy costs, other events such as geopolitical turbulence and threats of any kind to the oil infrastructure create uncertainty and also affect prices. Uncertainty results in a security premium being placed on oil prices. According to the international energy consultant Dr Gal Luft, 'whether perpetuated for political or criminal reasons, assaults on oil infrastructure have added a "fear premium" of roughly US$10 per barrel of oil'. Thus a single energy 'event' can create 'shockwaves through the world energy order, push prices up or down, and set off tectonic shifts in global wealth and power'.

Thus, while energy infrastructure has been targeted for many years in various countries, the effects of attacks have only recently generated more attention.

Grasping the Trends

Elements of energy infrastructures, such as oil pipelines and electrical pylons, are easily accessible and present the perfect 'soft' target that can result in economic damage and losses if attacked. Various armed groups have now incorporated energy infrastructures into their attacks. In Asia, since the 1980s the Kurdistan Workers' Party (PKK) has threatened and carried out sporadic attacks on oil and gas pipelines in Turkey and northern Iraq –most recently against the newly constructed Baku-Tbilisi-Ceyhan (BTC) pipeline–. In Pakistan, Baluchi militias have also carried out numerous attacks against power transmission lines and gas installations resulting in disruptions to electricity in the Punjab, while in India the United Liberation Front of Asom (ULFA) claimed responsibility for a series of pipeline attacks in 2006. Russia is not immune, as shown in 2004 when Chechen terrorists attacked several pipelines near Moscow, Volgograd and Stavropol. In America, the Revolutionary Armed Forces of Colombia (FARC) and the National Liberation Army (ELN) have carried out repeated attacks on Colombia's Cano Limón-Covenas oil pipeline, which transports an average 35,000 barrels per day (bpd) from Arauca province to the Caribbean coast. The most recent attack occurred in June 2008 and resulted in a temporary suspension of production. Further north, in Mexico, a string of oil and gas pipeline attacks were carried out in 2007 by EPR militants and resulted in supply shortages, economic losses and damages, while news of the attacks caused natural gas futures to increase.

But it is the threat posed by violent Islamist groups that reveals the increasing appeal of energy infrastructure attacks. In February 2003, members of a violent Muslim extremist group who had realised the value of attacking energy infrastructures issued an online call to the 'mujahideen of all Arab and Muslim countries in which the West has military bases or are involved in the energy industry, to rise against these interests in the name of the Muslim Ummah'. Al-Qaeda, which had previously opposed targeting oil in the Middle East, followed suit and announced a major shift in the group's strategy in late 2004 by calling on members to 'Do everything you can to stop the biggest plundering operation in history –the plundering of the resources of the present and future generations in collusion with the agents and the aliens [...] Be active and prevent them from reaching the oil, and mount your operations accordingly, particularly in Iraq and the Gulf'. This is in stark contrast to previous calls by Osama bin Laden, who acknowledged the strategic importance of the energy sector. In his 1996 'Declaration of War Against the Americans Occupying the Land of the Two Holy Places', bin Laden rejected attacks on energy infrastructures and called on followers 'to protect this (oil) wealth and not to include it in the battle as it is a great Islamic wealth and a large economical power essential for the soon to be established Islamic state, by Allah's Permission and Grace'. However, al-Qaeda had already begun exploring the possibility of attacks on energy infrastructure in 2002, when it attacked the *Limburg*, a French oil tanker off the coast of Yemen carrying 397,000 barrels of crude oil. In its statement claiming credit for the attack, al-Qaeda made sure to point out that the incident 'was not an incidental strike at a passing tanker but [...] on the international oil-carrying line in the full sense of the word'.

By 2005, a jihadist website featured a 'Map of Future al-Qaeda Operations', that essentially called for more attacks on energy infrastructures and stated that such targets should be a priority for al-Qaeda. With the presence of such a strategic resource in their own neighbourhood, al-Qaeda and other violent groups realised that they did not need to carry out all their attacks in Europe or North America in order to generate global attention and cause economic damage to their enemies. The change in strategy and the call for more attacks against energy infrastructures, coupled with increased volatility in the Middle East and elsewhere, has resulted in a jump in security premiums from US$2 to $15 per barrel depending on the event. For instance, following an attack in April 2008 on a Japanese oil tanker off the coast of Yemen, sweet crude rose to a record US$117.40 per barrel. Shortly after, another attack in May 2008 on an oil refinery in Aden resulted in prices increasing to US$122.80 per barrel. When al-Qaeda attacked the Abqaiq oil facility in Saudi Arabia in February 2006, the attempt alone drove oil prices up by US$2 per barrel. More recently, al-Qaeda affiliates have carried out attacks on oil installations in Yemen, including a June 2008 attack on the Safir oil refinery (a video of which was posted online).

Al-Qaeda's shift in targeting selection has implications for the North African energy security market. North Africa provides much-needed energy resources to its European neighbours: the EU receives 30% of its gas needs from Algeria alone. Thus even the threat to these resources can create future market insecurity and, in a worst case scenario, disrupt supply. With al-Qaeda affiliates operating throughout the region and other politically-motivated armed groups seeing the value of energy infrastructure attacks, the threat to the energy sector is real and in many cases has already been tested through attacks aimed at the energy sector in Algeria and Sudan. The following paragraphs examine the situation in Algeria and the growing jihadist threat against the energy sector. Sudan will also be discussed as it a good example of another regional case where armed groups have attacked energy infrastructures as a platform to air their grievances to a larger audience.

Algeria

From 1991 to 2002, civil war raged in Algeria between the government and several Islamic insurgent groups, such as the Islamic Salvation Front (FIS). Foreign workers were killed during the war, and Muslim extremist rebels warned foreign companies investing in the oil sector to withdraw from the country or face serious damage to their installations. Nevertheless, until 1995, the 'government-owned Sonatrach hydrocarbon company had escaped the violence that has killed an estimated 30,000 Algerians in three years of strife, largely because its oil and gas operations represent the economic lifeblood of all sides in the conflict. Both the government and the Muslim extremists trying to topple it acknowledge that 95% of Algeria's foreign exchange earnings come from the petroleum sector'. Another group, the Armed Islamic Group (GIA), had little chance of threatening energy infrastructures since at that time it did not control the territory through which the pipelines run. Starting in 1995, however, rebels began to attack energy infrastructure assets. As one Western oil executive at the time commented on the insurgent groups: 'Something has changed [...] It could be they are trying to raise the stakes'. Despite a seeming increase in the number of attacks against energy infrastructure and production sites, Algeria's hydrocarbon industry grew rapidly. As indicated by the *Financial Post,* Sonatrach had signed more than a dozen lucrative exploration agreements with international oil companies, which have already spent roughly US$400 million on them.

The heavy protection of pipelines and facilities and the location of oil and gas fields have provided much of the deterrent for attacks and/or served to limit any damage. The stream of revenues provided by hydrocarbon resources convinced the Algerian government that extensive protection of infrastructure was needed given the climate of political instability. Also, most of the country's oil and gas reserves are located in the far south or in the eastern Sahara, while most of the fighting took place in the north and the government controls all travel to the oil and gas producing region by requiring special permits. As Porter notes, 'Unlike southern Iraq or Nigeria's delta states where insurgents attack those countries' important oil sectors in order to call attention to their grievances and advance their political agenda, the key oil and gas producing areas in Algeria are in the south of the country and are far from population centers'. However, ports –located in heavily populated areas such as Algiers, Oran, Arzew and Skikda–, where oil and gas is stored for transport, and Algeria's main gas liquefaction facility at Skikda remain vulnerable.

The 2006 merger of the Salafist Group for Preaching and Combat (GSPC) with al-Qaeda, now known as al-Qaeda of the Islamic Maghreb (AQIM), marked a revival in the Algerian Islamist militant movement. In 2006 and 2007, respectively, suspected AQIM militants bombed a natural gas pipeline –with the earlier attack temporarily cutting off supply–. Other related attacks have involved bombing buses carrying oil sector employees. Overall, this points to an emerging trend within Algeria to target the energy sector by attacking soft, mobile targets in line with al-Qaeda's call to attack energy resources. However, the attacks on energy infrastructures are relatively few compared to campaigns in other states and analysts suspect that this may be due to a split within the group between those that 'want to bring the group's objectives into line with the broader global al-Qaeda movement and those who want to retain the group's "Algerianist" orientation'. In the short-term it appears that while sporadic attacks will occur, mainly on softer objectives, most attacks will focus on government targets.

Nevertheless, as energy supply channels tighten and global demand surges, the threats to Algeria's energy sector have a great potential to create the perception of vulnerability which will in turn influence pricing. In addition, non-state armed groups, like AQIM, continue to change, innovate and prove their ability to circumvent security measures by carrying out asymmetric attacks. The Nigerian-based Movement for the Emancipation of the Niger Delta (MEND) has carried out repeated attacks (an estimated 60 to 70 annually) on energy infrastructures in Nigeria since 2006, gaining international notoriety and causing production to be cut by 20%-25% (around 4-600,000 barrels per day). The North African groups, who operate within this energy-rich region, might see the effects of such attacks and in turn step up and launch more organised and systematic blows at the energy sector. As noted in a 2007 Rand Corporation report, 'Chaos and anarchy could threaten production or give rise to short-term strategies of disruption, including terrorist attacks on production facilities and pipelines'. Algeria's increasing significance as a European and US energy supplier makes such threats of even greater concern.

Sudan

Since its independence in 1955, the Sudan has experienced intermittent civil war as a result of economic and political inequalities fuelled by the divisions between the dominant Arab-Muslim population to the north and a non-Arab, mostly Christian population to the south. Temporary peace in the 1970s, which allowed oil development and exploration to commence, was followed by a resumption of hostilities in 1983 that quickly halted production. The discovery of oil, while not the root cause of conflict in the Sudan, added another dimension of conflict to a volatile region that is torn over economic resource distribution. As aptly noted by Kot, 'Since oil, like all strategic resources, is a source of power, it illogically becomes an important element in the conflict' (Kot, 1992, p. 104). In the case of the conflict in the Sudan, the oil region lies in the coveted territory dividing the north and south of the country. Due to the civil war, oil development was suspended until 1997 when temporary peace was achieved. However, it did not take long for conflict to resume, and the energy sector took centre stage and soon became a valuable target for the Sudanese People's Liberation Army (SPLA), the main rebel group based in the south that fought the government until 2005.

Compared with the campaign of violence in Nigeria, attacks on Sudanese energy infrastructure have been modest, primarily due to a concerted effort to protect facilities situated in the midst of the conflict zone. But while armed groups have not been able to cause major disruptions, they have managed to limit exploration and development through a sustained campaign to destabilise the oil-producing southern region. The first attack was recorded in September 1999 –shortly after the Sudan began exporting oil– when SPLA rebels bombed a large pipeline that carried oil to a Red Sea coastal facility. While the attack caused no major damage, it was intended to 'deprive the Sudanese government of funds with which to keep itself in power and to finance its war effort against rebels in the south of the country', according to an SPLA spokesman.

Following the initial attack in 1999, the SPLA continued to carry out smaller attacks, all of which were either unsuccessful or resulted in little damage. Between 2000 and 2001, the SPLA managed to launch five successful attacks on energy installations in the Western Upper Nile. Following a June 2001 warning to oil companies advising them to withdraw from the region, the SPLA ambushed a government-escorted convoy that was carrying oil company equipment. Shortly after the attack, the SPLA claimed credit for a raid on the Heglig oil field, stating that 'extensive damage was inflicted [...] the production and flow of the oil came to a complete halt. The main central pumping station and fuel stores were destroyed'. While the government denied it, Talisman confirmed the attack but noted that little damage had been caused.

From 2001 to 2004, the SPLA continued its campaign with an intensified effort to cause disruption to the energy sector by firing rockets, bombing pipelines, kidnapping oil workers and ambushing convoys. In one attack, the SPLA had reportedly blocked the route between Juba and Malakal, 'making the eastern area of Unity State non-operational [...] to all traffic, whether oil companies or government of Sudan security'. In a 2004 attack, the Sudanese rebels targeted an oil field and stated that they 'chose the oil fields because this is the wealth of Sudan, which this government is not sharing with all of its people'.

The SPLA has also repeatedly accused the central government in Khartoum of using oil revenues to finance the war; however, in response to this claim, Sudan's first vice-president, Ali Osman Taha, said: 'We do not use the proceeds from petroleum in the civil war'. Instead, he claimed that the government was 'directing those revenues towards development and services'. However, in 2000, a government official in the south resigned over the mismanagement of funds and the lack of resources to address development needs, noting that 'oil revenues were intensifying the war in the south'. Today, the Sudan is once again attempting to maintain peace. However, such efforts are highly sensitive and in many regions violence continues –especially in Darfur–. The oil industry is still a major target as demonstrated in an October 2008 attack when Darfur rebels abducted nine Chinese workers at an oil field operated by the Greater Nile Petroleum Operating Company near Abyei in the southern Sudan. The rebels, who have accused China of indirectly helping the central government fund military operations with oil revenues, demanded a share in the oil wealth. Oil resources will continue to be a major issue in this region and drive it back into war if the socio-economic situation does not improve.

Terrorist attacks carried out by radical Islamist groups within the EU's borders are a concern and measures to prevent future catastrophic attacks must continue. However, as North Africa becomes a more significant supplier of energy to Western Europe, threats to the energy infrastructure in the region must also be considered. As discussed above, attacks or threats against energy infrastructures can lead to uncertainty amongst market players and overall insecurity, thereby raising global energy costs and placing additional budgetary pressures on states and consumers. The worst-case scenario is that of attacks affecting supplies along a key route. The natural gas of the Maghreb is of particular importance to its European neighbours as it is a regional commodity: disruptions that originate in the Maghreb affect the entire regional supply chain. The events in Algeria show that AQIM is interested in attacking the energy sector although there has not been a broad campaign as seen in the Sudan or, in a more extreme form, in Nigeria and Iraq.

To counter this trend and the inflexibility of the current energy environment, states need to adopt a multifaceted approach. In the long-term, the EU needs to make a concerted effort to diversify its energy portfolio, develop domestic energy sources and invest in alternative energies so as not to rely so heavily on oil and gas from unstable neighbourhoods. In the short-term, however, not only should states address the issue of disruption to energy flows by assisting in protecting facilities, but they must also work with the media and the financial markets that react to such threats. Energy security can also be improved by increasing global strategic stockpiles in consumer countries; hence, the international community –led by the US and the EU– must press for capacity increases to mitigate the consequences of disruptions.

In addition, oil and gas importing countries can allocate much-needed aid to producing countries –such as the Sudan and Algeria– who struggle to secure their energy resources. European countries, for instance, could provide funding for costly technology to enhance the security of pipelines and facilities. Other assistance can come in the form of military training, funding police and community patrols, and strengthening capacity and facilities. In Iraq, the US helped fund 14,000 security guards that were placed in critical locations along major pipelines and at facilities. Similar efforts are underway in the Gulf of Guinea and off the Somalian coast where NATO, the EU and the US Navy have provided assistance in maritime security. Southern Europe, which relies on gas supplies from North Africa, might also require the assistance of NATO to help protect key installations in the Maghreb.

While important, military support can inhibit violence aimed at energy infrastructures but cannot remove it completely from the equation, since community engagement is also a key element. For example, the Algerian extremist groups rely heavily on community support to continue their violent campaign. Should attacks on energy infrastructure be deemed to be unfavourable within the community, then AQIM might continue to avoid serious attacks on it. Communities can also serve as the eyes and ears of intelligence officials and alert them when such attacks are being planned or, in some cases, inform them as to who perpetrated the act. In closing, with many new energy sites being discovered offshore and oil tankers traversing uncertain waters, such external state support will continue to be an important element in securing supplies located in unstable regions.

U.S. COUNTER-TERRORISM POLICY AND ORGANIZATION

The foundation of current United States counter-terrorism policy and organization is found in three recent Presidential Decision Directives (PDDs). PDD-62 addresses the weapon of mass destruction (WMD) threat, PDD-63 is concerned with the cyber threat and PDD-67 focuses on continuity of operations and government contingency planning.

The rationale for PDD-62 is that in the future the United States will face asymmetric threats in the form of attacks with WMD or attacks on our critical infrastructure. US counterterrorism policy is composed of ten elements:

1. Apprehension, Extradition, Rendition and Prosecution of Terrorists
2. Disruption of Terrorist Operations
3. International Cooperation
4. Preventing the Acquisition of WMD
5. Consequence Management
6. Transportation Security
7. Protection of Critical Infrastructure
8. Continuity of Government
9. Countering Foreign Terrorist Group Threat in the US
10. Protecting Americans Overseas

Most of these elements relate to law enforcement or intelligence community functions necessary to combat terrorism.

The CIA, for example, has established a Counter-Terrorism Center (CTC) that integrates intelligence and operations personnel working in this field and coordinates international cooperation against terrorists.

A key aspect of the counter-terrorism program management is the designation of specific organizations as lead agencies for implementing different parts of the US counter-terrorism program. The lead agency concept is intended to create accountability in a system not known for this characteristic.

In addition, PDD-62 established a National Coordinator for Counter-Terrorism within the National Security Council (NSC) who integrates the efforts of individual agencies, identifies and resolves issues, and is responsible for crisis management coordination. The National Coordinator also reviews departmental budget submissions and works with the Office of Management and Budget (OMB) to make adjustments as deemed necessary. This type of authority is rare within the executive branch and is similar to that exercised by the director of the Office for National Drug Control Policy.

The National Coordinator is also one of the few non-Cabinet officials to be a member of the NSC's Principals Committee composed of the heads of various departments and agencies with a role in national defense. During a crisis, the National Coordinator chairs the Counterterrorism Security Group (CSG) that reports directly to the Principals Committee.

The day-to-day coordination of counter-terrorism programs is conducted through four interagency working groups, all chaired by the National Coordinator. The threat of a WMD terrorist attack within the United States has led to the inclusion of several agencies, such as the Department of Health and Human Services and Department of Transportation, into the counter-terrorism decision-making structure.

The NSC divides primary terrorist threats into three categories. The current Tier I threats are bin Laden's Al Qida organization, Iran, and Iranian-sponsored terrorist groups such as Hamas and Hezbollah. The priority threats include the PKK in Turkey, 17 November in Greece and the FARC/ELN in Colombia. The FARC and ELN are being closely monitored because these groups reportedly view United States' $2 billion in aid to Columbia as a declaration of war against them. During the countdown to the millennium, the US was confronted simultaneously with domestic and foreign terrorist threats, a unique situation. A major terrorist plot was disrupted in Jordan while an individual carrying explosives and affiliated with a terrorist group was intercepted at the US-Canada border crossing in Washington. In response to these threats, the US issued public warnings and warned the Taliban. In addition, the US deployed crisis management teams overseas and alerted domestic and military response assets. Lastly, the United States drew up plans to respond to any terrorist attack with the use of force.

The United States drew several lessons from the millennium experience. First, greater international cooperation is required to disrupt bin Laden's Al Qida. This organization has a global reach thanks to a network of Sunni extremists in over 50 countries recruited from the jihads in Afghanistan, Bosnia, Kosovo and Chechnya. Second, enhanced cooperation among domestic law enforcement agencies is needed to address the presence of foreign terrorist groups within the United States. These "cells" are engaged in widespread criminal activity to finance a support infrastructure within the United States as well as to provide funding to terrorist groups abroad. In response to this challenge, the FBI is expanding the number of cities with Joint Terrorism Task Forces to improve the coordination of counter-terrorism efforts among federal, state and local law enforcement agencies. Third, the events surrounding the millennium demonstrated that border security between the US and Canada, while effective, needs to be strengthened.

Another area that has received increased focus within the NSC is disrupting the financing of terrorist groups. These groups have developed sophisticated fund-raising mechanisms employing legitimate non-governmental groups and non-bank financial entities that greatly complicate US law enforcement efforts. To rally international support for its initiative, the US supports the International Convention for the Suppression of Terrorist Funding-Raising.

There has been a distinct shift from state-sponsored terrorism to diffuse networks of activists. Generally, state-sponsored terrorism is easier to deal with. Afghanistan has become the epicenter of terrorism by providing sanctuary to bin Laden, among others. Al Qida is more than just bin Laden. The removal of bin Laden from the organization will not cripple it. In a manner similar to a corporate CEO, he has installed good mid-level management that could carry on without him.

This new type of terrorist group is also quite sophisticated. Computers captured in Jordan when the terrorist plot there was foiled contained documents and disks with sophisticated encryption. These groups are also becoming more lethal. The terrorist plot in Jordan that was disrupted shortly before the millennium involved simultaneous attacks on multiple tourist sites with truck bombs, grenades and automatic weapons. With the hardening of military and diplomatic sites abroad, terrorists are turning to soft targets that are even more difficult to defend.

Iran continues to pose a potential terrorist threat. The Iranian intelligence agency and Islamic Republican Guard Corps have developed contingency plans to conduct terrorist attacks against US targets in the event of a US-Iranian conflict in the Persian Gulf.

Overall, the United States record in combating terrorism is good but this is a tough race and it never ends.

6

Global Terrorism

International terrorism involves violent acts, or acts dangerous to human life, that are a violation of the criminal laws of the United States or any state, or that would be a criminal violation if committed within the jurisdiction of the United States or any state, and which are intended to intimidate or coerce a civilian population, influence the police of a government, or affect the conduct of a government. Acts of international terrorism transcend national boundaries in terms of the means by which they are accomplished, the intended persons they appear to intimidate, or the locale in which the perpetrators operate.

The United States continues to face a formidable challenge from international terrorism. The prevention of planned terrorist plots in the United States, Jordan, and Pakistan in December 1999 and the bombing of the U.S. S. Cole in Yemen in October 2000 underscore the range of threats to U.S. citizens and interests posed by international terrorists. In general terms, the international terrorist threat can be divided into three categories: loosely affiliated extremists operating under the radical international jihad movement, formal terrorist organizations, and state sponsors of terrorism. Each of these categories represents a threat to U.S. citizens and interests, both abroad and at home.

Loosely affiliated extremists. Loosely affiliated extremists, motivated by political or religious beliefs, may pose the most urgent threat to the United States. Within this category, Sunni Islamic extremists, such as Usama bin Laden and individuals affiliated with his Al-Qaeda organization, have demonstrated a willingness and capability to carry out attacks resulting in large-scale casualties and destruction against U.S. citizens, facilities, and interests, as demonstrated by the August 1998 bombings of U.S. Embassies in East Africa. Al-Qaeda is a well organized and financed criminal network comprised of structured, hierarchical cells in numerous countries around the world.

However, the threat from Al-Qaeda is only part of the overall threat from the radical international jihad movement. This movement is comprised of individuals from varying nationalities, ethnic groups, tribes, races, and terrorist group members who work together in support of extremist Sunni goals. One of the primary Sunni goals is the removal of U.S. military forces from the Persian Gulf area, most notably Saudi Arabia. The single common element among these diverse individuals is their commitment to the radial international jihad movement, which includes a radicalized ideology and agenda for promoting the use of violence against the "enemies of Islam" in order to overthrow all governments which are not ruled by Sharia, or conservative Islamic law. A primary tactical objective of this movement is the planning and carrying out of large-scale, high-profile, high-casualty terrorist attacks against U.S. interests and citizens and those of our allies, worldwide.

Formal terrorist organizations. The second category of international terrorist threat is made up of formal terrorist organizations. Typically, these autonomous, generally

transnational organizations have their own infrastructures, personnel, financial arrangements, and training facilities. These organizations are capable of planning and mounting terrorist campaigns on an international basis. A number of these organizations maintain operations and support networks in the United States. For example, extremist groups such as the Palestinian Hamas, the Irish Republican Army, the Egyptian Al-Gama Al-Islamiyya, and the Lebanese Hizballah have a presence in the United States whose members are primarily engaged in fund-raising, recruiting, and low-level intelligence gathering. In July 2000, an FBI Joint Terrorism Task Force investigation led to the arrests of 23 individuals alleged to be supporters of Hizballah in Charlotte, Concord, and Lexington, North Carolina. These individuals were charged with a variety of offenses, including providing material support to a foreign terrorist organization, immigration and visa fraud, bribery of government officials, and money laundering.

Hizballah is responsible for the deaths of more Americans than any other terrorist group, including the terrorist network of Usama bin Laden. Among the notorious acts committed by this group are the 1983 truck bombings of the United States Embassy and United States Marine Corps barracks in Lebanon, the 1984 bombing of the United States Embassy Annex in Beirut, and the 1985 hijacking of TWA Flight 847, during which United States Navy diver Robert Stehem, a passenger on the flight, was murdered by the hijackers. To date, however, Hizballah has not carried out a terrorist act in the United States.

State sponsors of terrorism. The third category of the international terrorist threat is comprised of state sponsors of terrorism, or countries that view terrorism as a tool of foreign policy. Presently, the Department of State lists seven countries as state sponsors of terrorism: Iran, Iraq, Sudan, Libya, Syria, Cuba, and North Korea. Of these, Iran represents the greatest terrorist threat to the United States. Despite a moderation in its public anti-U.S. rhetoric since the election of Mohammed Khatemi as president, the Government of Iran remains controlled by conservative clerics opposed to reform and normalization of relations with Western countries. The Government of Iran continues to target dissidents living outside the country and supports financially and logistically anti-Western acts of terrorism by others. Syria has not been directly involved in conducting terrorist activities for a number of years; however, the country still provides safe haven to international terrorist groups and rogue extremists. Cuba and North Korea appear to have significantly reduced their direct involvement with terrorism due to the rapidly diminishing capacity of their economies to support such activities.

The Domestic Terrorism Threat

Domestic terrorist groups represent interests that span the full spectrum of political and economic viewpoints, as well as social issues and concerns. It is important to understand, however, that FBI investigations of domestic terrorist groups or individuals are not predicated upon social or political beliefs;

rather, FBI investigations are based upon information regarding planned or actual criminal activity. The FBI views domestic terrorism as the unlawful use, or threatened use, of violence by a group or individual that is based and operating entirely within the United States or its territories without foreign direction and which is committed against persons or property with the intent of intimidating or coercing a government or its population in furtherance of political or social objectives. The current domestic terrorist threat primarily comes from right-wing extremist groups, left-wing and Puerto Rican extremist groups, and special interest extremists.

Right-wing extremist groups. Fight-wing terrorist groups often adhere to the principles of racial supremacy and embrace antigovernment, antiregulatory beliefs. Generally, extremist right-wing groups engage in activity that is protected by constitutional guarantees of free speech and assembly. Law enforcement becomes involved when the volatile talk of these groups transgresses into unlawful action.

On the national level, formal right-wing hate groups, such as World Church of the Creator (WCOTC) and the Aryan Nations, represent a continuing terrorist threat. Although efforts have been made by some extremist groups to reduce openly racist rhetoric in order to appeal to a broader segment of the population and to focus increased attention on anti-government sentiment, racism-based hatred remains an integral component of these groups, core orientations.

Right-wing extremists continue to represent a serious terrorist threat. Two of the seven planned acts of terrorism prevented in 1999 were potentially large-scale, high-casualty attacks being planned by organized right-wing extremists. In December 1999, individuals associated with an anti-government group and who were planning to attack a large propane storage facility in Elk Grove, California, were arrested by the Sacramento Joint Terrorism Task Force. When arrested, these individuals were in possession of detonation cord, blasting caps, grenade hulls, weapons, and various chemicals, including ammonium nitrate. Also in 1999, the FBI interrupted plans by members of the Southeastern States Alliance — an umbrella organization of militias in Florida, Georgia, South Carolina, Alabama, and other southern states - to steal weapons from national guard armories in Central Florida, attack power lines in several states, and ambush federal law enforcement officers. The goal of this group was to create social and political chaos, thereby forcing the U.S. Government to declare martial law, an act the group believed would lead to a violent overthrow of the Government by the American people.

Left-wing and Puerto Rican extremist groups. The second category of domestic terrorists, left-wing groups, generally profess a revolutionary socialist doctrine and view themselves as protectors of the people against the "dehumanizing effects" of capitalism and imperialism. They aim to bring about change in the United States through revolution rather than through the established political process. From the 1960s to the 1980s, leftist-oriented extremist groups posed the most serious domestic terrorist threat to the United States. In the 1980s, however, the fortunes of the leftist movement changed dramatically as law enforcement dismantled the infrastructure of many of these groups and the fall of communism in Eastern Europe deprived the movement of its ideological foundation and patronage.

Terrorist groups seeking to secure full Puerto Rican independence from the United States through violent means represent one of the remaining active vestiges of left-wing terrorism. While these groups believe that bombings alone will not result in change, they view these acts of terrorism as a means by which to draw attention to their desire for independence. During the 1970s and 1980s numerous leftist groups, including extremist Puerto Rican separatist groups such as the Armed Forces for Puerto Rican National Liberation (FALN – Fuerzas Armadas de Liberacion Nacional Puertorriquena), carried out bombings on the U.S. mainland, primarily in and around New York City. However, just as the leftist threat in general declined dramatically throughout the 1990s, the threat posed by Puerto Rican extremist groups to mainland U.S. communities decreased during the past decade.

Acts of terrorism continue to be perpetrated, however, by violent separatists in Puerto Rico. Three acts of terrorism and one suspected act of terrorism have taken place in various Puerto Rican locales during the past three years. These acts, including the March 1998 bombing of a super-aqueduct project in Arecibo, the bombings of bank offices in Rio Piedras and

Santa Isabel in June 1998, and the bombing of a highway in Hato Rey, remain under investigation. The extremist Puerto Rican separatist group Los Macheteros is suspected in each of these attacks.

Anarchists and extremist socialist groups — many of which, such as the Workers' World Party, Reclaim the Streets, and Carnival Against Capitalism — have an international presence and, at times, also represent a potential threat in the United States. For example, anarchists, operating individually and in groups, caused much of the damage during the 1999 World Trade Organization ministerial meeting in Seattle.

Special interest extremists. Special interest terrorism differs from traditional right-wing and left-wing terrorism in that extremist special interest groups seek to resolve specific issues, rather than effect more widespread political change. Special interest extremists continue to conduct acts of politically motivated violence to force segments of society, including, the general public, to change attitudes about issues considered important to their causes. These groups occupy the extreme fringes of animal rights, pro-life, environmental, anti-nuclear, and other political and social movements. Some special interest extremists — most notably within the animal rights and environmental movements — have turned increasingly toward vandalism and terrorist activity in attempts to further their causes.

In recent years, the Animal Liberation Front (ALF) — an extremist animal rights movement — has become one of the most active extremist elements in the United States. Despite the destructive aspects of ALF's operations, its operational philosophy discourages acts that harm "any animal, human and nonhuman." Animal rights groups in the United States, including ALF, have generally adhered to this mandate. A distinct but related group, the Earth Liberation Front (ELF), claimed responsibility for the arson fires set at a Vail, Colorado, ski resort in October 1998 that destroyed eight separate structures and caused $12 million dollars in damages. In a communique issued after the fires, ELF claimed that the fires were in retaliation for the resort's planned expansion that would destroy the last remaining habitat in Colorado for the lynx. Eight of the terrorist incidents occurring in the United

States during 1999 have been attributed to either ALF or ELF. Several additional acts committed during 2000 and 2001 are currently being reviewed for possible designation as terrorist incidents.

CURRENT TRENDS

In addition to the activities of individuals and groups, two other factors, the growing interest in the acquisition of weapons of mass destruction by terrorists and other groups and the potential use of the Internet and cyberspace to commit acts of terrorism, are factors that contribute to the current terrorist threat to the United States.

Weapons of mass destruction. The trend toward high-profile, high-impact attacks comes at a time when interest is growing among both international and domestic terrorist groups in acquiring weapons of mass destruction (WMD). Currently, there is no credible information that a terrorist group has acquired, developed, or is planning to use chemical, biological, or radiological agents in the United States. However, there has been an increase in the number of cases or incidents involving use or threatened use of such agents in the United States. Between 1997 and 2000, the FBI investigated 779 WMD-related reports, generally involving individuals or small groups. The vast majority of these cases were found to be false or fabricated reports. The biological toxin ricin and the bacterial agent anthrax are emerging as the most prevalent agents involved in investigations. In 2000, 90 of II 5 biological threats investigated by the FBI involved threatened use of anthrax. While actual ricin toxin has been involved in a limited number of cases, anthrax agents have not been uncovered in any law enforcement investigation in the United States to date. Given the potential for inflicting large-scale injury or death, the efforts of international and domestic terrorists to acquire WMD remains a significant concern and priority of the FBI.

Terrorist use of emerging technology. Terrorist groups are increasingly using new information technology and the Internet to formulate plans, recruit members, communicate between cells and members, raise funds, and spread propaganda. Last year, in his statement on the Worldwide Threat in 2000, DCI Tenet testified before Congress that terrorist groups, "including

Hizballah, Hamas, the Abu Nidal Organization, and bin Laden's Al-Queda Organization are using computerized files, e-mail, and encryption to support their operations." While these terrorist groups have not employed cyber-tools as a weapon to use against critical infrastructures, the reliance, accessibility, and expertise of these groups with computer and information technology networks and systems represents a clear warning sign.

Other terrorist groups, such as the Internet Black Tigers, who are reportedly affiliated with the Tamil Tigers, have engaged in attacks on foreign government web-sites and e-mail servers. During the unrest on the West Bank in the Fall of 2000, Israeli Government sites were subjected to e-mail flooding and "ping" attacks. These attacks allegedly originated with Islamic elements and were an attempt to inundate the systems with e-mail messages and degrade or deny services.

The FBI believes cyber-terrorism, the use of cyber-tools to shut down, degrade, or deny critical national infrastructures, such as energy, transportation, communications, or government services, for the purpose of coercing or intimidating a government or civilian population, is clearly an emerging threat for which its must develop prevention, deterrence, and response capabilities.

FBI Counterterrorism Jurisdiction and Role

The FBI is the lead federal agency for investigating terrorism. Under statutory authority granted by Title 28, United States Code, Section 533, the Attorney General has specifically assigned the FBI "lead agency responsibilities in investigating all crimes for which it has primary or concurrent jurisdiction and which involve terrorist activities or acts in preparation of terrorist activities within the statutory jurisdiction of the United States". In the United States, this would include the collection, coordination, analysis, management and dissemination of intelligence and criminal information as appropriate. If another federal agency identifies an individual who is engaged in terrorist activities or acts in preparation of terrorist activities, that agency is requested to promptly notify the FBI.

In addition, the FBI's role as a lead agency for investigating terrorism matters is supported by various Presidential Decision Directives (PDD). For example:

- PDD-3 9 sets forth the U.S. counterterrorism policy and outlines the FBI's jurisdictional responsibilities in relation to terrorism: "unless otherwise specified by the Attorney General, the FBI shall have lead responsibility for operational response to terrorist incidents that take place within U.S. territory or that occur in international waters and do not involve the flag vessel of a foreign country. Within this role, the FBI functions as the on-scene manager for the U.S. Government." Moreover, "the FBI shall have lead responsibility for investigating terrorist acts planned or carried out by foreign or domestic terrorist groups in the U.S. or which are directed at U.S. citizens or institutions abroad."
- PDD-62 grants the Department of Justice, acting through the FBI, lead agency or operational response authority to a incident.
- PDD-63 directs that the National Infrastructure Protection Center (NIPC) serve as a national critical infrastructure threat assessment, warning, vulnerability, and law enforcement investigation and response entity and that its mission "will include providing timely warnings of intentional threats, comprehensive analyses and law enforcement investigation and response." Under the directive, the Department of Justice/FBI have been given the responsibility for the Emergency Law Enforcement Services Sector. Helping assure the security of law enforcement agencies across the United States greatly increases preparedness to deal with terrorist incidents.
- PDD-77 set forth requirements for returning suspected terrorists to stand trial in the United States.

Various statutes give the FBI authority to investigate terrorist crimes committed overseas. Chief among these are the Comprehensive Crime Control Act of 1984, which created a new section in the U.S. Criminal Code for Hostage Taking, and the Omnibus Diplomatic Security and Anti-terrorism Act of 1986, which established a new statute pertaining to terrorist acts conducted abroad against U.S. nationals and/or its interests (Extraterritorial Terrorism Statute).

FBI Counterterrorism Strategy

The strategic goal of the FBI's Counterterrorism Program is to identify, prevent, deter, and respond to acts of terrorism. In the area of responding to terrorist incidents after they occur, the FBI, with the support of the Congress and the Administration, has greatly improved its crisis response capabilities since the World Trade Center bombing in 1993 and the Oklahoma City bombing in 1995. One can look to such investigative successes, as the indictment of 22 individuals in connection with the bombings of the U.S. Embassies in Kenya and Tanzania in 1998 to understand the FBI's far reaching capability to respond to terrorist incidents abroad as well as at home.

Even though the FBI has realized successes in responding to acts of terrorism, the FBI recognizes that the underlying political/religious/social movements which produced recent acts of terrorism are beyond its control- therefore, the FBI will never be able to prevent all acts of terrorism. International terrorists have demonstrated their willingness and ability to strike against citizens and facilities of the United States not only in foreign lands, but also here at home. Fast-paced global changes, such as the widespread growth in international trade and commerce; greater international openness and exchange of ideas brought about by improvements in communications and the Internet; shifts in the balance of political/social/economic forces in developing and established countries; and a growing international financial dependence, among others, continue to present the FBI with new challenges in the area of terrorism prevention.

In an effort to keep pace with the changing terrorist threat to the United States, the FBI is implementing a new management and operational initiative to further strengthen its ability to combat terrorism. This initiative, referred to as MAXCAP05, has as its goal the achievement by Fiscal Year 2005 of five core competencies or capacities for its Counterterrorism Program: investigative, intelligence, communications, liaison, and program management.

- Investigative Capacity is the extent to which each FBI Field Office is appropriately staffed, trained, equipped, and managed to prevent and effectively respond to acts of terrorism based on the known terrorist threat in that field office.

- Intelligence Capacity is the ability to produce, use, and appropriately disseminate on a timely basis strategic, operational, and tactical Counterterrorism intelligence products.
- Communications Capacity is the capability to fully utilize and integrate FBI resources throughout the Bureau in support of Counterterrorism programs and initiatives through the use of appropriate information technology.
- Liaison Capacity is the capacity to prioritize, establish, and maintain sound and productive relationships with external counterparts in the intelligence community, law enforcement communities, other federal agencies, defense establishments, foreign services, private industry and non-governmental organizations, State and local agencies, legislative and executive bodies, the media, and academia to obtain maximum information and support.
- Program Management Capacity is the capacity to effectively direct, measure, and manage the Counterterrorism Program's progress toward identifying and achieving its core competencies.

The FBI recently completed a field-wide assessment of investigative capacity. This assessment has been used to establish operational priorities. More importantly, the baseline assessments can serve as a starting point upon which progress towards achieving core competencies can be measured. Field office assessments will be updated semiannually.

2002 COUNTERTERRORISM BUDGET REQUEST

For FY 200 1, the FBI is requesting increases totaling $32,059,000 and 42 positions (8 agents) to improve and enhance existing counterterrorism capabilities and operations.

2002 Winter Olympics Preparation. The 2002 Winter Olympic Games have been designated a National Special Security Event. Consistent with FBI lead-agency responsibilities for intelligence collection and crisis management as contained in PDD-39 and PDD-62, the FBI is working closely with the United State Secret Service and other federal, state, and local law enforcement and consequence management agencies to plan for security and public safety issues for the 2002 Winter Olympic Games that will be hosted by Salt Lake City, Utah.

For FY 2002, the FBI requests increases totaling $12,302,000 for 2002 Winter Olympic Games deployment. The funding requested will cover travel, per diem, vehicle lease, utilities, telecommunications, and FBI overtime costs for the planned deployment of over 800 FBI personnel for the event period. The Salt Lake City games will be conducted at 20 official Olympic venues spread over a 6,000 square mile area. Olympic competition will take place simultaneously at 10 venues in 3 major cities and 6 remote mountain resort areas.

Recurring Security Services. The FBI is committed to implementing the security standards contained in the June 1995 Department of Justice report entitled, "Vulnerability Assessment of Federal Facilities." For FY 2002, the FBI requests an increase of $2,020,000 to acquire contract guard services for six stand-alone field office facilities where GSA does not provide such service ($1,600,000), replace an outdated closed-circuit television (CCTV) security system at FBI Headquarters ($320,000), and replace three guard booths at FBI Headquarters to facilitate new visitor identification procedures ($100,000).

Incident Response Readiness. Consistent with the provisions of PDD-62, the FBI initiated a long-term program in FY 2000 to develop law enforcement capabilities for the technical resolution of a weapons of mass destruction incident involving chemical, biological, or radiological threats or devices. Initial funding for this effort was provided through an interagency agreement with the Department of Defense. For FY 2002, the FBI requests 42 positions (8 agents) and $17,737,000 to support ongoing efforts in the areas of threat assessment, diagnostics, and advanced render safe equipment.

In addition to the FBI's Counterterrorism initiative for FY 2002, there is funding proposed within another Department of Justice program that is considered important to the FBI's ongoing counterterrorism efforts.

State and Local Bomb Technician Equipment. Within the funding proposed for the Office of Justice Programs (OJP), $ 10,000,000 is included to continue an FBI Laboratorymanaged program of training and equipping approximately 386 accredited State and local bomb squads located in communities throughout the United States.

Continuation of funding for this program will ensure State and local bomb squads are properly trained and equipped for dealing with traditional improvised and explosive devices, as well as the initial response to devices that may be used by terrorists or others to release chemical or biological agents. Through this program, the FBI has provided State and local bomb squads with weapons of mass destruction (WMD) protective search suits, real-time x-ray devices, multi-gas monitoring systems, portable radiation detectors, and computers to access the Chemical and Biological Organisms - Law Enforcement database through the Law Enforcement On-line (LEO) program. This initiative compliments the State and local bomb technician training and accreditation program that the FBI Laboratory provides at the Hazardous Devices School, Redstone Arsenal, Alabama.

SUMMARY

Combating terrorism is a priority of the FBI. Through the support of the Administration and the Congress, the FBI has been able to greatly improve its crisis response capabilities to respond to such acts when and wherever they occur. The management and operational strategy that the FBI is implementing will further improve its capacity to counter terrorism. We believe this strategy will allow the FBI to continually refine, adjust, and upgrade our response capacities in the face of new threats and groups. Also, this strategy recognizes and emphasizes the importance of the capacity for gathering and sharing intelligence on a timely basis with other agencies involved in countering terrorism. The strategy places a premium on the importance of establishing and maintaining communications and liaison with our federal, State, and local partners. Finally, the strategy emphasizes the effective management and allocation of program resources provided by the Congress.

7

Suicidal Terrorism

Traditionally viewed as a problem affecting the Middle East and South Asia, the threat posed by suicide terrorism is spreading around the globe. Rohan Gunaratna assesses the nature of the threat, preventive and reactive security measures, and examines future trends.

The enhanced international and domestic threat of suicide terrorism from terrorist groups in the Middle East and South Asia was the focus of the First International Conference on Countering Suicide Terrorism, held in Israel between 21-23 February 2000. The conference brought together some 80 police, military, intelligence and security specialists to share their national experiences, and was prompted by the growing need for governments to identify the threat and co-operate at strategic and tactical levels to disrupt suicide terrorism.

THE THREAT

Suicide terrorism is the readiness to sacrifice one's life in the process of destroying or attempting to destroy a target to advance a political goal. The aim of the psychologically and physically war-trained terrorist is to die while destroying the enemy target.

In the 1980s suicide terrorism was witnessed in Lebanon, Kuwait and Sri Lanka. In the 1990s it had spread to Israel, India, Panama, Algeria, Pakistan, Argentina, Croatia, Turkey, Tanzania and Kenya. With enhanced migration of terrorist groups from conflict-ridden countries, the formation of extensive international terrorist infrastructures and the increased reach of terrorist groups in the post Cold War period, suicide terrorism is likely to affect Western Europe and North America in the foreseeable future. There are now 10 religious and secular terrorist groups that are capable of using suicide terrorism as a tactic against their governments and/or foreign governments. They are: the Islam Resistance Movement (Hamas) and the Palestinian Islamic Jihad of the Israeli occupied territories; Hizbullah of Lebanon; the Egyptian Islamic Jihad (EIJ) and Gamaya Islamiya (Islamic Group - IG) of Egypt; the Armed Islamic Group (GIA) of Algeria; Barbar Khalsa International (BKI) of India; the Liberation Tigers of Tamil Eelam (LTTE) of Sri Lanka; the Kurdistan Worker's Party (PKK) of Turkey; and the Osama bin Laden network (Al Quaida) of Afghanistan.

There were also four pro-Syrian, Lebanese and Syrian political parties engaged in suicide terrorism in the 1980s, but they are currently inactive in the terrorist front. These groups staged around 25 suicide attacks in Lebanon. As more than one group claimed some of the attacks, perhaps to diffuse the threat to the group, it is difficult to identify the group responsible. The groups engaged in suicide operations in Lebanon alongside Hizbullah were the Natzersit Socialist Party of Syria; the Syrian Nationalist Party; the Lebanese Communist Party; and the Baath Party of Lebanon.

There are two types of suicide operations: battlefield and off the battlefield. In battlefield operations, suicide bombers are integrated into the attacking groups. Most off-the-battlefield operations have involved single suicide bombers. In the case of the LTTE and Hamas, there have been multiple suicide bombers. The targets have been static and mobile, against infrastructure and humans. Suicide bombers have destroyed military, political, economic and cultural infrastructure. They have committed terrorist attacks by killing civilians in buses, crowded places and in buildings. Suicide bombers have also assassinated political and military VIPs.

KEY CHARACTERISTICS

Examination of suicide terrorism across a range of groups has revealed that terrorist groups use suicide bombers when they are both strong and weak. In terms of military and economic power, Hizbullah and the LTTE lead the list of suicide operations. In terms of numbers, the LTTE has conducted the largest volume of suicide operations, followed by Hizbullah,

Hamas and the PKK. In terms of range, only some of the groups have operated beyond their territories.

As well as abortive attempts to conduct suicide operations in Israel, Hizbullah has successfully conducted suicide operations in Argentina. The LTTE has conducted one suicide operation in India. It is the only group to have killed two world leaders - the former prime minister of India, Rajiv Gandhi, and the president of Sri Lanka, Ranasinghe Premadasa - using male and female suicide bombers.

The Egyptian groups have conducted suicide operations in Croatia against a police station and in Pakistan against the Egyptian embassy. Al-Quaida used at least one Egyptian suicide bomber in the 1998 East African embassy bombings. All the other active groups have conducted suicide operations within their own territory. The PKK has threatened to conduct suicide operations in Germany where there is a large Kurdish diaspora.

All the suicide terrorist groups have support infrastructures in Europe and in North America. Leaders and members of these groups are known to travel to the West, and key activists live either in Europe or in North America distributing propaganda, raising funds, and in some instances procuring weapons and shipping them to the various theatres of conflict.

Suicide-capable groups differ in form, size, orientation, goal and support. A review of the key characteristics of the 10 suicide-capable groups reveals that any group can acquire suicide bomb technology and engage in suicide terrorism:

- Al Quaida is a mix of several associate groups that are internationally dispersed. From Afghanistan, Bin Laden provides the overall direction to the organisation. Al Quaida efforts are primarily directed against the USA ('Great Satan') and Israel ('Little Satan'), and their allies. More recently, Al Quaida has directed its efforts against India on the issue of Kashmir, a territory disputed between India and Pakistan. The USA has directed its resources to disrupting Al Quaida support operations in the USA, especially after the 1998 embassy bombings in Kenya and Tanzania.
- The Indian counter insurgency specialist, K P S Gill, broke the backbone of the Sikh insurgents in Punjab,

northern India. BKI is fighting for an independent 'Khalistan' in the predominantly Sikh state of Punjab. It has a small presence in the target country - India - but enjoys a significant presence in the diaspora - UK and Canada. In January 2000, when BKI was planning to conduct its second suicide operation, the Indian security forces apprehended the bomber.

- The GIA has staged only one suicide operation as part of its fight to establish an Islamic state in Algeria.
- Hizbullah, responsible for suicide bombing the US Marine Corps barracks and the headquarters of the French paratroopers in Lebanon in 1983, is fighting to oust the Israelis from southern Lebanon. Hizbullah is supported by Iran, a steadfast state sponsor. Today, Hizbullah is also a political party.
- Hamas and PIJ, operating in Gaza and West Bank, have vowed to destroy the 'Zionist state of Israel'. Currently, Hamas and PIJ are controlled by the Palestinian Authority under its President, Yasser Arafat. Shin Bet (the Israeli security agency) and the Mossad (the Israeli external intelligence agency) have regulated the efficacy of these two groups by removing their key operatives and military leaders.

In a deep-penetration operation, Shin Bet agents placed a micro explosive device in the mobile phone of the Hamas suicide bomb maker, Yahiya Aiyyash, killing him. Due to the efficiency of the countermeasures adopted by Israeli police, military, intelligence and security organisations, the number of fatalities and casualties caused by Hamas, the PIJ and Hizbullah bombing has steadfastly declined. Towards the last few bombings, the explosions only killed the bomber. Although Hamas is likely to retain a military capability, the group will probably join the political mainstream in the foreseeable future. The PIJ became weak after the Mossad assassinated Shikaki, its military and political commander in Malta.

- The two Egyptian groups - IG and EIJ - are fighting to establish an Islamic state in Egypt. The leader of the EIJ, Dr Ayman Al-Thawaheri, lives in Afghanistan and works closely with Bin Laden.

- Until the capture of PKK leader Abdullah Ocalan, the PKK fought for an independent Kurdistan in southeastern Turkey. Today, the PKK is demanding autonomy and equal cultural rights.
- The LTTE is fighting for an independent Tamil state in northeastern Sri Lanka. As the quality of targets chosen by the LTTE is high, it has a sophisticated training programme that lasts for about a year. As well as training the bomber, the LTTE research unit tests the effects of explosives on dogs and goats to ensure that the attack is successful. The list of Sri Lankan VIPs killed in suicide attacks includes one president, one presidential candidate, the State Minister of Defence, the Navy Chief and various area commanders. No country has lost so many leaders in such a short period of time as Sri Lanka has to the LTTE suicide bombers.

MOTIVATION

Some of suicide groups are motivated by religion, religious/ ethnic nationalism, or ethnic nationalism. Al Quaida's religious philosophy transcends territorial borders. Hamas, the PIJ and Hizbullah are primarily religious groups, but they are also driven by ethno-nationalism. BKI is the only non-Islamic religious group. While the LTTE and the PKK are driven by ethno-nationalism, the PKK is also infused with Marxist-Leninist ideology. As such, the motivation of Hamas, the PIJ and Hizbullah suicide bombers is primarily Islam. The motivation of the LTTE and the PKK suicide bombers is mainly Tamil and Kurdish nationalism respectively.

Dependent on the political environment and potential and actual donors, a new ideological orientation can be built into a group. With the end of the Cold War, most groups are abandoning Marxist, Leninist and Maoist ideologies and embracing ethno-nationalist and/or religious ideologies.

There are some constraints that affect the deployment of female suicide bombers. An examination of the groups driven by religious ideology reveals that Islam has constrained the use of women suicide bombers. Nevertheless, about five of the suicide operations in Lebanon were women. Although the PIJ once planned to use a woman to suicide bomb the Israeli prime minister's residence in Jerusalem, the operation was thwarted. About 30% of the suicide operations in Sri Lanka have been conducted by women.

A higher percentage of women have featured in off-the-battlefield suicide operations, which requires infiltration, invisibility and deception. A woman staged the suicide operation that killed Rajiv Gandhi in India. Most suicide operations in Turkey are by women. For many reasons, women are the preferred choice of secular groups when it comes to infiltration and strike missions. First, women are less suspicious. Second, in the conservative societies of the Middle East and South Asia, there is a hesitation to body search a woman. Third, women can wear a suicide device beneath her clothes and appear pregnant.

MODUS OPERANDI

The organisation of suicide operations is extremely secretive. The success of the mission depends on a number of elements: level of secrecy; thorough reconnaissance; and thorough rehearsals. Secrecy enables the preservation of the element of surprise, critical for the success of most operations.

Thorough reconnaissance enables the group to plan, often by building a scale model of the target. Thorough rehearsals allow the bomber to gain stealth and speed. There are other elements, such as getting the bomber to the target zone and then to the target itself. The bomber is usually supported by an operational cell, responsible for providing accommodation, transport food, clothing and security to the bomber until he/she reaches the target. Resident agents help generate intelligence for the operation, from target reconnaissance to surveillance. The cell members confirm the intelligence. Often, immediately before the attack, the bomber conducts the final reconnaissance.

As a comprehensive knowledge of the target is essential for the success of a suicide operation, terrorist groups depend on building solid agent-handling networks. Some security and intelligence agencies have succeeded in penetrating the agent-handling network of various terrorist groups. In some cases, the only form of defence is to penetrate the terrorist group itself. This is because bombers penetrate governments or societies as sleepers and gradually gain acceptance as a trusted member. Thus the bomber can reach and destroy a valuable target - human or infrastructure.

In such cases, even the presence of a few hundred bodyguards or guards assigned to protect sensitive installations cannot serve as a counter measure. As such, penetration of the terrorist group is the first line of defence. The last line of defence is hardening the vulnerable and likely targets.

There are six types of suicide improvised explosive devices (IEDs). These are: the human-borne suicide IED, also known as the suicide bodysuit; the vehicle-borne suicide IED; the motorcycle-borne suicide IED; naval craft-borne suicide IED; scuba diver-borne suicide IED; and aerial- (microlight, glider, mini-helicopter) borne suicide IED. All these categories have been used in South Asia and the Middle East.

The largest number of suicide IEDs used has been the suicide bodysuit. As terrorists are cost conscious, there have been only a few cases of bombers using aerial-borne suicide IEDs. Yet these are the most difficult to thwart. Their small size makes them hard to detect on radar, but the range of a light aircraft is limited, weather sensitive and lacks accuracy.

The traditional concept of security is based on deterrence, where the terrorist is either killed or captured. The success of a suicide terrorist operation is dependent on the death of the terrorist. The suicide terrorist is not worried about capture, interrogation (including torture), trial, imprisonment and the accompanying humiliation.

Furthermore, in suicide attacks, there is no need to provide an escape route, or for the extraction of the attacker/attacking force. The group does not have to concern itself with developing an escape plan, often the most difficult phase of an operation. Therefore, a suicide terrorist could enter a high security zone and accomplish his/her mission without worrying about escape or evasion. The certain death of the attacker enables the group to undertake high quality operations while protecting the organisation and its cadres. As every prisoner has a point of breaking under psychological or physical pressure, the certain death of the attacker or attackers prevent the captor extracting information.

LIKELY DEVELOPMENTS

The development of counter measures has led to a decline in the number of suicide attacks. In Israel, several rings of security prevent the suicide bomber from reaching the intended target. In response, groups try out novel methods of infiltration. In this game of 'cat and mouse', one side can learn from the other in an attempt to 'checkmate' the opponent. While most groups can improvise, only a few are innovative.

To detect persons carrying explosives, security authorities have used sniffer dogs, with a maximum attention span of 30 minutes. One terrorist group has hired the services of a dog handler from France to monitor the ability of sniffer dogs. It is likely that this group will develop a suicide body suit with a repellent to evade the attention of sniffer dogs. With these developments, it is likely that the role of the sniffer dog will diminish with time and more innovative mechanisms will be necessary to detect the bomber.

The suicide body suit has evolved to improve concealment and is becoming increasingly small. Initially, the device was a square block of explosives worn in the chest and the belly area. Gradually, the device evolved into a heart shaped block of explosives placed just above the navel. As body searchers for suicide devices are usually conducted around the abdomen, a group is also developing breast bombs.

Most suicide body suits have no/little electronics, making it difficult for security agencies to develop counter-technologies to detect these devices. A suicide body suit can be made from commercial items. With the exception of the malleable plastic explosives and detonator, all the other components can be purchased from a tailor shop (stretch denim) and an auto shop (steel ball bearings, wires, batteries and switches). Furthermore, when a device is sophisticated it becomes difficult to operate, as well as fixing it when it fails to function. Suicide devices will thus remain simple.

However, there are likely to be variations of suicide devices. Terrorists tend to select from a repertoire of tactics. This is to retain an element of surprise and to evade the attention of security authorities directed at countering a standard set of tactics.

STATE RESPONSES

Terrorist groups learn from one another. Unlike in the 1970s and the 1980s, post-Cold War groups share resources intelligence, technology, expertise and personnel.

However, due to the need to preserve counter-technologies or political rivalry, there is either a lack of co-operation or no co-operation at all between affected countries. For instance, the British do not share counter remote-control bomb technologies against the Provisional IRA (PIRA) with their US counterparts. This is, primarily due to suspicion of access or infiltration of the US military and security industries by PIRA activists and supporters. Similarly, there is no co-operation between Israel and Sri Lanka, the most affected countries. During the Cold War, Indian pressure, and subsequently, the Sri Lankan Muslim lobby led to a rupture of Israeli-Sri Lankan ties that included Israeli technical co-operation in training Sri Lankan bomb technicians. An example of how a lack of co-operation between the VIP security divisions of India and Sri Lanka affected security was the failure of the Sri Lankan Presidential Security Division to estimate the kill radius of the suicide device. In India, over 18m is maintained between the political VIP and the public. The distance between the LTTE female suicide bomber and President Chandrika Bandaranaike Kumaratunge, who was partially blinded by an explosion in December 1999, was less than 12m.

Other than co-operation at strategic and tactical levels between VIP security divisions, the lack of research into the technical capability of terrorist groups has gravely weakened the ability of security divisions to protect their VIPs.

Strategic and tactical countermeasures can be used against suicide operations. They could be preventive and reactive. Preventive measures range from propaganda directed against potential suicide bombers, to infiltrating the suicide organisations of terrorist groups. Reactive measures range from the hardening of targets, to using dummy cars to protect VIPs. Yet security agencies agree that suicide terrorism is hard to fight. The US secret service argues that if an assassin is willing to die, it is impossible to protect the president. Nonetheless, affected governments have tried to protect their VIPs and critical infrastructure.

GROWING THREAT

The threat of suicide terrorism is likely to spread with time. As many second-generation operations have been conducted away from the theatre of war, it is likely that suicide terrorism will affect Western Europe and North America in the future.

Terrorist groups are increasingly providing intensive training to their bombers, with the intention of increasing their endurance. For instance, the suicide bomber who destroyed the US embassy in Nairobi in 1998 had been resident in Kenya for four years. He had married in Kenya and lived in the capital before carrying out the suicide operation. Similarly, the suicide bomber who assassinated President Premadasa of Sri Lanka had lived in the capital, Colombo, for three years before carrying out the attack.

Terrorist groups are setting a dangerous trend of using suicide bombers to destroy targets far away from their theatres of war. Many groups are likely to use suicide bombers to infiltrate target countries and conduct suicide attacks against Western VIPs and critical infrastructure in the foreseeable future.

8

The Tools for Managing Risk

INTRODUCTION

Terrorism like global climate change is not a new phenomenon. Terrorism in the guise of the violent assertions of political action, liberation movements, and pseudo-criminal blackmail, has probably been around for the entire period of developed human existence. Terrorism and global climate change however also have another feature besides longevity in common; they are both very much in the public mind, and for many seem like recent inventions or the latest manifestation of the Wrath of God.

The public perception that terrorism is an invention of recent times is a result of the short memory span of most human beings and particularly the popular press. That terrorism has been shaping human life, governance and economics for a long time is not easily explained on the evening news, and in fact is not really news in terms of the lack of immediacy of the concept.

To develop a strategy for managing the risk of terrorism, the social and the technological aspects of terrorism must be considered in terms of the national/political context in which they occur, the level of technological skill of the perpetrators, and the resolve to cause harm by those individuals. In terms of looking into the future, the political and social causes behind terrorism need to be examined, as well as the technological advances that will increase the effectiveness of terrorism.

The development of terrorism in the Philippines is an example and a warning of what may be seen in the future. The differences that may be expected from terrorism that originates in a developing country as against a developed country need also be examined. Towards minimising the threat of terrorism the means must be found of reducing the level of hate that produces a terrorist's resolve to do harm as well as the flow of technology that facilitates terrorism.

MECHANISMS OF TERRORISM

The first mechanism is the creation of an individual or group with a reason to take terrorist action. William Eubank and Leonard Weinberg[2] discuss this lack of recognition as being a cause for terrorism in their article, Democracy and Terrorism. The desire to be noticed is a strong incentive, and one that drives many individuals and groups with a cause. This desire to be noticed comes from the frustration that common and readily available means recognition, for example access to the media, are not available to individuals and groups with a cause. This desire for recognition is the underlying cause of terrorism. Revenge, jealousy, retribution and criminality are secondary causes.

The second mechanism is the opportunity and social justification for a terrorist act. The opportunity may be the trigger for an act that may be quite spontaneous or may be the result planning with a measured analysis of the effect and possible retribution or consequences (a cost/benefit analysis) to the perpetrator.

The third mechanism is the availability of the means to undertake a terrorist act that will have sufficient impact to mitigate any negative response. It has an implied connection between the sophistication of the terrorist and the chosen technology.

LEVELS OF TERRORISM

State Terrorism, its Causes and Attributes

The emergence of a single military superpower, with weaponry that cannot be seriously challenged by any other state is one of the present and developing causes of state sponsored terrorism. The fact that one state, The United States of America, has gained an overpowering military advantage (hegemony) has not and will not necessarily bring peace. It may well prevent open major warfare as was seen in the first half of the twentieth century, but conflicts where the United States has little interest (eg the Sudanese civil war, Bougainville and East Timor) will be allowed to continue without superpower intervention.

In essence, Pax Americanum may satisfy the close allies of the United States, and those states that can live with the fact of an economic, social, as well as military hegemony. That hegemony may however not sit well with states of widely differing social and political values. Small and weak nations are increasingly having difficulty in having their causes and indeed their very existence acknowledged by the superpower.

The ability of smaller nations and national groups to seek solace, help or just to take a counter position with an alternative superpower has disappeared with the demise of the Soviet Union. Since no small stick is effective against US might, then indirect methods of action are the only choice for the disgruntled small and weak nation. The indirect methods will be supporting direct violent terrorism or more subtly using economic (including Information Technology disruption) and social (including criminal) terrorism.

The 11 September attacks were in all probability the result of neo-state sponsored terrorism. The disruption of the US Postal Service by anthrax could possibly also prove to be an act of state (foreign supported) terrorism. Both have hit the target with serious economic and social impacts. The involvement of the previous Panamanian government in the cocaine trade was an example of individual terrorism (fired by the personal greed of Manuel Noriega) combined with state terrorism (the government agencies of Panama reacting against the former neo-colonial power).

Cause Driven Terrorism: Religious, Social and other Cause Driven Terrorism

Cause driven terrorism is not new, although it has been given new impetus. Terrorist acts were carried out by those involved in such causes and organisations as, anarchism, International Workers of the World (IWW), the Women's' Suffrage Movement, and Zionism. All those involved believed that the 'End Justified the Means', and many are now considered martyrs, heroes or if still alive, freedom fighters. They received recognition of the World through their actions and in turn achieved their goals. Either in life or death they received the accolades of their contemporaries and future generations.

Some modern examples of cause driven terrorism are:

Islamic/Christian conflict in Indonesia and the Philippines, which is coupled with ethnic cleansing,

Social conflicts such as the Huk uprising[3] (Philippines 1949 - 53) that was based on resistance to entrenched poverty and oligarchic nepotism, and

Aum Shinrikyo (Supreme Truth), Radical Animal Liberation and Eco-terrorism that are based on the development of philosophy of empowerment for social causes but which are too extreme to be taken seriously by the majority.

The Huks are still considered with great affection by many in Central Luzon (Philippines) although their reputation was damaged by association (truly or falsely?) with the Philippine Communist Party. The creation of martyrs in the inter-communal fighting in Indonesia is going on with increasing ferocity. The Aum is waiting for its martyrs to be created by the hangman. In each situation there is or was a cause, and in each situation the terrorists acts bring (have brought) recognition by the local, national and international communities.

Individual and Criminal Terrorism

Such terrorism is essentially the result of a selfish need for recognition, amusement or gain. It does include, acts of arson for pleasure, systematic brutalisation of individuals and communities, and repayment for past real or imaginary wrongs. The Uni-Bomber had a 'beef' with the US Government and the academic community, the arsonists that lit the Christmas 2001 fires in Australia received a thrill, and the brutalisation of communities in East Timor during 1999 by militias was essentially criminal (inspired by a few militia leaders) backed by elements of the Indonesian state.

In each case of individual and criminal terrorism, the perpetrators received recognition for their action, although in the case of the militia leaders in East Timor, they eventually found that their mentors, the TNI (Indonesian military), were forced to denounce their actions and remove support. For individuals and criminals terrorism is far less likely to bring accolades, and more likely to bring retribution from the state or from the communities that are the victims.

THE TERRORIST THREAT TO INFRASTRUCTURE AND CONFIDENCE

The threat to infrastructure is significant and increasing. Some examples are:

- Hard targets hit by physical weapons, The World Trade Buildings, the Pentagon and the Federal Building in Oklahoma,
- A soft target, The US Postal Service brought to a near standstill by the anthrax threat, and
- An even softer target, The Internet hit by the Loveletter computer virus (a case of individual terrorism; just for fun, from the Philippines).

Examples of infrastructure exist in every facet of human endeavour and all are vulnerable. Jennifer Caplan, in her article entitled 'Terrorism: The Ultimate Wild Card' describes how corporate Chief Financial Officers, fear terrorism. The fear is rooted in the knowledge that there is no bottom-line to the damage that a terrorist act could do to a corporation. The threat to confidence comes with the knowledge that risk transfer, which is taking out insurance against a terrorist act, is becoming impossible to organise or excessively expensive.

THE TECHNOLOGY OF TERRORISM

In 1993 Paul Wilkinson asked the question 'does modern technology tilt the balance in favour of the terrorists?' Paul answered that question in the affirmative. Since that question was first asked, the opportunity for sophisticated terrorism has certainly increased, with 11 September and the development of cyber-terrorism being confirmation of the continuation of that tilt.

The threat to infrastructure is great because the tools available to terrorists are very considerable. Furthermore as the tools that are available to terrorists are increasing in number and sophistication, then the list of possible targets is also increasing. A terrorist with an imagination will have no problem in finding a juicy target and the appropriate terrorist tools. Three generic types of terrorist tools are considered below.

Much is made of the possibility of a terrorist producing and using a nuclear weapon. It is a faint possibility but such a weapon would in reality have little interest to a terrorist. An 'A Bomb', built by a non-national organisation using power reactor grade or degraded plutonium, would be awkward to construct, difficult to successfully detonate and require a small ship or large mobile cement mixer to transport. It would not be a weapon of choice. A variation on a nuclear weapon would be a radiological device consisting of high level nuclear waste packed with conventional explosive. Again this weapon would have drawbacks to the terrorist in that great personal risk would be had in its manufacture, whilst its detection is probable before detonation, and products post detonation would be detectable and relatively removed from the environment.

Bio-weapons are a class of weapon that terrorists will find increasingly attractive. They are in the realm of technology available to, state, cause driven groups and possibly technically gifted criminals. If a third rate power, in a time of conflict was to unleash a bacteria such as a genetically modified anthrax, then there is the scenario for taking out a large percentage of the world's population. The microbe for such a catastrophic event would need the following characteristics: have long survival rate outside a host, be infectious on human-human contact, be carried by other vectors (species), have a reasonably long infectious period before the on-set of symptoms, be genetically stable and be releasable such that its spread would quickly cross borders and regions. Such a weapon was the goal of Aum Shinrikyo; they only needed a little more time to develop it.

The technology for manufacturing such a lethal bacteria or other microbe is common and well understood. Any country with a basic research facility for disease monitoring and control can turn those facilities over to disease causing agent synthesis and distribution. The facilities to produce a biological weapon also exist in many commercial laboratories, and can be purchased in kit form for as little as a few tens of thousands of pounds or dollars. Such countries or cause driven groups do not need the expensive infrastructure for nuclear weapons to cause mayhem, just a 'bug bomb' kit. 'Bug bombs', such as the anthrax containing letters used recently in the US, may have been developed by a non-national organisation or individual who had the means to steal biological material from the national arsenal. Where national security is weakened by economic or political crisis, as in parts of the former Soviet Union, then such theft is increasingly possible. It would be possible for a talented individual to develop and deploy a bug bomb of mass destruction potential. Its physical effectiveness would depend on the type and strain of microbe, the quantity of biological material and most importantly the method and place of its deployment. The weapon would not need to be very effective in its lethality to cause panic and the loss of confidence in control measures.

A cause driven group, such as Aum Shinrikyo[8], can likewise call upon its own dedicated members to undertake a chemical weapon development programme took years to produce their desired weapon. Their research and development occurred in both Japan and Australia, with testing on the effectiveness of their chemical agent (Sarin) being first undertaken on Australian sheep (1993/4) and then Japanese civilians in 1994. In this case Australia's keenness to invite Japanese businesses to set up in Australia without seriously questioning their intent, origins and credentials, led to an unwelcome involvement of the group with Australia. (Thankfully it only cost Australia a few sheep!)

A computer virus that has the following features would have the ability to destroy the internet and cause great disruption to commerce, transport and industry. The features would be:

1. Non-detectable to anti virus software at the time of its creation,
2. On a time (or other) delay system,
3. Spreadable by the internet,
4. Compatible to all major operating systems and
5. Introduced in a friendly and wanted format, that will be desired by many users.

The obvious way to 'deliver' such a virus would be initially to incorporate it in a major piece of software (e.g. a systems upgrade). The scenario would be a software release (over say three months), a timed relay to an email system, thence a timed (or program) triggered systems infection. The Loveletter if incorporated in a software package with a timing protocol could have been such a virus.

Who could create such a terrorist weapon? The answer is that such a virus could be created by a state, a cause driven group or an individual. In the case of the Loveletter, the suspected perpetrator was a Philippine student who had the desire to be noticed. Was he a criminal; was he a hero? That depends on his intent and the stance of those that sit in judgement (his victims) and his own community.

The creation of computer virus depends on knowledge, skills, and the dedication to undertake such an activity. In the case of the Philippine student, the possible damage to his own country and countrymen would have been relatively little, since the Philippines is not a strongly computer dependant country or society. The damage done to the United States, the former colonial power in the Philippines, was considerable. The collateral damage to other developed economies was also considerable. Did the student have a desire to hurt the former colonial masters and their allies? The question to that answer is probably still in the head of the perpetrator.

THE RESOLVE OF THE TERRORIST

To match the tools available to terrorists, is the new level of resolve being found in such groups as the 11 September perpetrators. Their action was founded on four basic pillars, these being: a cause great enough to attract people with education to a suicide mission, patience and resolve, resources (money, organisation and facilitators), and time. The actions of 11 September were an excellent example of project management, with achievable aims and superb organisation with high security. (Intelligence agencies such as MI5, CIA and KGB probably could not have provided better organisation, and would have been lucky to find nineteen/twenty zealots to undertake the mission.)

On an individual scale, the Uni-Bomber, Theodore Kaczynsk, showed resolve (his campaign of terror lasted 17 years) and skills at, victim selection, weapons manufacture, delivery systems and in hiding his identity. On capture,

Kaczynsk, has had his manifesto published, and has probably achieved his main goal, recognition.

The resolve, coupled with intelligence, of groups such as the 11 September hijackers and individuals such as Theodore Kaczynsk, makes preventing terrorist acts by such people very difficult, and in some cases impossible. Such people have time on their side as well as ability to keep their secrets till the time they choose to act. Groups and people of lesser intelligence and resolve will be easier to detect, and deter or remove.

RISK MANAGEMENT AS A TOOL FOR REDUCING THE HAZARD OF TERRORISM

The most vulnerable infrastructure is that which is obvious and is considered a key element in an economy or a corporate structure or is an icon of a target culture. Transport and communications systems, utilities, activities that attract wide participation of a big audiences, or symbols of a nation or culture are all prime targets. Military infrastructure, which usually a very hard target, is relatively immune from terrorism, given its high level of security.

The removal of the threat to infrastructure is not really feasible in a broad sense, since the targets are as diverse as the terrorists' imagination. Specific precautions can be taken where copycat actions are considered possible, and for very high profile targets. The financial cost and the social dislocation caused by counter-terrorism (security) measures will be a very significant in the future, and may be seen by terrorists (including those involved in state sponsored terrorism) as part of their success.

Some simple tools can be developed to examine the hazard to infrastructure and specific human activities of terrorism. These are based on a modified HAZOP (Hazard and Operability) system, where a series of question are posed, and thence answered by appropriate personnel.

The cost of the attacks on the World Trade Centre will and can never be fully calculated. Besides the loss of life and structures, the loss of confidence to the business community and society is great, and will be on-going. Other major costs of 11 September, are the faltering of confidence in the ability of man to be able to minimise hazard, creation of uncertainty in the ability of emergency services to cope with major crises, and spiralling cost of additional security, whether that security be effective or not. For the Sydney Opera House, a conclusion is drawn that 'immediate additional security is not warranted', despite the building being a cultural icon in Australia, having a very large movement of people through and around it, and having a very high replacement value. The reason for not seeing additional security as a priority for the Opera House, is that Australia still has a relatively low international profile, there have been no major incidents at the site till now, and that Opera House is only one of many possible targets throughout the country.

A company by using such a tool would be able to prioritise its response to the terrorism hazard. It could consider transferring some risk by insurance or by divesting of riskier parts of the business (e.g. the share of the Middle Eastern pipeline mentioned in the table). Other ways of hazard reduction may include the decision to take lower profile in particular regions or in their approach to business.

The tool is an extension of an occupational health and safety (OH&S) HAZOP exercise, with questions on the terrorism potential being included in the OH&S suite of considerations. It would use an extended employment of local resources in its application, with the terrorism expertise coming from the local emergency services.

At the level of small and middle, enterprises, entities and events (SMEs), Risk Management offers more relevance and likelihood of success in preventing terrorist attacks than examples given in Tables 1 and 2. SMEs will have less need for reliance on 'big-picture intelligence' and more reliance on local interaction of industry, commerce, government and the community. There is less to lose, less to save and less to interest the terrorist who is desires to be recognised. The threat in this case is likely to come from disgruntled employees, contractors, and other service providers, for whom revenge, jealousy, retribution and/or simply criminality are the reasons for their actions.

Risk Management (RM) may be more or less useful at some levels, in some areas and in some instances at combating terrorism in some forms and from some sources. It will never provide full security. Further, RM with hazard reduction will come at a cost. A cost/benefit analysis will in many cases point to inactivity with regard to hazard reduction as being the most appropriate form of response, in other cases the exercise will result in considerable expenditure being warranted.

TO STOP A TERRORIST (OR TERRORIST GROUP)

Returning to the three categories of terrorism, possibly the easiest to stop or curtail is State Terrorism. The means for doing this are:

1. Wave and use a big stick after publicly proclaiming the Terrorist State to be the work of Satin. The need for producing non-ambiguous and verifiable evidence is crucial in this approach,
2. Very privately take covert action (political, military, social and economic) to disarm the state, and/or
3. Publicly accommodate (appease) the desires of the State's rulers and elite so as to encourage them to shun terrorist practices.

The choice of the curtailment measure would be dependant on the situation, and may change as the threat increases or diminishes (as with 1992 and 2003 the North Korean nuclear stand-offs).

For Cause Driven Terrorism the following may work to some extent:

1. Discredit the cause and/or its leaders (accuse the leadership of, graft and corruption, being associated with outside bodies such as the Communist movement, and being involved in anti-social activity, eg child pornography), and
2. Offer alternatives to the cause (greed in place of fundamentalism).

Those individuals and groups with cause driven terrorist intent would be the hardest to dissuade from their goals. Either tireless physical prevention of terrorist acts or very long-term social re-orientation would be needed to prevent such individuals and groups from planning and committing such acts.

For Individual Terrorism:

1. Remove the opportunities (and tools) for a terrorist act,
2. Improve surveillance of those with a recognised propensity for terrorism (those with prior convictions and mental health records) and
3. Use education to dispel notions of martyrdom and heroics associated with terrorism.

The jeopardy of individual and criminal terrorists is recognised by anti-terrorist groups, in that they try and make cause driven terrorism appear as criminally inspired. (The Israeli Government spokespeople regularly refer to Palestinian actions as criminal acts. Israel further uses the word terrorist to describe Palestinian individuals who are casualties, either as active participants or bystanders, in an attempt to remove any martyr status that could come to those casualties.)

Risk Management and Terrorism Containment

It is demonstrated in the above pages how a modified HAZOP system could be used for 'testing' the likelihood of terrorist action on a particular target. A series of questions are posed, and thence answered by appropriate personnel sitting in a panel. But who would be these appropriate personnel?

To look at any situation that could be under a threat, local knowledge combined with skills in terrorism detection and containment would be needed. People that know a facility, work place or social situation (eg a sports or cultural function) would need to be matched with trained counter-terrorist personnel. The 'test' would either be undertaken at regular intervals or on an as needs basis. If threats were encountered or strong suspicions raised, then the appropriate civil authority would be informed. If national interests were threatened, the civil authority could refer the situation to the military or intelligence forces.

The effectiveness of using HAZOP in occupational health and safety management has been often demonstrated. A problem with HAZOP is that boredom sets in with the panel when during repeated OH&S HAZOP sessions nothing is found to report. In the case of using HAZOP like tools of Risk Management in counter terrorism measures, the boredom will very quickly set in, since most of the time the panel will be reporting no activity or cause for concern. This boredom is essentially a management problem and will need to be addressed by those leading the panels.

THE HUMAN DIMENSION

Terrorism and the threat of terrorism will cause a diversion of funds from other activities, and will thus reduce living standards. Bill Bogart10, produced estimates that 11 September cost the World between 0.75 and 1.25% Global GDP, with developing countries experiencing a loss of 2.9 5% growth. Thus a significant effect of terrorism on the community and individuals will be the loss of opportunity because of resources being directed to counter terrorism

Intelligence agencies, policemen and other law and security services do not create wealth; they are an expense on any balance sheet. To be able to stop another 11 September would be worth a considerable allocation of resources, but unfortunately such an allocation of resources will in many instances be a futile exercise, for the counter terrorism dollar will be spent on chasing hoaxes, myths and shadows.

The response of humans to terrorism as expressed by leaders (politicians) is to express outrage at the thought that terrorists can continue to create mayhem at will. Peter Sandman11, has defined Risk as being a function of outrage and hazard, with hazard being in turn a function of magnitude and probability. Another definition of risk is that it is a function of likelihood and safeguards. Politicians (partially through self interest) will dwell on reducing outrage, and will want to be seen to be emplacing safeguards. The effect that the application of the counter terrorism dollar will be misplaced, and will be directed towards highly visible activities (organising and conducting a second Gulf War with dubious links to terrorism) and not directing resources into intelligence gathering, an activity that can produce real results.

THE DEVELOPING SCENARIO

In an article published 1 September, 2001, Bruce Hoffman pointed out that despite the damage 'a seriously or potentially catastrophic CBRN attack might pose, it is highly unlikely that it will undermine national security and less threaten the survival of a nation like the US ..' Bruce Hoffman was proved right by 11 September in his proposition, in that the US strengthened its national security, and from all indications became a stronger nation. For Europe, Japan and other developed nations terrorism has little chance of seriously affecting the national resolve to maintain business as normal and not let terrorists threaten the populace or government.

For developing countries like the Philippines, the positive scenario of national security strengthening and the development of a stronger national will to survive, following a major terrorist action, may not always be the case.

The end of the Huk rebellion (circa 1954) occurred because of the input of State resources (Philippine and US) into fighting the Huk military wing, the disillusionment of many Huk supporters because of the bad behaviour of Huk fighters, the passing (and partial implementation) of legislation that remedied some of the Huk grievances and the simple exhaustion of the Huk fighters and supporters. The same will not necessarily happen to groups involved with the current rebellions in the Southern Philippines. The involvement of many external players in the Southern Philippine rebellions[14] will prolong the fighting and the economic cost. This coupled with innate weaknesses in the Philippine economy, a legitimacy question over the current president, and the failure to undertake social reform, has left that country open to the possibility of a terrorist triggered financial and political collapse.

Small internal conflicts will occur in many developing nations, will fester for a time, and will die out. There is the possibility that some internal conflicts will continue, and develop into mass revolts, as occurred in the European Peasants Revolts of the middle ages and in early years of the Russian Revolution.

The likelihood of this scenario is increasing and will be the result of widespread grinding poverty related to over population. This will be the doomsday scenario for some nations, and may be too late to prevent in terms of acceptable (and equitable) human intervention. In that extreme situation 'to be cruel is to be kind actions' may or may not be taken by the nations themselves, or by trans-national bodies.

Bruce Hoffman1 stated in 1997 'every new generation learns from its predecessors, becoming smarter, tougher and more difficult to capture and eliminate'. The continual need for vigilance from terrorist attack adds up to a great human effort with a great cost in resources and probably lives.

The expanding selection of technologies available to terrorists, the 'success' of recent terrorist actions, and the limitless variety of targets makes countering terrorism increasingly difficult. It will not be possible to patrol and otherwise provide physical protection for every possible target. It will be necessary to rely increasingly on civil and military intelligence agencies for stopping terrorists at an early stage in the development of a terrorist initiative. In essence people will be needed to think like a terrorist to possibly stop a terrorist (and hence individuals with mild social paranoia may be in great demand by counter-terrorism agencies).

For people living in developed economies the greater risk to life and limb will be, motor accidents, falling whilst drunk, and being hit by a stray golf ball, than by encountering a terrorist or being caught-up in a terrorist act. The prospects for government and commerce to overreact to outrage and expend excessive resources on counter-terrorism actions are great. Hopefully this overreaction must be tempered by common sense.

Paul Wilkinson referring to 11 September, commented that the vulnerability of the USA to terrorist attack was from intelligence failure that was responsible for the lack of a preliminary warning. How true. May we put more into intelligence gathering, and as Paul goes on to recommend, use the United Nations' diplomatic efforts to resolve conflict.

INTERRELATIONSHIPS IN ENGINEERING AND TERRORISM

September 11th 2001 was probably the first instance of a concerted attack on iconic infrastructure and a civilian population that had members of the engineering profession as primary perpetrators. Those engineers used engineering methods and techniques from project management to achieve their destructive ends.

Recently the key Australian engineering institution, the Institute of Engineers, Australia, has produced a report on securing critical built infrastructure. This report although very useful and thorough, does not take into account the threat to the environment from terrorism, or the use of the environment as a terrorist weapon.

Cause driven terrorism is not new. Terrorist acts were carried out by those involved in such causes and organisations as, anarchism, syndicalism, International Workers of the World (IWW), the Women's' Suffrage Movement, and Zionism. The study of countering terrorism however has been given impetus following the terrorist attacks of September 11, 2001 on New York. The study has taken many paths.

These include looking at: the sociology/ psychology of the terrorist or terrorist group, the understanding of underlying themes of terrorist organisations, the use of risk management techniques to identify targets that may be of interest to terrorists, the design of security infrastructure (barriers) to counter or ward off terrorism, the consideration of how the built infrastructure/ environment may be strengthened to mitigate the effects of terrorism and recovery strategies following terrorism.

In the case on September 11, the terrorist attack was on an icon of the built environment in a city that is in itself an icon to a way of life. Terrorism can also effect the natural environment. It can attack the environment directly, indirectly or use the environment as a weapon. The result of an attack may be temporary or permanent alterations to the natural environment and changes to human society that is part of the environment.

Terrorism can be defined as, a criminal act that has planning, the use of a technology and a socio/political cause, and is designed to foster fear and dread outside the immediate impact area. Terrorism is a tool to create terror in some population. It creates a very human response that may include: fear, dread, hate, disorientation, confusion, disillusionment and finally apathy. It may also inspire in part of the population the desire and resolve for: counter action, retribution and restitution. It may be designed to create a cycle of hatred that will be self-perpetuating and will mimic the continual improvement concept of total quality management and human betterment with continual destruction and human degradation.

When terrorism is most effective it will cause: dislocation of infrastructure, the non-productive use of resources and infrastructure, economic and market distress (often lasting far after all physical damage has been repaired), strategic dislocation (from the reassigning of resources and the disorientation of government and business) and operational disorientation (for example the loss of focus on a national, corporate or organisational goal).

TECHNOLOGY, ENGINEERING AND TERRORISM

The events of 11th September 2001 showed how terrorism did use technology and project management to achieve a very serious outcome. The fact that some of the perpetrators of that attack were engineers, or other technocrats, (Engineers Australia, 2003, 14/15) shows how an understanding of technology, project management and the psychology of fear and dread can be used together to create a continuing market instability, and in the case of the airline and tourism industries, on-going disruption and losses.

That engineers partake in terrorism action should not be surprising. In the definition of terrorism provided above, the combination of a technology, project planning and a socio/political cause includes two key areas in which engineers excel. Engineers that come from societies that are in themselves under threat from internal and external influences, and where alternate (and legal) means of expression are either banned or methodically suppressed will have the third terrorism necessity, a socio/political cause, and will be recruited by (or be found offering their services to) terrorist organisations.

With the third essential requirement for terrorism being a socio/political cause, university education in a radicalised part of the World and/or amongst radical students will expose engineering students to the realities of inequality, corruption and governmental ineptitude. In societies where engineering attracts students with superior abilities (and in many cases strong financial resources), the combination of cause, technological ability, and management training will make a serious combination, as is (was) the case with the engineer, Osama Bin Laden.

Engineers with their understanding of technology, risk management and project management will be a serious threat, since they will be looking to analytically and efficiently use the reverse of what an engineer is trained to do (that being to change the physical world to the betterment of mankind) to destroy what has been created. In particularly they will use risk management tools, such as consequence analysis to select targets, plan their projects and maximise the physical and psychological harm of their actions.

The countering of the attractiveness of terrorism to disillusioned and angry engineers will be awkward. The use of risk management tools to try and identify possible extremists amongst the ranks of engineers seeking entry into a country or region, or who are undergoing some other security or skills check, may be of some use. The Risk Management (RM) tools that would be used would include an analysis of: the country (and ethnicity) of origin, the university and educational majors, current employment and work history, political and social orientation, an age/sex profile and resources used to migrate and/or travel and reside in new destinations. The tools may identify some potential or actual terrorists but a high correlation of results obtained from using such tools and a significant reduction in the terrorist threat appears unlikely and would be very difficult to verify.

THE RESPONSE OF THE ENGINEERING PROFESSION TO TERRORISM

In February 2003, The Institution of Engineers, Australia (IEAust. 2003), announced its response to global events that have drastically changed Australia's security environment by initiating a project called "Engineering a Safer Australia" (Engineers Australia, 2003). The project consists of:

- A Policy Report: Maximising the contribution of engineering to national security Report:(June 2003),
- An Engineering practice guideline: Secure infrastructure & built environment engineering design: (June 2003) and

- A Homeland Security Edition of the Multi-Disciplinary Transactions: (October 2003).

From a detailed study of the Policy Report, the immediate theme is to provide guidance on securing critical (built) infrastructure. The report begins with definitions of critical infrastructure and the challenges to it, and then goes onto examine: should be the response of the Australian Government, the required response from industry and professional bodies, and the ethical and professional responsibilities of engineers who are concerned with securing infrastructure.

There are also occasions for specific branches of the engineering profession to respond to terrorism. A paper delivered at the Asia Pacific Confederation of Chemical Engineers (Viswanath, 2002) discussed the response of the chemical engineering profession in the United States to the terrorist threat, with specific reference to weapons of mass destruction. Another area of specific interest in counter terrorism is the question of aircraft engineering and the terrorist threat. The securing of access to flight-decks, and improved detection devices at airports have been to examples of the use of engineering to prevent another September 11.

On Friday 23rd May, 2003, the Australian Prime Minister, John Howard, announced, in a news cast carried by the Australian Broadcasting Corporation (ABC 2003), that there would be formed a new division in his department to oversee defence, security, intelligence and border protection. The division would be less than a Department of Homeland Security (eg the USA approach). Further, in March the National Counter-Terrorism Committee, a committee made up of representatives of the Australian security services, was promulgated to 'undertake the nationally accepted roles, responsibilities and definitions of critical infrastructure'. The Government has gone on to create a National Infrastructure Advisory Council, on which engineers and other technocrats will have seats, and thus be able to have an 'engineering input' into security and counter terrorism measures.

The above activities of the Australian Federal Government point to a strong move towards developing a national/Federal response to the 'chronic' terrorism threat, with considerable emphasis on securing critical infrastructure. This new venture into Federal involvement in security comes in the light of the Bali bombings with references made by PM in his announcements of departmental changes to those bombings. The Bali incident obviously having a major impact on the Government and its response to the 'acute' terrorist threat.

The IEAust (and its individual members) is and should offer its assistance to the Australian Federal Government in its efforts to counter terrorism. The Institution should however be aware that a knee-jerk reaction only lasts for as long as the press is interested and politicians are feeling the heat of public opinion, and that an on-going measured response is required in the long-term.

As the fear and dread of terrorism become less 'acute' and more 'chronic' the response of engineers will go from seeking immediate solutions to infrastructure protection to a measured cost to benefit analysis of terrorism counter measures, as is practiced in risk management applied other hazards. That measured response should include an element of preserving human capital, in that if terrorism acts do occur, then the minimisation of human loss should be a priority.

Planning for the preserving of human life (capital) is part of emergency management. The use of consequence analysis to identify hazards subsequent to an initial event, and then put in place secondary loss prevention plus response and recovery strategies, is well understood and is part of emergency management. The planning involved in emergency management should take into account the possibility of terrorism, vandalism and other criminal activity as well as natural and other man-made hazards. The Institution of Engineer's Code of Ethics states 'that the primary responsibility of engineers is to the community.' Specifically, its first tenet is that, 'members shall at all times place their responsibility for the welfare, health and safety of the community before their responsibility to sectional or private interests, or to other members'. By that very basic tenet, engineers should not participate in terrorism, and further should actively assist in countering terrorism.

A corollary to this tenet is that they should also participate in informing the community of risks. Given that weaknesses in infrastructure (in terms of the terrorist risk) will often be readily apparent to engineers, then the question is, should engineers actively inform the community of those risks even at the chance of causing community anguish or panic? Questions of the appropriateness and timing of whistle-blowing could be raised here.

THE PLACE OF THE TERRORISM THREAT IN ORGANISATIONAL RISK MANAGEMENT

In 2000, the Australian National Audit Office (ANAO 2000) produced the Business Continuity Management Guide, see Figure Risk Classification Framework. The guide categorised risks under two main groupings, these being External and Internal.

In 2003, the Institution of Engineers Australia requested submissions for their SafeAustralia programme. In their draft report they utilised the ANAO's categorisation of risks, and placed the terrorist risk firmly in the External/Technological category. On reflection, terrorism should be placed in each sub-category of external and internal risk. The reasoning for the inclusion of terrorism all categories outside the strict technological risk focus, goes back to the very nature of terrorism and its differentiation from other criminal activities. Terrorism can be found both outside an organisation and within, and in both cases it can affect the working of that organisation.

In the figure below, threats may arise from both external sources and internally. These threats may include terrorism, with the internal terrorism coming for staff or management who have an agenda originating outside that of the organisation.

External risks to an organisation: Technological, e.g. Telecommunications failure; computer and systems hacking; explosion; marine pollution; hazardous substance incidents; food / water supply contamination; vandalism; and terrorism.

In the broader sense, the Figure represents how terrorism can effect or be part all parts of an organisation. (NB. To examine the full range of terrorist risk threats in terms of the figure would require the development of a Lexicon of Terrorism.) Some terrorist threats and risks in the order provided in the above Figure are:

Political / regulatory:

- Threats and actions against key personnel
- Actions against law enforcement bodies

Environmental / natural:

- The use of bushfire (wildfire) as a terrorist weapon
- The release of exotic pests and diseases
- Acts against natural levees and watercourses

Economic / Market:

- Corporate terrorism
- State terrorism (as purposeful market disruption of another state)

Technological:

- Maritime terrorist actions
- The use of aircraft in suicide terrorist attacks
- The use of aircraft to spread bio-aerosols

Strategic:

- The reassigning of resources to non-productive activities (eg security and excessive over-engineering of infrastructure to lessen vulnerability to terrorist attack)

Operational:

- The loss of focus by key personnel on a corporate or organisation goal
- The use of resources to non-productive activities (e.g. security)
- Excessive government regulation that causes public resentment

That the Institution of Engineers, Australia, is placing emphasis on the external/technological aspects of terrorism is understandable, since engineers are technocrats who understand plant, structures and systems. They can also (and should appreciate) the human aspect of terrorism and counter terrorism. Although Risk Analysis (RA) is at best a 'sloppy science', and Risk Management (RM) by its very nature requires the understanding of such factors as Human Reliability Analysis, Human Error Response and Human Reliability Quantification, engineers use RA and RM. The use and adaptation (Clarke, 2003) of these tools is part of the training of many engineers and hence should be included in the IEAust's response to the questions of how engineers can be involved in countering terrorism.

In an editorial in US Journal, 'The Bridge' 1998, George Bugliarello examines the Engineering response to terrorism. He states that engineers can put terrorism into perspective. He advocates that engineers assist in avoiding over-reaction, and that engineers should help in placing the terrorist threat in context in terms of other threats such as natural hazards and accidents at home and on the highways. Bugliarello goes on to recommend that engineers have a place in counter-terrorism in detecting threats and in the improvement in the design of structures. He further goes onto to recommend that the detection methods (sensors) and infrastructure design improvements be part of the general move to improve safety from all threats, and that the public be encouraged to 'intelligently assess issues of cost versus risk'.

THE EVER EXPANDING TERRORIST THREAT

A recently recognised threat to infrastructure, and the built and natural environments is from maritime terrorism. Direct threats, such as the suicide attack on the USS Cole (Oct. 2000) are spectacular, but probably not of global importance. The use of a ship as the vector in a terrorist attack, where the ship is the weapon of mass destruction (WMD) is quite possible if not likely. Such a possibility has been recognised by the International Maritime Organisation (IMO 1, 2003), the US Maritime Transportation Security Act of 2002 ("Act, 2002") and in International Code for the Security of Ships and Port Facilities. Existing ships must comply with this requirement by the first scheduled dry-docking after July 1, 2004, and 'newbuilds' by July 1, 2004 (IMO 2, 2003).

The terrorist threat from the use of shipping as a WMD is great. The weapon could take many forms, including nuclear, radiological, chemical and biological. It could be delivered with relative ease (and security to the perpetrators) to many parts of the World, including inland cities and industrial complexes by waterways, canals and rivers. It could destroy cities, industrial complexes and seriously damage the environment by destroying ecology and habitat.

The accidental cyanide spill at Baia Mare gold re-treatment plant in Romania, January 2000, where the cyanide contaminant travelled via tributaries into the rivers Somes, Tisza and finally into the Danube before reaching the Black Sea (UNEP 2000) showed how the ecology of a vast stretch of a river system was seriously damaged by the release of a toxin. Such a poisoning could be perpetrated by terrorists by destroying a cyanide delivery barge on any one of numerous river systems that are transport links to the gold mining industry.

A ship or a ship container is the most likely (albeit highly improbable in any specific location) delivery system for a (sub-national) terrorist nuclear weapon, given that such a weapon would be cumbersome and large (from using non-weapons grade fissile material or weapons grade material that had been degraded/contaminated with time). It would need a considerable amount of conventional explosive for detonation (greater than that used for the Nagasaki bomb), a large tamper, and be of a size and weight that would require a small ship, of say a few thousand tonnes for delivery, containment and self destruction. The 'bomb' could be a fizzer as a nuclear weapon (i.e. not achieving a completely sustainable chain-reaction), but would be a sizeable radiological weapon in any case. It would create great terror in the communities immediately affected, and in the World at large.

Engineering and Maritime Counter-Terrorism

The IMO has recognised the threat of a maritime terrorist attack, and has utilised engineering solutions to counter it. These include the compulsory inclusion of a ship identification beacon on all shipping, the use of satellite tracking, port to ship monitoring systems and the use of electronic data management for manifest, destination and port of origin checking. This is a good example of putting in place engineering (technological) barriers and systems to counter a terrorist threat.

For Australia, with respect to in-bound shipping, what would be needed to put the IMO's shipping security project into place would be an efficient and very extensive Coastguard. That service would need to approach, challenge, board and check any ship, at a safe distance from shore, that is detected either not having a beacon, or being in the wrong place at the wrong time as determined through the interception of the beacon signal and after reference to itineraries and manifests. The implication for Australia, with its very extensive and sparsely populated coastline, would be a very costly redirection of more resources into security. Engineers involved in shipping, ports, defence and communications would be needed in significant numbers for this project good for engineers but not necessarily good for the community.

The difficulties and costs to Australia in complying with the new IMO edicts for out-bound shipping to the US have recently been discussed in the Sydney Morning Herald, August 3, 2003. The present challenge is to meet the July 2004 deadline for 'to meet stringent new security arrangements for ports and container shipping. After that, vessels sailing from ports, that have not complied with the new code may be liable to be turned away from United States ports'.

On a world-wide basis the IMO's initiative will however offer good security against the collective threat of maritime terrorism in time. As the provisions for ship monitoring come into effect and given the ever growing capacity for computer aided data analysis, the movements of suspect vessels would become more obvious and thus interdiction of sea-going terrorists become more likely.

(Of note is that President Jacques Chirac has indicated in an article by Philip Webster, Charles Bremmer and Roland Wilson, of Evian Agencies in The Australian, Tuesday, June 3, 2003 that France does not like the idea of the US having the right to police the World's shipping lanes and seize suspicious vessels at will. In this case the engineering may be appropriate but the politics of national sovereignty needs to be worked on!)

Terrorism and the Environment

Terrorists can use the environment in delivering and developing a terrorist threat. Three examples mentioned previously were: the use of bushfire as a terrorist tool, the release of exotic pests and diseases, and releasing the stored energy of a river system following attacks against natural levees and watercourses.

The bushfire (wildfire) threat can apply to many parts of the world. In recent times bushfires have ravished parts of Australia, the Western parts of the United States and Southern France. The bushfire/ wildfire threat is a threat to, human life, the economy and the environment (flora, fauna, the atmosphere and water). Economic terrorism through the use of wildfire could include the loss of: plantation and old growth timber, cereal crops, national icons (e.g. national parks of California and Oregon) and areas of tourist interest. The effects of environmental terrorism using wildfire could include: the loss of biodiversity in the areas burnt, soil erosion enhancement, the loss of water quality in creeks and rivers by contamination from ash and partially burnt material and the destruction of environmental amenity.

The introduction and spread of exotic diseases and pests to unaffected flora and fauna is a major threat that could be used by terrorists. This form of terrorism could be employed by foreign national agencies as an extreme form on economic terrorism. The release of a plant virus, such as the wheat streak mosaic virus, could be used by one nation (that has the virus in its cereal crops) to counter the competitive advantage of another nation that does not have the virus. The threat of the purposeful release of foot and mouth disease in the feral pig populations of Australia and New Zealand would have wide and serious economic consequences, with the collapse of meat and livestock exports to most developed countries being a certainty.

Australia has either by accident or by design imported exotic pests that have caused or have the potential to cause great environmental damage. Three specific pests of interest have been/are: prickly pear (imported by the First Fleet, 1788), cane toads (1935) and S. American fire-ants (late 1990s). There are still many pests waiting for a chance to enter Australia or New Zealand, and what better way than in the pocket of an economic terrorist (they would be undetectable by airport scanners!).

Attacks on natural and man-made levees have occurred in the past. The Nationalist Chinese Army blew the levees on the Yellow River to prevent the Japanese advance in 1938 (Gleik, 2000). During periods of flooding many levees become sodden and are often close to being topped. In this situation only a small charge of conventional explosive would be required for starting a levee rupture that could have very serious economic and environmental effects. In times of high rainfall many towns in United States, Europe and Australia could be under threat from a terrorist attack on town levees and dykes.

Terrorist attacks using natural hazards will take patience, knowledge and planning to succeed, as did the attacks on the built environment of the World Trade Centre. A terrorist cell would need to monitor the natural environment to know when and where to light a fire, release a pest or dynamite a levee.

The reward to the terrorist is that their attacks using natural hazards could produce more widespread and devastating results than attacks on urban and industrial infrastructure. (NB: The use of wildfire as a weapon of war was attempted by the Japanese in World War II. They launched over 9,000 'fire-balloons' against the United States and Canada (Canadian War Museum). The results were not spectacular; a death toll of six with few fires. Unfortunately (for the Japanese) the best wind conditions for balloon carriage only existed in the winter months when forests were too wet to burn or snow covered.

CONCLUSION

Engineers have a role in countering terrorism. Their knowledge and skills in carrying out Risk Assessments and in applying Risk Management to countering the terrorism threat will be valuable. They will be able to advise on security orientated infrastructure projects, as well as devising physical barriers to ward off terrorism from infrastructure in some cases. For threats to the environment they will be able to devise prevention, control and recovery strategies for many terrorist incidents.

As the immediate fear and loathing of terrorism becomes blunted for the great majority of the community, engineers will have a role in providing wise counsel to the community on how to live with terrorism and the terrorist threat. They will be able to provide good and honest advice on how to avoid, minimise and recover from terrorism. They will also have a role in putting the terrorist threat into perspective and help ensure that resources are not wasted on chasing phantoms.

Lastly in a recent class exercise presented to budding final-year environmental engineering students, the security of the great Australian icon, The Sydney Opera House, was raised. The consensus for providing near total security for the structure took the following form:

- Remove the concrete sails and use the crushed concrete and recovered reinforcing bar to provide a thick shield over the forecourt and theatres,
- Paint the newly created shield in camouflage paint, and plant a few gum trees in flowerbeds on the top for environmental amenity,
- Install new exits facing the adjacent unattractive rockface,
- Ban all ferries, ships and dinghies from coming within fifty metres (on pain of being obliterated by constantly manned hidden machineguns and guided missiles just like the US White House and its anti-aircraft measures),
- Provide for multiple levels of security on the doors (including full body searches) and
- Rename the structure, the Sydney Opera Bunker.

May we counter terrorism with planning, common sense and technology, without having to live, work and play in a bunker.

Until recently, the pipeline industry has been preoccupied primarily with environmental, safety and maintenance issues. Beyond occasional cases of vandalism, the human factor was hardly perceived as a threat to the world's vast web of oil and gas pipelines, which, all told, carry roughly half of the world's oil and most of its natural gas.

This has changed since September 11. With the threat of terrorism looming, pipeline operators in the industrialized world have taken action to prevent terrorism from harming energy infrastructure with steps that include:

- Increasing system redundancy,
- Deploying state-of-the-art surveillance equipment,
- Deploying aerial and ground patrols, and
- Fortifying pipeline systems against cyber-security breaches.

All these have made the pipeline system in places like North America and Europe relatively secure. But since most U.S. oil and a growing portion of its natural gas come from abroad our energy system cannot be protected unless similar security measures are applied at the generating points of oil and gas in the Middle East, the Former Soviet Union, Africa and Latin America.

Unfortunately, the security situation in those parts of the world where terrorists are known to operate leaves much to be desired. In fact, terrorists no longer need to come to the U.S. in order to wreak havoc in our energy system. They can achieve the same degree of damage by going after energy targets in their home base where they enjoy support on the ground.

In mid-December 2004, Arab satellite channels aired an audiotape message by Osama bin Laden in which he called on his cohorts to take their holy war to the oil industry and to disrupt supplies to the U.S from the Persian Gulf.

Two days later a follow-up statement by the Saudi branch of al Qaeda was published, calling on "all mujahideen ... in the Arabian Peninsula" to target "the oil resources that do not serve the nation of Islam." These statements reflect the reality of the post-September 11 world in which terrorist groups have identified the world's energy system, "the provision line and the feeding to the artery of the life of the crusader nation," in the words of al Qaeda, as the Achilles heel of the West. Throughout the world the jihadist message is gradually being heeded and it is becoming increasingly apparent that a new chapter in the war on terror is looming on the horizon and that its primary targets are oil and gas pipelines.

WEAPON OF CHOICE

Pipelines are very easily sabotaged. A simple explosive device can put a critical section of pipeline out of operation for weeks. This is why pipeline sabotage has become the weapon of choice of the insurgents in Iraq.

Since President Bush declared the end of major hostilities in April 2003, there have been close to 200 pipeline attacks. According to the Iraq Pipeline Watch at the Institute for the Analysis of Global Security, most of the attacks took place in northern Iraq, primarily on the pipeline running from Kirkuk to the Turkish Mediterranean terminal of Ceyhan.

In addition, there have been dozens of attacks on oil and gas pipelines leading to the refineries around Baghdad, primarily near the Bayji refinery complex 125 miles north of Baghdad. In March 2004, terrorists began striking at oil installations in the south near Basra as well, where more than two-thirds of Iraq's oil is produced. The attacks have exacted a heavy price from the new Iraqi government— it is estimated that pipeline sabotage costs the country more than $10 billion in oil revenues — and have undermined the prospects of Iraqi construction.

Such attacks also have a corrosive influence on the morale of the Iraqi people and their attitude toward the presence of U.S. forces in their country. Iraqis are growing increasingly vexed by the coalition's slow progress in the reconstruction effort and its inability to guarantee a reliable supply of electricity, which is primarily derived from oil. Worse, the sabotage campaign has created an inhospitable investment climate in Iraq and scared away oil companies that were supposed to develop its oil and gas industry.

Emulating the success of the saboteurs in Iraq, terrorists in many oil-producing countries have set their sights on pipelines and other oil installations. In December 2004, Sudanese rebels attacked an oil field, killing 15 people. "This was our first military operation and we chose the oil fields because this is the wealth of Sudan, which this government is not sharing with all of its people," said Ali Abd al-Rahim al Shindy, leader of the group that carried out the attack.

Chechen guerrillas fighting to sever themselves from Russia are going after the country's gigantic pipeline web of roughly 31,000 miles. Russia is the world's second-largest oil exporter and 40% of its revenues are derived from oil. There is no better way for the Chechens to hurt the Russian economy than hindering Russia's capability to export crude. In 2004, pipelines were blown up in Volograd, Dagestan, Stavropol as well as in and around Moscow.

In India, a separatist rebel group called United Liberation Front of Asom (ULFA), which fights for independence for oil-rich Assam state, has taken responsibility for a number of pipeline attacks. Assam is the source of some 15% of India's onshore crude oil production and, as the country's oil demand grows, the implications of disruption of the flow of oil from there will become increasingly noticeable.

In southeast Turkey, Kurdish guerrillas belonging to the Kurdistan Workers Party (PKK) have staged a campaign of bomb attacks on an oil pipeline.

In Colombia, terrorist groups, primarily the Revolutionary Armed Forces of Colombia (FARC) and the National Liberation Army (ELN,) have attacked the 480-mile Cano Limon-Covenas oil pipeline so many times that it became known as "the flute."

The campaign against the world's vulnerable pipelines is likely to continue to spread to new territories. Terrorists have already indicated interest in the nearly completed 1,000-mile Baku-Tbilisi-Ceyhan (BTC) pipeline, slated to transport 1 million barrels of oil a day from the Caspian Sea to Western markets through the Turkish port of Ceyhan. The pipeline is expected to be operational by the end of 2005 but even before construction ends, terrorist elements may already be planning attacks on it. According to Azerbaijan's National Security Minister, Namiq Abbasov, the country's special services had obtained information that regional insurgents and members of al Qaeda are planning acts of sabotage against the pipeline.

Another problematic area in the pipeline's path is Georgia, where separatists in South Ossetia and Abkhazia provinces often clash with the Georgian government. In addition, there is increasing threat by Islamist groups operating in the Caucasus such as the Islamic Party of Eastern Turkestan, the Islamic Movement of Uzbekistan (IMU), Chechen separatists and Hizb-ut-Tahrir al-Islami. The latter group seeks to seize power and supplant existing governments with a sharia-based caliphate for the purpose of jihad against the West.

China, the world's fastest growing energy consumer, is also vulnerable to terrorist strikes against oil. To satisfy its growing energy needs, China has decided to run pipelines connecting the northwest district of Xinjiang with neighboring Kazakhstan. This means China's oil will be at the mercy of increasingly hostile Muslim Uighur minorities trying to break away from the central regime in Beijing.

But in no oil and gas domain could pipeline sabotage do more damage than in Saudi Arabia, home to one-fourth of the world's oil. Over 10,000 miles of pipeline crisscross Saudi Arabia, mostly above ground. Were concerted pipeline attacks to spread to Saudi Arabia, repeatedly interrupting the Saudi oil supply, the implications for the global economy could be profound.

Not all pipeline sabotage is politically driven. Thieves often pilfer fuel from pipelines for personal use or to sell on the black market. Such activity sometimes ends tragically. In 1998, more than 1,000 villagers in Nigeria died when a ruptured gasoline pipeline exploded as they scavenged fuel.

FEAR PREMIUM

Whether perpetuated for political or criminal reasons, assaults on oil infrastructure have added a "fear premium" of roughly $10 per barrel of oil.

The cause and effect are not lost on terrorists whose goal, feasibility aside, is to bankrupt the U.S. "The killing of 10 American soldiers is nothing compared to the impact of the rise in oil prices on America and the disruption that it causes in the international economy," exhorted one jihadist website. For the U.S., which imports more than 10 million barrels a day, the spike in oil prices due to oil terror cost close to $40 billion in 2004.

Governments, oil companies and pipeline operators are seeking to put in place mechanisms to reduce the impact of the scourge. The most effective way to address the scourge of sabotage is to confront terrorists wherever they are. This is already being done by most countries as part of the global war on terror. By pursuing jihadists and separatist groups, denying them freedom of operation and destroying their infrastructure, governments can reduce the number of attacks.

The most obvious way to increase pipeline security is the use of patrols and the creation of buffer zones along the pipeline routes into which unauthorized personnel are prohibited from entering. In Iraq, close to 14,000 security guards have been deployed along the pipelines and in critical installations. But ground patrols are only effective to a certain degree, especially in areas of inclement weather and forbidding terrain.

Another way to reduce pipeline sabotage is by paying tribes and powerful warlords to protect the pipes on their territory. This method was tried in Iraq with limited success. Rival tribes would often blow up a pipeline and then claim to be more deserving of the protection money.

Sensing Systems

Technology could also play an important role in the effort to secure pipelines. Sophisticated surveillance systems to enhance infrastructure security can be deployed in critical locations.

New technologies for seismic sensing of underground vibrations can provide early warning when saboteurs approach the protected area. Such systems may be expensive, but by making possible the remote monitoring of much of the pipeline network, governments can eliminate the need for large numbers of troops and instead rely on smaller numbers of rapid-response teams.

Such systems can also be complemented by air surveillance. As a result of progress in high-resolution remote sensing and image processing technology, it is now possible to deploy small and medium-size unmanned aerial vehicles (UAVs) and unmanned helicopters for pipeline inspection purposes.

These UAVs can stay in the air up to 30 hours at medium-to-low altitudes, and can send images to a central control station where they can be reviewed by security teams. Some defense contractors are developing UAVs mounted with automatic weapons to be used against saboteurs.

Unfortunately, many of the countries where such technologies would be most effective are too poor to afford them. Under such circumstances governments and pipeline operators that cannot prevent attacks altogether should invest in mechanisms to minimize the damage attacks can cause. The cheapest and most effective way to protect an existing pipeline is to prevent easy access by surrounding it by walls and fences. New pipelines should be buried. While this may substantially increase construction cost, in areas where saboteurs are known to operate the investment will quickly pay for itself. This is the reason the BTC has been completely covered from the outset.

New technologies can fortify pipes with external carbon fiber wrap that can mitigate the affects of explosive devices. Equally important is to shorten the lead time between the attack and the repair. The quicker it takes to repair the damage, the lower the cost of the disruption. Pipeline saboteurs often target pipelines at critical junctions or hit custom-made parts that take longer to replace. To reduce the lead time, pipeline operators should be equipped with sufficient inventories of spare parts.

It is important to realize that none of the approaches discussed here is likely to put an end to the problem. As long as oil and gas continue to be essential to the functioning of the world's economy, pipeline sabotage is likely to remain one of the industry's risks. No matter what remedy is applied, it will add a surcharge to the price of a barrel, which is already unusually high.

9

The Changing Nature of Terrorism

Australians are confronted as never before by terrorism. Our sense of vulnerability to attack is new. So are the force, global reach and ambition of the distinctive threat from transnational terrorism now perpetrated in the name of a Muslim extremist cause. Understanding these changes is the first challenge. That is not easy for a nation neither expecting nor used to being targeted like this. But it is essential to maintaining an effective national response.

Open and pluralist societies like ours are now confronted in fundamental ways. These terrorists seek to undermine our security and prosperity. They feel threatened by the values and aspirations that make us an open, tolerant and creative country with a confident future. Australians know that preserving these qualities is vital to our health as a community in all its diversity. It is central to our resilience in the face of this threat. It is the key to our appreciation of the many Muslims who are part of us and to the continuing strength of our links with Muslim-populated countries overseas.

But, naturally enough, we struggle to come to grips with the dimensions of contemporary terrorism. It is not easily understood as a nationalist or political campaign such as Irish, Basque or Tamil separatist terrorism. It bears little resemblance to familiar examples in the public memory when Australians were occasionally incidental victims. While these previously known forms of terror continue, they are peripheral to the nature and scale of the security challenge Australia now confronts.

We find it hard to comprehend the rhetoric of these terrorists, who condemn anyone who does not agree with their approach to Islam. For us, the terrorists' assertions of an international conspiracy to repress and defeat Islam makes no sense. It has no connection to everyday reality, however much we understand and sympathise with the plight of Muslim and other communities in distress. We cannot easily relate their assertions to a territorial dispute, political ideology or historical injustice.

For Australia, these are no longer issues of global distance - or ones that can be left for others to contemplate. The terrorists' challenge is now direct and immediate. Their goals confront us. They want to drive the West's presence and influence from Muslim lands. They want to replace governments there with regimes that reflect their extremist interpretation of Islam. Ultimately, they want to reshape the international order to accommodate a pan-Islamic super-state. Their objectives are inherently political regardless of their religious trappings. To achieve this they are set on intimidating those who do not support them - Muslim and non-Muslim alike.

For the first time, Australians are having to come to terms with a security threat neither constrained nor defined by national borders, traditional power structures or formed armies - one that is neither dependent on sponsoring nation states, nor responsive to traditional deterrence. Rather, it is driven by an ideology that is inaccessible to reason, and with objectives that cannot be negotiated.

DEFINITION OF AN ACT OF TERRORISM

There is no internationally accepted definition of terrorism. Not even the United Nations has been able to achieve consensus on this contentious issue. The old adage that 'one man's freedom fighter is another man's terrorist' goes to the root of the ongoing debate. Individual states, therefore, have been compelled to develop their own definitions for the purposes of enacting legislation to counter the threat.

In Australia, what constitutes an act of terrorism is defined in Commonwealth legislation. The Criminal Code Act 1995 states that a terrorist act means an action or threat of action where the action causes certain defined forms of harm or interference and the action is done or the threat is made with the intention of advancing a political, religious or ideological cause. Further, the Act states that 'the action is done or the threat is made with the intention of:

i. coercing, or influencing by intimidation, the government of the Commonwealth or a State, Territory or foreign country, or part of a State, Territory or foreign country; or
ii. intimidating the public or a section of the public; and where the action
   (a) causes serious harm that is physical harm to a person; or
   (b) causes serious damage to property; or
   (c) causes a person's death; or
   (d) endangers a person's life, other than the life of the person taking the action; or
   (e) creates a serious risk to the health or safety of the public or a section of the public; or
   (f) seriously interferes with, seriously disrupts, or destroys, an electronic system including, but not limited to:
      (i) an information system; or
      (ii) a telecommunications system; or
      (iii) a financial system; or
      (iv) a system used for the delivery of essential government services; or
      (v) a system used for, or by, an essential public utility; or
      (vi) a system used for, or by, a transport system.

The Criminal Code makes it an offence if a person commits a terrorist act, provides or receives training connected with terrorist acts, possesses a thing connected with terrorist acts, collects or makes documents likely to facilitate terrorist acts, or does any act in preparation for or planning of terrorist acts. The penalty for engaging in a terrorist act is life imprisonment.

The penalty for other terrorism-related offences outlined above ranges from ten years to life imprisonment.

We have to adjust to a threat that is not only alien, but unconventional and unpredictable. Its presence is largely unseen and unknown. But it commands frequent headlines and commitment of our resources on a national scale. We seek to protect and defend ourselves in the knowledge that there can be no guarantees from successful attack in open societies like ours. This is an 'asymmetric' threat with disproportionate advantage to the smaller but determined aggressor operating beyond any accepted rules of behaviour.

Our exposure is magnified by globalisation. An interdependent world allows terror to be transmitted to remote victims. Borders and distance offer little protection to a terrorist enterprise proficient at using technology to recruit, communicate and operate transnationally. With more extensive international interests than ever before, we must increasingly work with international partners to protect ourselves. Our economy is linked to global systems that are exposed to terrorist sabotage.

The networks we rely on for transportation, energy, finance and communication can be protected, but not made immune. More so than in the past, Australia's people, its economic links and its contributions to international security and prosperity have spread to parts of the world where the terrorist danger is even more direct - and where we have less control over how we are protected.

We must adapt to living in a more dangerous world. These new terrorists have used aircraft as weapons. They have used public transport to kill indiscriminately. They have made bombs from materials used in farming and mining. They have experimented with chemical and biological weapons. They are limited only by imagination and opportunity.

And we must adapt to these harsh new realities in a changed strategic environment. These changes began with the end of the Cold War and the new strategic uncertainties that followed. The emergence of the United States as the pre-eminent military and economic power remains the overwhelmingly dominant factor in the global strategic balance today. The balance it struck with other big powers brought advantages and opportunities for countries like Australia, open and capable, and committed to the benefits of international cooperation in an increasingly globalised world.

The deadly and unprovoked terrorism of 11 September 2001 has further recast these international settings - for the United States, Australia and the broader international community. Not only did a potent new enemy demonstrate strategic reach, but it wrought unprecedented damage on the homeland of the world's biggest power, exposing unimagined vulnerabilities. In doing so, it instantly created an adversary determined not only to remove terrorist enemies but to confront existing and potential security threats with great vigour and resolve.

The menace to Australia of weapons proliferation has also been compounded by this new form of terror. We must address the possibility that these transnational terrorists may acquire and use chemical, biological, radiological or even nuclear capability. This prospect presents us with dangers of grave proportions. These twin dangers remain key drivers of United States strategic policy, as they do for Australia and other key partners.

The asymmetric nature of the threat posed to Australia demands a disproportionate scale of response. National security is higher on the Australian Government's policy agenda than it has been for decades. The national resources deployed to counter the threat are major - and still growing.

The transnational terrorist capacity to inflict harm disproportionately, without restraint or warning, means Australia's response must be broad-spectrum. It has demanded adjustment to the conventional defence posture we maintain to fight conventional wars. And it has put a new cast on our broader security policies, including our approaches to other transnational issues, such as people smuggling, money laundering and organised crime. Good intelligence has become an even more vital element to our protection. So too has better law enforcement and improved counter-terrorist legislation.

Our counter-terrorism response has meant changes to the environment in which Australians lead their everyday lives. Protection against terrorism is essential to preserving the right of each Australian to security. This allows us to participate freely in a society based on shared values of freedom and respect for the dignity of human life. We need to recognise this-

and to make sure the inevitable cost of our preparedness does not also tax our values, our tolerance and our fundamental way of life.

AUSTRALIA'S PAST EXPERIENCE OF TERRORISM

The extent to which Australia has been affected by terrorism significantly changed with the 11 September 2001 attacks in the United States and the Bali bombings of 12 October 2002, in which a combined total of 98 Australians were killed.

In the past, few Australians had been killed as a result of terrorism. Most of those few were killed overseas and not deliberately targeted as Australians. Two Australians killed by the Irish Republican Army (IRA) in the Netherlands in 1990 were the victims of mistaken identity, the terrorists believing them to be British.

In Australia, past acts of terrorism have generally involved attacks against foreign interests - including those of Turkey, Iran, India and Israel. Although Australians were killed in these attacks, Australia was not itself the target. Rather, Australia was the venue for the expression of extremist violence directed at other nations' governments in reaction to events overseas. The bombing of the Hilton Hotel in Sydney on 13 February 1978, in which three Australians died, was targeted at Indian officials attending a Commonwealth Heads of Government Meeting (CHOGM).

Australia is now a target of transnational extremist-Muslim terrorism and Australians are being targeted overseas.

The threat Australia faces is enduring. It requires a sustained national response. While we have already made many changes in order to better protect ourselves, we may need to make more. We can expect our national resilience to be put to future tests. The dynamic nature of the threat will continue to demand heightened awareness and vigilance of all Australians.

A NEW KIND OF FOE

Transnational terrorism confronts us with a new kind of foe. It is diverse, complex, adaptable and continually evolving. It is uncompromising, global in reach, and its operations are highly networked. Its approach is asymmetric, using unconventional and unexpected means to wreak maximum damage. It is of a previously unknown scale.

It is being perpetrated in the name of an extremist Muslim cause but it is a type which, in a future world order, could be applied by others. It signals a new era of conflict.

ASYMMETRIC WARFARE

Terrorism is a form of asymmetric warfare: an approach that uses non-traditional methods to counter an opponent's conventional military superiority. It uses unconventional means to attack unexpected targets. It turns perceived strengths into weaknesses and exploits vulnerabilities to deadly effect. It may also involve the capability to attack an adversary with means for which they are unprepared or incapable of responding in kind.

The new transnational terrorists have adopted a strategy that responds to the unprecedented dominance of the United States and other highly developed Western countries in all aspects of conventional military power. The terrorists therefore seek means other than conventional warfare with which to confront the West.

Terrorism pits clandestine methods against open societies. It uses small teams whose operations are cheap, but demands a response that is enormous in scale and expensive in resources. It exploits the foundations of civil society, such as principles of human rights, efforts to avoid civilian casualties, and adherence to the rule of law - including the laws of armed conflict.

The terrorists' asymmetric approach demands a sustained, comprehensive and coordinated response at national and international levels, incorporating a wide range of Australia's assets.

An Extreme Ideology

As with most previously known forms of terrorism, extremist ideology is the driver. The threat we face today is driven by an extremist interpretation of Islam. This form of extremism is absolutist. It leaves no room for compromise and it seeks no place at the negotiating table. It uses violence to signal its committed path to a final end. It is not bound by social norms, laws or values.

These terrorists justify and feed their ideology through skilful exploitation of dynamics within mainstream societies. They use adverse political, social and economic conditions as a rallying cry to recruit and motivate their members. They exploit distrust of the West and feelings of humiliation and anger. They invoke events that resonate with most Muslims, such as the Israeli-Palestinian conflict and the war in Iraq, as justifications for their ideological cause.

They are also driven by a need for continued action. Militant jihad - as interpreted by transnational extremist-Muslim terrorists - is a process of constant struggle against their enemies. They therefore seek to constantly strike their enemies to maintain the momentum of their cause.

Global Goals and Scope of Operations

Although they act in the name of a religious cause, these terrorists have political goals. They want ultimately to establish a caliphate - a pan-Muslim super-state that unites all Muslims and all lands now or ever part of the Islamic world. This includes the Middle East and North Africa from the Red Sea to the Atlantic coast. It includes Andalusia in Spain, parts of the Balkans, Central and South Asia through to the Indonesian archipelago, and parts of the Philippines in South-East Asia.

They seek to drive the West's presence and influence from these lands. They oppose governments in Muslim countries - criticising them for being 'un-Islamic' and therefore illegitimate - and seek to replace them with ones that accord with their extremist views. Their operations are global in scope. They do not limit their attacks to previous theatres of 'militant jihad'. Al Qaida's so-called fatwa (religious decree) of February 1998 called on supporters everywhere to attack the United States and its allies - including civilian targets - anywhere in the world. Terrorism previously directed against Western interests in other countries has since spread to Western countries themselves.

This illustrates the global reach of the new terrorism since 1992. The network of these terrorists is also global. There are extremist-Muslim terrorist elements and supporters - with varying degrees of connection - in the Middle East, South, Central and South-East Asia, North Africa, Europe and North America.

This network extends to Australia. Some terrorist groups have small numbers of supporters in Australia and some Australians have trained in extremist camps in Afghanistan, Pakistan and Kashmir. We know the terrorists have considered planning attacks in Australia.

The new enemy also recruits globally. That means Western countries are a source. There is no simple 'terrorist profile' based on nationality or ethnicity.

TERRORIST OPERATIONS - SOME FEATURES

A Network of Networks

Transnational terrorist operations are highly networked. Small, dispersed teams and individuals work semi-autonomously to achieve a general goal. Leaders communicate their intentions periodically and non-specifically, including through public pronouncements.

Groups are affiliated through both formal and informal links. Decision-making and operations are often highly decentralised.

Al Qaida is the most visible manifestation of the terrorist threat, but the new transnational terrorists are not organised as a hierarchy with Al Qaida at their head. The threat comes from a 'network of networks', made up of dispersed groups and movements. Some of these groups are themselves a network, with limited central command and control.

The autonomy of small teams within this loose structure helps the terrorists survive. Even if the heart of a network is destroyed, the small teams can survive, operate independently, and tap into another part of the network. When a terrorist group is destroyed or its capability degraded, other groups or teams can take over their functions relatively easily.

Networked operations make it more difficult to identify indicators and forewarnings of terrorist attacks. They also make it harder to target the threat. But understanding how the networks operate is critical to devising a strategy to deal with them.

A Skilled Enemy

Many of the methods applied by these transnational terrorists are sophisticated. The New York and Washington attacks of 11 September 2001 showed an ability to plan, coordinate and execute multiple, simultaneous attacks. We have seen further examples in East Africa, Riyadh, Casablanca and Madrid.

Many are technically skilled, intelligent and educated people. Some have received professional military training, including in Western forces. Many more have had professional instruction in advanced terrorist methods in training facilities in Central, South and South-East Asia and the Middle East. They are good at planning and logistics. They use modern technology to their advantage.

Their security practices are also well developed. Their cell structure, combined with good counter-intelligence tradecraft, keep their identities, operations and methods secret. Not everyone in a team knows the plan or the mission (e.g. the target and the exact method or timings). This is sometimes only revealed at the last moment - lessening the risk that the exposure of part of a plan, or the capture of one terrorist, will undermine an operation.

They are often knowledgeable about Western countries, customs and culture. Some were born or live in the countries they target. Their knowledge and familiarity helps them maximise physical harm and psychological impact. It also allows them to live in target countries without arousing suspicion and plan for terrorist attacks undetected.

They use converts to Islam for terrorist operations - including those from European backgrounds. People from such backgrounds can attract less security scrutiny than those who meet certain nationality and ethnic profiles used in some countries.

Above all, the new transnational terrorists are patient. They strike at times and by means of their own choosing. They conduct meticulous long-term planning. There may be years between conceiving and conducting a major attack. Plans that in the past proved impractical are often revisited. Targets are pursued with great persistence, and planning is developed and refined - we know this from examples like the World Trade Centre in New York, which was first targeted in 1993.

Resources are sometimes moved to target locations well before an attack - in some cases years ahead. These terrorists may infiltrate and obtain the necessary documents, vehicles, weapons and explosives well in advance.

The Targets of Terrorism

These new terrorists deliberately attack civilian targets to cause, where they can, mass casualties. The September 11 attacks in the United States caused human casualties on an unprecedented scale for a terrorist attack. The 2002 Bali attacks presented terrorism of a scale previously unknown in our region. The more recent Madrid attacks deliberately targeted a crowded urban public transport system. Based on recent experience and terrorist statements, we can expect more attempted mass casualty attacks in the future.

As defences improve, the terrorists have demonstrated a willingness to widen their focus from well-protected, or 'hard', targets to also include less well-protected, or 'soft', targets. 'Soft' targets such as restaurants, bars and clubs also afford the potential for causing mass casualties.

'Hard' targets, however, remain attractive to terrorists. Destroying well-protected high-value targets - such as diplomatic missions and military facilities - has great symbolic value. Table 1 illustrates the scale of impact of global terrorism since 1992 in terms of loss of human life.

We know that terrorists have also sought to target critical infrastructure in a deliberate attempt to cause maximum damage and disruption to facilities and services vital to a nation's government and economy. Recent attacks in Saudi Arabia are examples of how the terrorists have targeted the oil industry sector. These attacks have served the multiple purposes of singling-out and killing Westerners, undermining confidence in the Saudi economy, and having a global economic impact on oil prices.

CRITICAL INFRASTRUCTURE

The Australian Government defines 'critical infrastructure' as physical facilities, supply chains, information technologies and communications networks which, if destroyed, degraded or rendered unavailable for an extended period, would significantly impact on the social or economic well-being of the nation, or affect Australia's ability to conduct national defence and ensure national security.

Critical infrastructure includes:

- communications (telecommunications, electronic media, postal services)
- finance (banking, insurance, trading exchanges
- transport (air, sea, road, rail
- utilities (water, waste water)
- energy (oil, gas, electricity)
- health (hospitals, public health, laboratories)
- food supply (bulk production, bulk storage)
- manufacturing (defence industry, heavy industry, chemicals)
- government services (parliament, defence, intelligence, law enforcement, fire services, also including foreign missions in Australia
- community assets (national icons, buildings, sports facilities).

Terrorist Methods

Transnational terrorism is highly lethal, using old and new weapons to devastating effect. Advances in weapons technology are making them more lethal than ever before. The range of weapons at the terrorists' disposal is wide and increasing.

TERRORISTS HAVE GREATER LETHALITY

Transnational terrorists have access to weapons of unprecedented lethality.

Access to a vast array of new, highly lethal weapons is spreading, aided by the transfer of knowledge, funds and weapons systems internationally. These include anti-aircraft and anti-armour missiles, and enhanced-blast explosive devices. Many of these weapons are cheap, readily available and can be carried, concealed and operated by a single individual. The terrorists have already used some of these weapons. The use of hand-held missiles to attack aircraft is an example of the greater lethality able to be posed by a single individual with sufficient training in their use. The transnational terrorists' preferred method of attack is bombings. They have hijacked aircraft and used them as weapons. Assassinations, kidnappings and hostage-taking are also used, although to a far lesser extent. Terrorists will use whatever methods suit their purpose at any given time. Training in techniques and tactics covers the use of a range of weapons and explosives, vehicles and other craft. One preferred method is the truck or car bomb. These enable terrorists to deliver substantial quantities of explosives to the target. They are often, but not always, conducted by suicide bombers. Terrorists also use remote control to detonate their bombs, demonstrating a degree of sophistication in their operations.

The transnational terrorists have demonstrated maritime attack capability. On several occasions they have used small boats packed with explosives. Since January 2000, there have been maritime attacks against the USS Cole in Aden in October 2000 and against the French-owned oil tanker MV Limburg off the coast of Yemen in October 2002. Further attacks have been planned but disrupted. Most attacks occur (or are planned) in coastal waters.

Use of 'stand-off' weapons such as rockets, missiles and mortars are also part of their methodology. They enable the attackers to keep a safe distance from any defensive countermeasures. These weapons are readily available in some parts of the world and have been acquired and used by these terrorists, including surface-to-air missiles against passenger aircraft.

Suicide tactics

Suicide tactics further boost the lethal reach of these terrorists. The willingness of extremists to die in the act of terrorism makes planning easier, because the attacker has only to reach the target. There is no need to plan for escape, one of the most difficult stages of an attack. Suicide tactics are not new, but they are a major feature of the new transnational extremist-Muslim terror.

Innovative forms of attack

Transnational terrorists are innovative in developing new forms of attack. They adapt their methods to specific targets. If a hard target is of high symbolic importance, the terrorists will build on experience and develop new methods of attack. They showed this by using several teams to breach the multi-layered defences of hardened targets in the Middle East. Innovative approaches turn everyday items into lethal weapons. For example, in the September 11 attacks individual terrorists used box cutters to seize control of passenger aircraft with full tanks of fuel, turning them into large flying bombs. They have also manufactured explosives from everyday chemicals and garden fertilisers.

Non-conventional weapons

Terrorists have shown a growing interest in chemical, biological, radiological and even nuclear (CBRN) terrorism - adding a significant new dimension to the threat. If the terrorists obtained chemical, biological or nuclear weapons or materials, there is little doubt they would use them.

Transnational terrorists have sought chemical, biological and radiological materials capable of causing human casualties and economic harm.

So far, all known large-scale chemical, biological or radiological attack plans initiated by the terrorists have failed or have been disrupted. We expect more such plans will surface. Any successful chemical, biological or radiological attack by these terrorists would be a grave development and would likely encourage others.

WEAPONS OF MASS DESTRUCTION

The terms weapons of mass destruction (WMD) and chemical, biological, radiological and nuclear (CBRN) weapons are often used interchangeably.

WMD refers literally to any device that causes large-scale destruction, but is commonly taken to mean weapons capability employing chemical, biological, radiological or nuclear materials.

Chemical and biological agents may cause mass casualties but this need not always be the case. Terrorists might equally use them to assassinate one, perhaps high-profile, individual. Radiological weapons cause no physical destruction as such. But radiological materials, in combination with conventional explosives, can contaminate an area (the so-called 'dirty bomb') and may have lasting effects which result in casualties. Radiological weapons are not a serious part of any country's weapons program. Transnational terrorist groups have ready access to information on chemical, biological or radiological materials and, to some extent, nuclear weapons, via publicly available information, including on the Internet. The spread of information from state programs producing CBRN materials has further increased the potential for terrorists to develop or acquire offensive CBRN capabilities. A range of terrorist plans involving chemical and biological capability have been disrupted in recent years. It appears that years of research and training were to be translated into practice in late 2001 when extremists in Italy discussed plans to transport 'a liquid that suffocates people'. This was reportedly with intent to attack a cathedral in Paris with 10 litres of an unknown chemical agent. In December 2002, French authorities disrupted a network and found materials suggesting it was planning a cyanide gas attack. And in January 2003 UK authorities arrested a group of extremists apparently planning a ricin attack in London.

Users of the Tools of a Globalised World

The tools available to a globalised world are used to great effect by transnational terrorists. The Internet, mobile telephones and satellite telecommunications give them a truly global reach. They can run their networked operations more smoothly and coordinate action between geographically dispersed groups. They use the Internet to collect information and for operational planning. They conduct research and reconnaissance, identifying targets and vulnerabilities. They have access to a wealth of public information they can exploit.

So one-time reassurances - such as distance and geographic isolation in the case of Australia - provide little or no protection against the new transnational threat. Attacks can be coordinated and launched 'virtually'. Theatres of operation are no longer limited by geography. Propaganda is an important weapon in the terrorists' arsenal. It helps them issue threats, spread disinformation and create terror. The threat of violence, to coerce or intimidate opponents, is a form of terrorism in itself. Terrorists have always used fear as a tactic, but modern technology has made it much more powerful. We see increasingly adept use by transnational terrorists of the mass media to get their fear-inducing headlines. Both the media and the Internet have proven similarly effective in conveying the terrorists' message to their supporters worldwide - and boosting their global recruitment efforts.

Globalisation has made financing transnational terrorism easier. Financiers can transfer funds electronically and rapidly to operational elements across international boundaries. International money-laundering to support terrorist operations is also easier. All these aspects of globalisation have helped reduce the terrorists' dependence on state sponsors. Past terrorists often relied on state sponsors for capability beyond geographic borders. Today's transnational terrorists do not. Before the fall of the Taliban, Afghanistan provided a useful base of operations and training. But it was not essential for the terrorist network's survival or its ability to plan for and conduct complex operations. Areas outside effective government control, such as tribally administered territories in parts of South Asia, or areas where civil government is weak, remain important to terrorists as a base for training and operations and a source of recruits. This is why failed and failing states pose such a risk - they may easily develop into safe-havens for terrorists.

While transnational terrorists are adept in using the tools of globalisation they also use 'low-tech' means that make them harder to detect. For example, in transferring money they use personal couriers and traditional banking networks that operate outside international financial controls. Using these methods, funds can be transferred rapidly and reliably with a limited or no audit trail. That makes it harder for government agencies to identify terrorist funding channels.

Cyber-terrorism

Muslim extremists call it 'cyber-jihad' - an actual or threatened attack on a computer network to coerce or intimidate governments or the public. While there have been no instances of cyber-attack by terrorists to date, this remains a potential threat against which we must protect ourselves. We know some extremists view computer network attack as a means of waging asymmetric warfare. Direct physical attack - which often results in human casualties and physical damage - will remain the terrorists' preferred method in the medium term. But computer network attack on critical infrastructure offers the potential for significant damage of its own kind.

Cyber attacks can be launched from anywhere in the world and from multiple locations at the same time. They could cause serious damage or disruption to critical infrastructure. Since our critical infrastructure is more and more interlocked with its underlying information infrastructure, that information infrastructure may be one avenue through which to attack a high-value target. The possible consequences include disruption to e-commerce resulting in financial and economic loss, and an undermined public confidence in information technology systems. Terrorists may seek to mount cyber-attacks in combination with a physical attack to intensify its effects. They could also use cyber-attack to provide a decoy or cover for a physical attack. Individuals and groups sympathetic to terrorist causes have engaged in cyber activities, including website defacement and multiple messaging intended to deny service for a period.

An Adaptable Enemy

These terrorists are highly adaptable to changes in the strategic environment. They shift regional hubs of operations in response to changes in political and security circumstances. Their networked mode of operations makes this easier for them. They understand their environment and readjust their strategy accordingly. They are particularly adept at responding to change in tactical circumstances. Their planning is flexible and unforeseen considerations are incorporated in the planning process. They have shown they can learn from experience and mistakes. They have demonstrated a capacity to identify and exploit weaknesses in security arrangements and they continually seek new methods to defeat countermeasures. The adaptable nature of these terrorists means that their past actions will not always be a useful indicator of their future plans.

10

Al Qaida and its Operations

Al Qaida has become the most recognised and evocative symbol of the new terrorist threat. It has provided the fanatical ideology, the operational example and the management model that other groups and individuals have followed. It is the foremost example of the wider phenomenon of transnational extremist-Muslim terrorism. To understand Al Qaida's evolution is to gain an appreciation of this new terrorism. And to understand Al Qaida we need to understand how its philosophy differs from that of mainstream Islam.

A Pluralist and Tolerant Tradition

Islam has played a vital role in shaping human civilisation. The classical period of its rich history nurtured and moulded much of our modern scientific knowledge and philosophy. It fostered a tolerant, diverse and pluralist tradition.

Like Judaism and Christianity, Islam traces its faith back to the Prophet Abraham. It accepts all the major Biblical prophets. It accords a special status to Jews and Christians, referring to them in the Quran as 'People of the Book'.

Mainstream Islamic scholars - whose views reflect those of the vast majority of the world's Muslims - have long stressed the Quran's clear endorsement of diversity, its prohibition of coercion, suicide and murder, its instruction to Muslims to act towards others with compassion, forgiveness and restraint. Tolerance of other beliefs has been a key element. Islamic tradition has long encouraged Muslims to respect the sanctity of human life. It encourages them to coexist peacefully with other People of the Book. It advises them to beware of extremism. It has also embraced a wide range of perspectives about ways to approach the faith: Islam is not monolithic. The Quran does contain verses calling on Muslims to defend themselves if attacked, which extremists cite in support of their views. But such verses are usually heavily qualified. It has long been a central tenet of mainstream Islamic scholarship that Quranic verses should not be considered in isolation or divorced from their moral and historical contexts. Mainstream Muslim scholars have argued that, in a time of war, Muslims are obliged to draw a distinction between combatants and non-combatants. Killing innocent civilians is forbidden.

ISLAM IN AUSTRALIA

Australia is threatened by transnational terrorism, perpetuated in the name of an extremist Muslim ideology. A radical but tiny minority of Muslims have twisted Islamic teachings to further their revolutionary ideals. The overwhelming majority of Muslims are peaceful and law-abiding. The Australian Muslim community continues to make a significant contribution to the struggle against terrorism.

In the early 16th century, Makassan fishermen from the Indonesian archipelago were the first Muslims to visit Australia. They traded with the indigenous Aboriginal community. In the 19th century, Afghan Muslim camel drivers played an important role in exploring and opening up the outback. Today, Islam is one of the fastest-growing faiths in Australia. Muslims are a vital part of the rich mosaic of Australian society.

In the past 25 years, the Australian Muslim community has grown significantly. The 2001 Census counted 281 578 Muslims living in Australia - an increase of 40 per cent since the 1996 Census and an overall rise of 91 per cent in the past decade. These figures may be conservative. Some recent estimates suggest Australian Muslims now number between 350 000 and 450 000. Australian Muslims are ethnically diverse. About 35 per cent of them were born in Australia. The rest immigrated to Australia from over 70 different countries, including Lebanon, Turkey, Indonesia and Bosnia-Herzegovina. There are over 100 mosques and at least 21 Muslim primary and secondary schools in Australia. Islamic community centres, student associations, halal butchers and restaurants are found in every major city in Australia.

Australian Muslims are doctors, lawyers, academics, sportspersons, journalists, diplomats, police officers, members of the Defence Force, entrepreneurs, shopkeepers and labourers. Muslims have contributed much to our political, economic and social life. They have cemented their place in our religious and cultural landscape. They occupy an increasingly important place in Australian life, and are embracing opportunities to participate in a tolerant, inclusive and culturally diverse Australia.

Extremist Ideology

The ideology and the methods of extremist-Muslim terrorists are far removed from mainstream Muslims' tolerance of other faiths. Only a tiny minority of Muslims support the terrorists' strategy of violence. Extremists cloak themselves in the language of Islam but, particularly in their advocacy of violence, flout what the overwhelming majority of Muslims accept as fundamental precepts of their religion.

SOME CONSERVATIVE MUSLIM REFORM MOVEMENTS

Salafism

Salafism is an approach to Islam based on reverence for the example of the 'righteous ancestors' (Al-Salaf Al-Saleh). Some Salafis advocate strict adherence to a literal interpretation of the Quran and the Sunna (the deeds of the Prophet and the Hadith), which they believe contain the source of all necessary guidance. They oppose attempts to interpret Quranic law from an historical, contextual perspective. They reject innovation in faith (bida). 'Wahhabism' is often associated with the Salafi orientation. Its adherents consider the term 'Wahhabism' derogatory; they see themselves as orthodox Muslims and draw heavily on the conservative tribal social customs of the Arabian Peninsula. Salafism is not of itself a doctrine of extremism but groups like Al Qaida draw on strands of an extremist interpretation of Salafism.

The Muslim Brotherhood

Hassan Al-Banna formed the Muslim Brotherhood in Egypt in 1928. It was at first a social and moral reform movement to revive Islam as a way of life and end the separation of religion and state. It complemented government activities by providing valuable community services. Offshoots of the Brotherhood still play an important and legitimate role in some Muslim countries' political processes. Al-Banna combined the Quranic descriptions of qital (fighting) and jihad (struggle) (Jihad does not mean 'holy war'. It means struggle or striving in accordance with the teachings of Islam. There are two forms of jihad: the 'greater' jihad - an inner struggle to better oneself for God - and the 'lesser' jihad - the taking-up of arms in defence of Islam, under strict conditions, when the religion is threatened. The terrorists espouse an aggressively violent or militant interpretation of the lesser jihad) to provide the basis of a call to wage war against non-Muslims who had taken overMuslim lands. Groups like Al Qaida are also influenced by a tradition of religiously based rebellion inspired by the teachings of Ibn Taymiyya and Sayyid Qutb. This contrasts with the more conservative and politically passive tradition of establishment Salafism or 'Wahhabism' found in countries like Saudi Arabia.

INFLUENCES ON MUSLIM EXTREMIST THINKING

Ibn Taymiyya

Ibn Taymiyya was an important fourteenth century theologian. He cultivated the idea that Muslim rulers who contravened Islam should be labelled kuffar (unbelievers). He developed his ideas at a time when the Muslim world was under attack by the Mongols, and was therefore concerned about defending the Muslim community. He argued that Muslims were obliged to overthrow kuffar rulers like the Mongols. He advocated amending the five pillars of Islam - the obligatory duties of all Muslims - to include militant jihad. His ideas have inspired the worldview of terrorist groups like Al Qaida.

Sayyid Qutb

In the 1950s, Sayyid Qutb expanded on the thinking of Al-Banna and refined the aims of the Muslim Brotherhood. He argued that artificial nation-states had allowed Muslim countries to lapse into a pre-Islamic state of ignorance and barbarism (Jahiliyya). He advocated the use of militant jihad as a revolutionary instrument to re-establish God's sovereignty on Earth.

Abdullah Azzam

Abdullah Azzam was a Palestinian activist and mentor to Usama Bin Laden. Drawing on the writings of Ibn Taymiyya, he argued that all Muslims had a compulsory duty to wage uncompromising war to reclaim all lands formerly ruled by the Islamic caliphate. His doctrine was absolute - his motto was 'Jihad and the rifle alone: no negotiations, no conferences, no dialogue'. Azzam helped fund and promote the cause of the mujahideen (fighters engaged in militant jihad) in Afghanistan.

Ayman Al-Zawahiri

Ayman Al-Zawahiri, an Egyptian radical, is another key ideologist for Al Qaida. Drawing on the works of Qutb, he sees democracy as a form of idol worship. It must be vanquished through warfare. He considers supporters of democracy to be kuffar. He was the driving force behind Al Qaida's 1998 edict instructing Muslims to kill Americans and their allies wherever they found them.

A Capacity to Harness Opinion and History

Al Qaida and its affiliates employ extremist and selective interpretations of Islam. They use the interpretations that validate their worldview and theologically rationalise their actions, no matter how vicious or out of kilter with mainstream Islam.

The extremists argue that 11 September 2001 victims were not innocent. Because they voted in elections and paid taxes, they were complicit in the acts of an 'evil' US Administration. By extension, any victims in any future attacks are deemed not to be innocent.

Usama Bin Laden, in particular, has been a consummate manipulator of certain frustrations and disillusionment felt throughout the Muslim world. He exploits the depths of resentment that underlie centuries of Muslim history. This resentment is rooted in a sense that the Muslim world has been humiliated by Western colonisation and political, military, economic and cultural dominance.

Other Muslim extremists advocate and take advantage of Bin Laden's assertion that the United States seeks to dominate the Muslim world. They cite the war against the Taliban in

Afghanistan and the US-led occupation of Iraq as evidence. The Israeli-Palestinian conflict is perhaps the rawest wound Bin Laden exploits. He demonises the United States by tapping into widespread pro-Palestinian sentiment within the Muslim world and denouncing US support for Israel. Bin Laden also plays on Muslim attitudes towards other theatres of militant jihad, such as Kashmir, Chechnya, Bosnia and the southern Philippines. Many Muslims identify with these causes, and by invoking them Al Qaida swells its pool of potential recruits. But this does not mean they are of themselves root causes of terrorism.

Al Qaida

All roads lead to and from Afghanistan

The 1979 - 89 war to expel the Soviet Union from Afghanistan was central to the development of Al Qaida. It became a rallying point for militant extremists. The 25 000 or so volunteers from abroad who joined the local Afghan resistance provided Al Qaida with its first recruits. Already susceptible, they were further radicalised in Afghanistan. They adopted the revolutionary visions of Qutb, Azzam and Zawahiri. The majority went home battle-hardened and well trained. Some resolved to spread their new ideas.

The liberation of Afghanistan was supported by a number of countries that opposed the Soviet occupation. The Afghan resistance received financial and logistical support from several countries, including the United States, Pakistan and Saudi Arabia. As well as doing his own share of fundraising, Bin Laden placed much of his own wealth at the mujahideen's disposal.

A BRIEF BIOGRAPHY OF USAMA BIN LADEN

Usama Bin Laden was born in Saudi Arabia in about 1957. His father, Mohammed, originally from Yemen, was a wealthy businessman with close connections to the ruling Al-Saud.

Usama Bin Laden was one of about 50 children. He had a strict religious upbringing. He attended university in Jeddah and graduated with a degree in administration.

Soon after the Soviet Union invaded Afghanistan in 1979, Bin Laden travelled for the first time to the border areas of

Pakistan. It was not until the early 1980s that he entered Afghanistan proper, bringing with him large amounts of cash and construction machinery. In 1984, he built in Peshawar (Pakistan) a guesthouse for militants who were on their way to participate in the resistance to Soviet occupation. Bin Laden and his guesthouse played an important role in the work of Azzam's Maktab Al-Khidamat (services office). They processed and trained large numbers of volunteers on their way to Afghanistan.

When victory over the Soviets looked imminent, Bin Laden created the movement now known as Al Qaida. The aim was to continue the militant jihad globally. Ten years later, with Ayman Al-Zawahiri and others, he formed the International Islamic Front for Jihad Against the Jews and Crusaders.

Bin Laden returned to Saudi Arabia. He used his high public profile there to draw attention to the Afghan victory. He began to criticise the Saudi government for failing to defend Islam.

When Iraq invaded Kuwait, Bin Laden offered to help defend Saudi Arabia using Saudi Afghan veterans. He was rebuffed. The Saudis accepted assistance from US forces.

Bin Laden fled to Sudan, which was governed by the National Islamic Front. He set up Al Qaida's headquarters in Khartoum. Financed by legitimate businesses, including Sudanese government construction contracts, Al Qaida set about establishing its global terrorism credentials. Its primary objective was the removal of US forces from the Arabian Peninsula and the overthrow of the Saudi regime. Eventually, Bin Laden returned to Afghanistan. There, Al Qaida accelerated its operations and intensified its opposition to governments in the West and in the Muslim world that did not meet its standards.

Bin Laden has no formal qualifications as an Islamic scholar. His value to the mujahideen movement - and his impact on it - has been due to his charisma, his leadership, the wealth he inherited through his father's business success, his connections and his administrative skills.

Azzam and others travelled widely, seeking financial support and recruiting volunteers to join the militant jihad in

Afghanistan. In effect, they established the global framework for what would become Al Qaida. Recruits came not just from the Middle East, but Central, South and South-East Asia, and parts of Africa, as well as Western countries.

After the Soviet forces were defeated, some mujahideen who had trained in Pakistani camps travelled to other locations, such as Kashmir and Chechnya, rather than returning to their home countries. They had been trained for militant operations beyond the Afghan resistance. Afghanistan was where the careers of Azzam, Bin Laden and Zawahiri intersected. For Bin Laden it was not just an opportunity to experience militant jihad. He also met key figures from other extremist groups and learnt about their causes. In particular, his developing association with Zawahiri gave him an introduction to the wider militant jihad movement. He could now develop his own ideas about the shortcomings of governments in the Muslim world.

Learning from Success

The mujahideen were just one factor in the defeat of the Soviet army in Afghanistan. But they claimed responsibility for it, and for the collapse of the Soviet system soon after.

In the militants' eyes, the Soviet withdrawal proved that a small group of religious extremists with limited resources could defeat a military superpower. For Al Qaida it was a lesson: it could take its fight to other theatres where it faced odds that had seemed impossible. As Zawahiri put it:

> The most important thing about the battle in Afghanistan was that it destroyed the illusion of the superpower in the minds of young Muslim mujahideen. The Soviet Union, the power with the largest land forces in the world, was destroyed and scattered, running away from Afghanistan before the eyes of the Muslim youth. This Jihad was a training course for Muslim youth for the future battle anticipated with the superpower which is the sole leader of the world now, America.

Al Qaida drew conclusions, too, about US resolve. They took the US withdrawal from Lebanon in 1983 after about 250 marines died in a truck bombing, and from Somalia in 1993 after a number of its soldiers were killed, as proof that the

United States was not prepared to engage in a fight with a determined enemy.

Al Qaida's Message

Al Qaida's fanatical interpretations of Islam place all Muslim societies that do not comply or agree in its sights. Its principal goal - ridding Saudi Arabia of US forces and replacing the Saudi Government (see Box on Usama Bin Laden) - was based on Bin Laden's view that the Saudi Government had forfeited its Islamic legitimacy. That goal has since been extended to the ejection from the entire Muslim world of US and Western influence.

Al Qaida's ultimate message is that all former Muslim lands must be recovered - no matter how long ago they were 'lost' - and their governments replaced by regimes reflecting Al Qaida's interpretation of Islam. All Jews, 'Crusaders' and 'idolaters of democracy' are to be expelled from those lands.

Al Qaida's strategic goals appear to have evolved but are not known to be set out in any consolidated form. Its aims are based on a selective and extremist interpretation of Islamic texts, under which the duty to wage war against the enemies of God is divinely ordained. Bin Laden's 'declaration of war against the Americans' of 1996 declared militant jihad against the United States. It gives a good insight into Al Qaida's worldview and aims. And his so-called fatwa issued in February 1998 at the establishment of an umbrella group called the 'World Islamic Front for Jihad Against Jews and the Crusaders' outlines clearly the true nature of the terrorists' ideology.

Al Qaida's battlefield is global. It will attack its enemies anywhere in the world - its attacks are no longer limited to previous theatres of militant jihad. In their 1998 fatwa, Bin Laden, Zawahiri and their associates tell Muslims that:

> *... to kill Americans and their allies - civilians and military - is an individual duty for every Muslim who can do it in any country in which it is possible to do it, in order to liberate the Al-Aqsa Mosque and the holy mosque [in Mecca] from their grip, and in order for their armies to move out of all the lands of Islam, defeated and unable to threaten any Muslim. This is in accordance with the words of Almighty God.*

This was the first time that Al Qaida identified civilians as legitimate targets. Al Qaida's inclination to take the fight beyond the Muslim world to Western countries has been unambiguously demonstrated in New York, Madrid and elsewhere. And Al Qaida does not consider itself constrained in its methods or choice of targets.

Al Qaida spokesman, Sulaiman Abu Ghaith, said in June 2002:

> *... we have the right to kill four million Americans, including one million children, displace double that figure and injure and cripple hundreds of thousands. We have the right to fight them by chemical and biological weapons ...*

The terrorists oppose secularism and single out democracy for particular criticism. Zawahiri has been notably critical of Muslim groups that have endorsed democracy. He argues that only God can exercise sovereignty over worldly communities. So, in his view, democracy - which renders human beings sovereign - is heresy. It allows mankind to usurp the role of God. Zawahiri characterises democracy as a false religion. For him, people who live in democracies, particularly in Muslim countries, are therefore legitimate targets because, by voting and paying taxes, they participate in the 'idolatrous' democratic process. Similarly, those who seek to promote democracy in Muslim countries are also deemed to be targets.

Al Qaida continues to strive for large-scale, coordinated, mass casualty, multiple attacks of the kind seen on September 11 and in the East Africa embassy bombings of 1998.

Disseminating the Message

Al Qaida skilfully conveys its message through the use of modern information and communications technology: pre-recorded video and audio tapes, DVDs, CD-ROMs and the Internet. In 2001, Al Qaida produced a recruitment DVD that was widely copied and made available on the Internet.

The Internet has become an important part of modern terrorism's arsenal. Al Qaida in particular uses it - through websites like the now-defunct www.azzam.com - to spread its ideology and propaganda, and to send messages to sympathisers and operatives. Announcements, edicts and ideological expositions by senior Al Qaida figures are made. Videos depicting terrorist attacks are screened. The Internet is also used for the passage of operational instructions. Certainly, terrorist websites regularly feature calls on Muslims to attack Western targets.

The World Wide Web is also used as a training tool. Various procedural and instruction manuals and general tactical guidance have been posted on extremist websites. Al Qaida also uses the media shrewdly. Bin Laden himself has taken advantage of increasingly globalised communications links to spread his message. His interviews with Time, Newsweek and CNN reached worldwide audiences. They give him opportunities to influence the actions and beliefs of Muslim extremists everywhere.

An Evolving, Inspirational Prototype

Because it is a highly adaptable and complex entity, understanding Al Qaida's structure and behaviour is difficult. During the late 1990s, Al Qaida in Afghanistan took on many characteristics of a hierarchical organisation. It had permanent installations, fixed structures, standardised methods and regular procedures. Since 2001, it has assumed more the character of an ideological movement. Decentralised, semi-autonomous remnants operate independently or follow broad general direction. It remains well funded and ambitious. Apart from the finances of Bin Laden himself, it draws on donors in the Gulf and elsewhere. It developed its own commercial ventures, particularly in Sudan in the early 1990s.

Through Al Qaida's capacity for change and regeneration, some characteristics have emerged over time. Al Qaida is a 'network of networks'. Each of them can operate independently, or with other networks. These networks cover leadership, planning and operations, financial, training and equipment support, as well as propaganda and several other functions. Some networks include a 'hub'. Others are diffuse and decentralised. Since the destruction of Al Qaida's Afghanistan base, many hubs have been shut down, or moved to nearby areas within South Asia. Other networks have evolved to function primarily through electronic media such as the Internet.

Just one Part of a Wider Network

For many Muslim extremists, Al Qaida has become more an idea or ideology than a physical entity. Bin Laden's propaganda skills, and his capacity to exploit Arab and Muslim antagonism towards the West, motivate and direct many militant groups and individuals that may otherwise have few tangible links with Al Qaida.

So, although Al Qaida has been the key influence on the development of transnational extremist-Muslim terrorism, it is not the only element. New adherents to its fanaticism have been attracted by Al Qaida's high-profile successes, its propaganda skills and its capacity to take advantage of deeply felt grievances in the Muslim world.

Some new players have taken up the extremist mantle of their own accord. Others have developed networks independently, and have in turn established links with Al Qaida. And existing, more localised extremist-Muslim terror groups, impressed by Al Qaida's achievements, have absorbed its broader ideological ambitions. They have added their networks to the mix. The shared Afghan experience has accelerated the development of this process. Some such groups share or have adopted aspects of Al Qaida's worldview and developed a similar style. Prominent among them are the Pakistani-Kashmiri terrorist group Lashkar e-Tayyiba, Jemaah Islamiyah and the Al-Zarqawi network.

In this way the Al Qaida experience has been replicated and reinforced. The result is a transnational extremist-Muslim terrorism at once more resilient, more extensive and more difficult to counter. So, as Al Qaida's leaders are eliminated, others will be ready to take their place. Even if Al Qaida itself were wiped out, networks set up in its image are probably capable of continuing its work.

Al Qaida's adaptive networks have helped it survive a sustained US-led military offensive. Since October 2001, a significant proportion of its leadership and rank-and-file has been either captured or killed. Much of the remainder has dispersed and is in hiding. Its communications links and operational capability have been seriously disrupted. But its links with other, similarly flexible networks show how

Al Qaida is just one aspect of a larger series of connections, so much so that it retains a potent capacity to strike in diverse locations.

Some Afghanistan veterans have become focal points in their own countries for new and revived groups. They in turn developed their own network structures - echoing the experience of Al Qaida. In other cases, local groups with few or no direct links to Al Qaidahave drawn inspiration, expertise and direction from the movement's public statements.

They act independently in their local areas. Some are attracted to the movement's ideology, some by what they see as its potency against what they resent, some by its propaganda. The aims of groups like Ansar Al-Islam in northern Iraq, Laskar Jundullah in Indonesia and the Abu Sayyaf Group in the southern Philippines have been supported by Al Qaida's global focus.

Irrespective of its own fate, Al Qaida has generated a system of self-sustaining and adaptable networks. It can maintain operational capability because of the autonomous nature of the networks' components. It is likely that some of these networks' functions - training, for instance - have shifted to new geographical and network locations. As Al Qaida's training facilities are damaged, the network is able to adjust. The training function can be continued by other groups. The same thing applies to other network functions, such as finance or operations. It is possible that no overall network for command and control even exists.

The loose links between these networks mean associated groups can operate without central control. Such arrangements are also more resilient to attack. Affiliated groups have adopted in some cases Al Qaida's flexibility and transformative capacities. This extends even more the terrorists' reach and makes their security harder to penetrate.

The networks that originally centred on Al Qaida have become more widespread and less interdependent - with varying degrees of connectedness to each other. They extend throughout the world. There are now active terrorist elements and supporters in the Middle East, parts of Africa, Western countries and in South, Central and South-East Asia.

THE SOUTH ASIAN CONNECTION

Many individuals and organisations within the complex terrorist 'network of networks' share links with extremist groups in South Asia. These links are mainly historical and ideological, but also include practical and organisational elements.

Historically, many key players within the global militant jihad movement fought the Soviet Union in Afghanistan in the 1980s. They kept in contact after coming home from the war. These links are still strong. For example, the Abu Sayyaf Group in the Philippines is named after a famous mujahideen commander of the Afghan War. Similarly, the Jemaah Islamiyah network draws on strong Afghan alumni links. Many individual terrorists know each other well based on shared Afghan experience.

Ideologically, the diverse transnational terrorist networks share a worldview based on the shared study, indoctrination and experience of the Afghan War. Operating patterns are based upon techniques learned in Afghanistan and then standardised and disseminated through the network. In practical terms, common operational methods have been refined through exchange of information between individuals and groups with shared Afghan experience.

Techniques that appear in one conflict or with one group may later appear in other conflicts. They may be passed via electronic communication or through mobile cadres who train terrorists in specific techniques. Much of this training is centred on Kashmir and the tribal areas of Pakistan. This makes South Asia a key geographical focus for terrorist networks today.

The well developed Al Qaida infrastructure inside Afghanistan was destroyed in 2001, but various South Asian groups have copied Al Qaida's organisation and methods. Dispersed groups continue to operate independently, or follow general guidance from key terrorist leaders, with a geographical focus on South Asia.

Of the Pakistani extremist groups, Lashkar e-Tayyiba is the most closely affiliated with Al Qaida. Formed in 1989, Lashkar e-Tayyiba, like Al Qaida, sprang from popular opposition to the Soviet presence in Afghanistan. Through shared experience in Afghanistan, many Lashkar e-Tayyiba leaders had links to Al Qaida. Lashkar e-Tayyiba transferred its efforts to the insurgency in Indian-held Kashmir in the early 1990s. Its activities later escalated from localised actions in Kashmir to international terrorism in India. Lashkar e-Tayyiba performs a critical function in the transnational network as a primary provider of training to the broader transnational terrorist movement, particularly following the destruction of Al Qaida's Afghanistan base in October 2001.

THE EVOLUTION OF TRANSNATIONAL EXTREMIST-MUSLIM TERRORIST GROUPS IN SOUTH-EAST ASIA

Islam in South-East Asia is predominantly moderate and tolerant. We need to understand the evolution of Muslim extremist terrorist groups in the region in that context. Islam arrived in South-East Asia peaceably, carried to the region in the thirteenth century by Muslim traders from South Asia and the Middle East. Over several centuries, as the religion spread across South-East Asia, it incorporated and adapted elements of pre-existing cultural and spiritual beliefs and traditions.

Reflecting its peaceful evolution, South-East Asian Islam has been traditionally open-minded and accepting of cultural diversity.

Every country in South-East Asia has a Muslim community - from five per cent of the population in the Philippines to around 90 per cent in Indonesia. Within these Muslim communities, Islamic identity or affiliation has grown in recent decades, in line with a global phenomenon. There is a greater observance of Islamic practices and dress codes, particularly among young Muslims. And Islamic organisations have become increasingly prominent and active on university campuses and in politics more generally.

Muslim political and social organisations play a positive role in the countries of the region. Indonesia's two largest Muslim organisations, Muhammadiyah and Nahdlatul Ulama, were central to the successful transition to democracy. They play critical roles in providing welfare and education to their fellow citizens. Both organisations are firmly opposed to terrorism. They expressed support for Indonesia's new anti-terrorism decrees in the wake of the Bali bombings.

The vast majority of South-East Asia's Muslims represent tolerant, mainstream Islam. In parliamentary elections in both Indonesia and Malaysia in 2004, Muslim political parties advocating a moderate and tolerant message outperformed those advocating a narrow conservative interpretation of Islam.

It is important to recognise that support for political Islam or a growth in Muslim piety does not translate into a greater likelihood of Muslim extremism and militancy.

An increase in identification with Islam should not be confused with the emergence of terrorist groups such as Jemaah Islamiyah, which was responsible for the Bali attack. Bali bomber Amrozi no more represents the views of the majority of Muslims in South-East Asia than Usama Bin Laden represents the majority of Muslims in the Arab world.

The vast majority of the population of South-East Asia rejects not only the callous violence of terrorist groups but also their goals and ideology.

Evolution of Militancy - Fusing Local and International Agendas

Terrorist tactics are not new in South-East Asia. Nor are they limited to a particular religious or ethnic group.

Militant separatist movements in South-East Asia since the 1940s have had a range of ethnic, political and religious motivations. And violence against civilians has been perpetrated by followers of a variety of political ideologies and religious faiths. Almost every armed nationalist and communist movement in the region has had such tactics in its repertoire. Across the region, militant sub-national groups have over past decades used terrorist attacks to advance their separatist, ethnic or religious interests.

But the emergence of systematically applied terrorism, associated with a virulent form of extremist Muslim ideology, has transformed terrorist attacks in South-East Asia. A seldom-chosen tactic has become an integral - even primary - choice for interconnected groups. Muslim militancy is not a new phenomenon in South-East Asia. In the post-colonial era, militant Muslim separatist groups formed in countries where Muslims are in the minority - Burma, the Philippines, Thailand-to fight for autonomy from national governments. In Indonesia, where Muslims make up the majority, Muslim militancy has been driven by two goals - to establish an Islamic state, governed by a rigid and doctrinaire interpretation of Islamic law, and to redress economic and political grievances.

A number of South-East Asian Muslim separatist groups have been prepared to use violence or terrorism against their governments. The Moro Islamic Liberation Front (MILF) and the Abu Sayyaf Group continue to operate in the Philippines. The Pattani United Liberation Organisation (PULO) is active in Thailand, and the Rohingya Solidarity Organisation in Burma.

These groups are not primarily anti-Western. Rather, they have had long-standing disputes with national governments based on local socio-political and economic grievances. But Muslim militancy in the region has undergone a dramatic evolution over the past decade. The historical grievances of radical Muslim groups were local in nature. Now, the predominant terrorist threat in South-East Asia is transnational. It draws inspiration and support both from other South-East Asian militant groups and from outside the region.

A volatile fusion of local and international agendas has emerged. Most troubling of all, for some extremist militants, terrorist attacks have become an acceptable part of their strategy. And terrorist attacks have become more lethal, more frequent, more widespread and more focused on targeting Western interests.

Jemaah Islamiyah exemplifies the evolution of Muslim militancy in South-East Asia. It has links to Al Qaida and is strongly influenced by Usama Bin Laden's terrorist ideology and methodology. The threat posed by Jemaah Islamiyah is compounded by its development as a network that ignores national boundaries. It stretches over several regional countries. It has formed links with existing extremist Muslim groups to further its own goals.

In the southern Philippines, elements of local militant Muslim insurgency groups, the MILF and the Abu Sayyaf Group, have established links with Jemaah Islamiyah and to some extent with Al Qaida. Links with elements of the MILF are very important to Jemaah Islamiyah. They give Jemaah Islamiyah access to training camps in Mindanao and a ready-made insurgency to give new recruits combat experience.

Dangerous sub-national groups, who can or want to use terrorism to further their causes, are also present in South-East Asia. Mujahidin KOMPAK, Laskar Jihad (supposedly disbanded) and Laskar Jundullah in Indonesia, and the Malaysian Militant Group (Kumpulan Militan Malaysia - KMM) started out with the ostensible aim of promoting the interests of political Islam. Their transition to more violent methods resulted from their greater identification with, and links to, other radical Muslim movements in the region, in South Asia and in the Middle East.

Driving the increase in terrorist activity in our region has been the exposure of South-East Asian militants to the thinking of Middle Eastern Muslim extremists. That includes the latter's message that terrorism is acceptable. Again, Afghanistan was the crucible. The most significant transmission of extremist ideology and military skills to South-East Asian militants took place in the 1980s, with their participation in the war against the Soviet Union in Afghanistan.

Origins of the Transnational Agenda: the Afghanistan Connection

South-East Asian extremism took a leap forward when militant Muslim groups - including the leaders of Jemaah Islamiyah - decided to send recruits to training camps in Afghanistan and in Pakistan from the mid-1980s. Their aim was to support their co-religionists in the fight against the Soviet Union.

The Soviet forces left Afghanistan by 1989. But the concept of militant jihad - in this case, a multinational armed struggle by Muslim believers - did not end with their departure. The Soviet - Afghanistan experience was a catalyst for radical activity in South-East Asia. There is an Afghanistan connection to many South-East Asian Muslim militant groups. Up to 1000 South-East Asian Muslims are believed to have received military training with the Afghan mujahideen in the 1980s. In some cases this included battlefield experience. Key leaders of radical Muslim groups in the region are all veterans of the Soviet -

Afghan war. They include Jemaah Islamiyah key operative Hambali, Abu Sayyaf Group leaders Khaddafy and Abdurajak Janjalani (now dead), and others.

In the camps in Afghanistan, South-East Asian volunteers were infused with a sense of brotherhood and common cause with those undertaking or supporting militant jihad from other parts of the Muslim world. They were introduced to more advanced terrorist and militant ideology and techniques. They brought them back to South-East Asia and passed them on at training camps in our region.

The returnees formed a natural, transnational network in South-East Asia that is now extensive and well entrenched. This network is at the heart of the terrorist threat in South-East Asia today.

Education and Advanced Technology

Other external forces are at work to spread extremism in South-East Asia. A significant number of young South-East Asians are studying at religious schools, or madrassas, in Pakistan, Afghanistan and Yemen. They have been influenced by some of the more doctrinaire versions of Islam - particularly the closely-related Salafi and Wahhabi streams. The financial power of Saudi Arabia has also helped promote Wahhabism in South-East Asia through the funding of educational institutions.

Many South Asian and Middle Eastern madrassas teach only a rigid and doctrinaire interpretation of the Quran, with a strong emphasis on militant jihad.

South-East Asia's information technology revolution has hastened the spread of external influences, including extremist ideology. International television and information available on the Internet have led to a greater identification with Muslims in conflict around the world. They have inspired and shaped the behaviour of radicals in South-East Asia. The Internet is not merely a communications mechanism for extremists. It is also an effective vehicle for global publicity and recruitment efforts.

Some madrassas - including those run in Pakistan by the militant group Lashkar e-Tayyiba - emphasise computer literacy, even while teaching few or no other secular subjects. Within

South-East Asia itself, large numbers of community-run Islamic boarding schools, or pesantren, operate outside the state control of formal Islamic education systems. Income disparity in many countries of the region has led to poorer youth taking up this option with governments unable to meet the educational needs of growing populations.

A small number of these schools have become a source of concern to regional governments as Jemaah Islamiyah has sought to use networks of pesantren across several South-East Asian countries as a vehicle to propagate extremist ideology and for recruitment purposes. Pesantren vulnerable to these approaches are few in number relative to the majority that emphasise the teaching of moral values. Al Qaida has also recruited and radicalised students with Western secular educational backgrounds. In South-East Asia some of Jemaah Islamiyah's leading operatives have had advanced technical and scientific qualifications from secular universities.

It is important to note that many leading advocates of pluralism and democracy in South-East Asia are graduates of Islamic education institutions. Former Indonesian President, Abdurrahman Wahid, and prominent Indonesian Muslim intellectuals including the Rector of the State Islamic University in Jakarta, Dr Azyumardi Azra, and the Rector of the Paramadina Mulya University, Nurcholish Madjid, are all graduates of Islamic education institutions.

Regional Vulnerabilities

Transnational terrorist groups, including Al Qaida and Lashkar e-Tayyiba, have demonstrated an interest in South-East Asia. They see it as a base for operations, a safe haven and a source of potential recruits. It is also a source of the kinds of services drawn upon by other transnational criminals. Terrorists look to exploit any vulnerabilities in the region's varied counter-terrorism capabilities. Areas of potential concern in some regional countries include limitations in institutional, governance and legislative frameworks; resource constraints; inadequate coordination arrangements, both internally and between countries in the region; and variable political will. Problem areas also include law enforcement, intelligence, transport security, defence and anti-terrorist financing.

Terrorist groups can also exploit long-standing socio-political and economic grievances that persist in some countries.

The lack of controlled border crossings in some South-East Asian countries is a major impediment to the monitoring and control of terrorist groups. Maritime piracy is a significant problem in the region. Porous borders, combined with massive inbound tourist and business flows, open immigration regimes, limited identity and document fraud detection, inadequately trained or corrupt officials, poor coordination between border control agencies and various security agencies, and limited immigration and customs control capacities all provide an environment in which terrorism can flourish.

All these problems can be compounded by inadequate legislation. Effective laws are important to put governments in the best possible position to investigate, detain and prosecute those involved in terrorism and its financing.

Al Qaida and other terrorist groups are known to have abused charitable organisations. They have used them for fund-raising and have diverted money donated to them towards support for extremist activities. Unregulated and unaudited Islamic charities in South-East Asia are vulnerable to misuse by extremist groups.

TERRORIST FUNDING IN SOUTH-EAST ASIA

South-East Asian terrorist organisations have received funding through covert means such as couriers, and legitimate and front companies and organisations. It is suspected that Al Qaida provided funding for the Bali bombings and it is known to have provided funding in the past to terrorist groups in the Philippines.

Some Islamic non-government organisations, particularly those based in the Arabian Peninsula are - both knowingly and unknowingly - used as conduits for terrorist financing in South-East Asia. The Australian Government is aware that, while predominantly engaging in legitimate humanitarian and religious activities, some of these organisations have been used by terrorists for the transfer of funds, the purchase of arms and other forms of logistic support. Terrorism has also been supported by other financial activities, including fundraising, extortion, kidnapping and ransom.

Jemaah Islamiyah and the Evolution of South-East Asian Terrorist Networks

Jemaah Islamiyah - origins and development

Jemaah Islamiyah has its origins in the Darul Islam separatist movement in Indonesia. Darul Islam was involved in regional rebellions in the 1950s and 1960s that sought to impose Islamic law or form Islamic states in parts of Indonesia. The movement was strongest in West and Central Java, South Sumatra and South Sulawesi, areas where Jemaah Islamiyah is most heavily represented today.

After the Darul Islam insurgency was suppressed in the mid-1960s, Darul Islam continued to exist as an underground political movement working for imposition of Islamic law in Indonesia. In the 1980s, in the wake of the Islamic Revolution in Iran, the movement became more active and was involved in covert opposition to the Soeharto Government. By the mid-1990s, several armed extremist groups had emerged from the Darul Islam movement, tracing their origins to the insurgencies of the 1950s.

Jemaah Islamiyah evolved as a secretive militant organisation from a faction of the Darul Islam political movement, led by Abdullah Sungkar, who died in 1999. Sungkar and Abu Bakar Ba'asyir, his long-time associate, established the Al Mukmin pesantren at Ngruki, in Central Java, in 1971.

This school became a centre for Muslim radical activity in the area. Many of the Jemaah Islamiyah leaders studied at the Ngruki school, as did Bali bombers Amrozi and Mukhlas. The terrorist who drove the bomb to the JW Marriott Hotel in Jakarta, killing 12 people in August 2003, was also a former Ngruki student.

Both Sungkar and Ba'asyir were jailed several times during this period by Indonesian authorities for seeking to establish an Islamic state. Sungkar and Ba'asyir fled to Malaysia to escape a crackdown by Indonesian authorities on Muslim militancy in the mid-1980s. Malaysia then became the centre of the group's activities. Jemaah Islamiyah - in the form in which it is known today - was established around this time, in the mid- to late-1980s. Sungkar led Jemaah Islamiyah from Malaysia, preaching a doctrine of attaining an Islamic state in

Indonesia through militant struggle on the three-fold basis of strengthening faith, Islamic brotherhood and military capability. The Luqmanul Hakim madrassa in the Malaysian state of Johor, since closed down by Malaysian authorities, was a base for Ba'asyir and Sungkar while in Malaysia. Bali bomber Mukhlas taught at the Luqmanul Hakim school during this period.

These Indonesian exiles developed a radical religious following in Malaysia. At the same time, they were developing links with the Muslim separatists in the southern Philippines. They adapted their preaching to their new circumstances. They began to promote a pan-Malay Muslim ideology calling for a unified South-East Asian Islamic state.

Probably the most important factor in the development of South-East Asian extremism was Sungkar's decision to send recruits to militant training camps in Afghanistan and Pakistan from the mid-1980s.

Both Sungkar and Ba'asyir returned to Indonesia in 1998 following the fall of President Soeharto. After the death of Sungkar, Ba'asyir took over leadership of the major Darul Islam faction in Central Java. Ba'asyir used it as a platform to launch the Indonesian Mujahideen Council (Majlis Mujahidin Indonesia - MMI) - a political organisation campaigning openly for the implementation of an Islamic state in Indonesia.

While the MMI has a broad membership, including many members who seek to bring about an Islamic state through peaceful, democratic means, its leadership core is closely linked with Jemaah Islamiyah and seeks to use the MMI as a political front.

Abu Bakar Ba'asyir

Abu Bakar Ba'asyir is the spiritual leader of Jemaah Islamiyah. Indonesian police arrested Ba'asyir on 30 April 2004 under Indonesia's counter-terrorism law, and declared him a suspect in the Bali and JW Marriott Hotel bombings.

Ba'asyir incites and supports terrorism. He has repeatedly stated his support for Usama Bin Laden.

In an interview on the SBS Insight program on 9 March 2004, Ba'asyir gave unflinching support to the Bali bombers, describing them as defenders of Islam and Indonesia. In an interview broadcast on Channel 7 on 17 March 2004, Ba'asyir claimed that 'sooner or later, America and the countries that assisted will be destroyed in the name of Allah'.

Jemaah Islamiyah - operations and training

Using the skills gained in the crucible of the war in Afghanistan, Jemaah Islamiyah has developed a formalised structure to provide systematic training for its new recruits from across the region.

Jemaah Islamiyah established Camp Hudaibiyyah within the MILF's Camp Abu Bakar in Mindanao, in the southern Philippines, from about 1998, using some of the original graduates from training in Afghanistan and Pakistan. Camp Hudaibiyyah was closed down by the Philippine military in 2000, but there is evidence that Jemaah Islamiyah training has continued in alternative locations in the southern Philippines.

While many of the more senior Jemaah Islamiyah operatives gained their terrorist training and expertise in Afghanistan and Pakistan, others have developed the bulk of their skills in South-East Asia.

Training camps are not required at all for competent individuals to pass on the bomb-making skills and techniques needed for terrorism. Graduates of Jemaah Islamiyah's militant training may well have the operational, logistic and administrative skills required to plan and stage another terrorist attack like Bali or the JW Marriott Hotel bombing.

ABU BAKAR BA'ASYIR

Abu Bakar Ba'asyir is an Indonesian cleric of Yemeni descent who was born in Jombang, East Java, in 1938. Ba'asyir was active in advocating an Islamic state in Indonesia from his student days, and he joined radical Islamic youth movements. He started, but did not complete, an Islamic legal studies course at a university in Solo. He appears to have gradually become attracted to more extreme ideas during his university days.

Ba'asyir met Jemaah Islamiyah founder Abdullah Sungkar - also an Indonesian of Yemeni descent - in Solo. Here the two established an Islamic radio station that, by 1971, had evolved into an Islamic boarding school, Al Mukmin, located at Ngruki, outside Solo. Ba'asyir and Sungkar both spent four years in jail (1978 - 82) on charges related to their ongoing covert agitation for the establishment of an Islamic state in Indonesia. Ba'asyir's original nine-year sentence was reinstated in 1985 and he fled to Malaysia with Sungkar. From exile, they directed their followers to the anti-Soviet militant jihad in Afghanistan. Jemaah Islamiyah - in the form in which it is known today - was officially formed during this period.

Ba'asyir took over the spiritual leadership of Jemaah Islamiyah after the death of Sungkar in 1999. In 1999 he helped found the Rabitatul Mujahidin (Mujahideen Association) in Malaysia. In 2000 he founded and was elected head of the Indonesian Mujahideen Council (MMI).

In April 2003 Abu Bakar Ba'asyir went on trial charged with attempting to cause the collapse of the Indonesian Government, forgery, perjury and immigration offences. He was not charged in relation to the Bali bombings. The first charge included allegations Ba'asyir had led a plot to assassinate Indonesian President, Megawati Soekarnoputri, and that he had authorised the Christmas 2000 church bombings in Indonesia.

In September 2003, Ba'asyir was convicted of treason and immigration offences and sentenced to four years in prison. This sentence was reduced on appeal and the treason conviction overturned. Ba'asyir was rearrested under Indonesia's counter-terrorism laws on the same day he was released from jail: 30 April 2004. He faces questioning and possible new charges as a suspect in terrorist activities, including the Bali and JW Marriott Hotel bombings.

Jemaah Islamiyah's emphasis on training has several benefits for the organisation. It provides a flow of extremists, bolstering Jemaah Islamiyah's ranks or replacing its losses. And coordinated training helps to cement transnational organisational bonds within Jemaah Islamiyah by throwing together recruits drawn from different geographic regions.

Jemaah Islamiyah - links to global terrorism

In looking for global partners to advance its terrorist campaign, Al Qaida has found a willing ally in South-East Asia in Jemaah Islamiyah. And now that Jemaah Islamiyah has global recognition as an actor in transnational extremist-Muslim terrorism, support from Al Qaida and other sponsors of terrorism in the Middle East is likely to continue to flow to South-East Asia.

Financial and operational links to Middle Eastern extremist groups, especially Al Qaida in the early 1990s, were important in the development of South-East Asian radical Muslim groups, including Jemaah Islamiyah.

While Jemaah Islamiyah and Al Qaida operate largely independently of each other, there are close and direct links. Jemaah Islamiyah leader, Hambali, who was captured in Thailand in August 2003, is widely understood to have been Al Qaida's South-East Asian operations chief, and certainly provided ongoing contact between Jemaah Islamiyah and Al Qaida. The relationship between Jemaah Islamiyah and Al Qaida is more a loose alliance forged through a shared ideology, rather than a hierarchical structure of command and control. But Al Qaida is a potent inspiration and example to South-East Asian Muslim militants, and has provided resources for their terrorist operations.

Jemaah Islamiyah's transformation from a radical Muslim organisation focused on local grievances and with local ambitions to a transnational terrorist network is of key concern to Australia and other governments in the region.

Jemaah Islamiyah - a distorted vision

Jemaah Islamiyah promotes its vision of a unified South-East Asian Islamic state encompassing Indonesia, Malaysia, Singapore, the southern Philippines and southern Thailand. Jemaah Islamiyah has also identified Australia as a region in which to expand its network.

But Jemaah Islamiyah's concept of a South-East Asian super-state, forming part of a global Islamic caliphate, governed by Taliban-style religious extremism, is flawed. The overwhelming majority of the population of Indonesia - and indeed of South-East Asia more broadly - appears to reject Jemaah Islamiyah's vision and its use of terrorist attacks to further its aims. There are other large obstacles to Jemaah Islamiyah achieving its goal, not least the fact that all governments in the region reject the idea. Nation-states and nationalism are obvious major hurdles. And Jemaah Islamiyah's attempt to provide a transnational framework for radicalism in the region is not always at one with the deep historical roots and distinct agendas of its potential allies in South-East Asia. Local agendas and the jealously guarded independence of partner groups get in the way.

Jemaah Islamiyah relies on operational cooperation with other extremist organisations in the region, based on shared values, family links and ties forged overseas or while waging militant jihad in inter-communal conflicts in Maluku and Sulawesi. But Jemaah Islamiyah does not command the obedience of these other organisations. The various extremist groups are beset by personal rivalries, differences over the appropriateness of targeting civilians, and the acceptability of traditional Indonesian Islamic practices.

Even within Jemaah Islamiyah there is division. Some elements focus almost exclusively on bringing about an Islamic state in Indonesia. Others work to an anti-Western or anti-US agenda.

The region has seen how Jemaah Islamiyah is prepared to damage regional economies in pursuit of its own ideological goals, regardless of the impact felt more broadly across society. The Bali bombings are estimated to have taken 1.5 per cent off Indonesia's gross domestic product.

The fall-out from terrorist attacks in Bali, Jakarta and the southern Philippines shows how Muslim-inspired terror strikes also at mainstream Islam and mainstream Muslim countries. The ultimate manifestation of the contempt that South-East Asian Muslim extremists have for the people of the region is their repeated, indiscriminate killing of citizens of South-East Asian countries. Westerners, Christians and Jews are priority targets, in line with Usama Bin Laden's so-called fatwa. But 34 Indonesians were killed in the Bali bombings and 11 in the JW Marriott Hotel bombing, among them both Hindus and Muslims.

Extremist-Muslim terrorism is likely to remain a feature of the security environment in South-East Asia for the foreseeable future. The major factors underlying the severity of the terrorist threat - the strong intention and capability of terrorist organisations to strike, and the varying counter-terrorism capabilities of regional governments, which in turn enhance the attractiveness of the region to terrorist groups such as Al Qaida - will not soon, or easily, change.

JEMAAH ISLAMIYAH STRUCTURE

Jemaah Islamiyah established a geographically based hierarchy with defined responsibilities and decision making procedures.

The leader (Amir), a leadership council (Markaz) and consultative councils (Shura) oversaw four geographic divisions (Mantiqi). Each Mantiqi divided into smaller sub-groups (as represented below) which administered Jemaah Islamiyah activity appropriate to their area.

- Mantiqi I and IV were focused primarily on fundraising.
- Mantiqi II was focused primarily on leadership and recruitment.
- Mantiqi III was focused primarily on training.

While parts of this structure have been disrupted since late 2001, including through the arrests of key leaders, Jemaah Islamiyah retains a flexible hierarchical administration. Amir Markaz Shura Mantiqi III Sabah, Sulawesi and South Philippines Mantiqi IV Australia and Papua New Guinea Mantiqi I Singapore and Malaysia Mantiqi II Indonesia Wakalah Wakalah Wakalah Kirdas Kirdas Kirdas Fiah Fiah Fiah

THE THREAT TO AUSTRALIA AND AUSTRALIA'S INTERESTS

Australia - a Terrorist Target

Australia is a terrorist target, both as a Western nation and in its own right. Intelligence confirms we were a target before the 11 September 2001 attacks, and we are still a target. Our interests both at home and abroad are in the terrorists' sights. Al Qaida leaders threaten publicly and frequently. Their declared rationale is often misleading, but their intentions are clear.

Before 11 September 2001, Usama Bin Laden referred to the United States and its allies, mentioning Israel and the

United Kingdom by name. Since then, he has more clearly identified those countries he considers to be 'allies'. Australia has been referred to in six separate statements issued by Bin Laden himself or his deputy, Ayman al-Zawahiri:

- On 3 November 2001, Bin Laden said: The Crusader Australian forces were on the Indonesia shores ... they landed to separate East Timor, which is part of the Islamic world.
- In an interview released in mid-November 2001 concerning the war in Afghanistan, Bin Laden said: In this fighting between Islam and the Crusaders, we will continue our jihad. We will incite the nation for jihad until we meet God and get his blessing. Any country that supports the Jews can only blame itself ... what do Japan or Australia or Germany have to do with this war? They just support the infidels and the Crusaders.
- Bin Laden made further reference to Australia in a videotape released in the United Kingdom in May 2002 in which he said: What has Australia in the extreme south got to do with the oppression of our brothers in Afghanistan and Palestine?
- On 12 November 2002, Bin Laden made a statement that gave more prominence to Australia than any other non-US Western country and reaffirmed Australia as a terrorist target: We warned Australia before not to join in [the war] in Afghanistan, and [against] its despicable effort to separate East Timor. It ignored the warning until it woke up to the sounds of explosions in Bali. Its government falsely claimed that they were not targeted.
- On 21 May 2003, in an audiotape, Ayman al-Zawahiri said: O Muslims, take matters firmly against the embassies of America, England, Australia, Norway and their interests, companies and employees.
- On 18 October 2003, in an audio message addressed to the American people concerning the war in Iraq, Bin Laden stated that: We maintain our right to reply, at the appropriate time and place, to all the states that are taking part in this unjust war, particularly Britain, Spain, Australia, Poland, Japan and Italy.

Another statement attributed to Al Qaida was issued through Al Jazeera television in December 2002. This statement reinforced the threat. It stated that Al Qaida would attack vital economic centres and strategic enterprises of the 'Jewish - Christian Alliance', including operations on land, at sea and in the air. Australia has also been mentioned in statements attributed to Al Qaida on the Internet.

Jemaah Islamiyah also has Australia in its sights. It perpetrated the October 2002 Bali bombings - a stark testament to the threat it poses to Australian people and interests. The bombings were a deliberate attempt to inflict mass casualties on Western civilians. Australians were clearly likely to suffer the heaviest impact. We do not know whether direct targeting of Australia was part of the original intent but this has been subsequently claimed by some of those convicted.

The Bali bombers - including Mukhlas and Amrozi - have spoken to the media about their actions. Mukhlas stated in an interview with Australian television in May 2004:

> *... In Australia ... this [is] a curse from God that they be afraid of their own shadow ...It's the victory for the terrorists.*

There are almost certainly other groups seeking to harm us, both in Australia and overseas. Most are likely to draw influence or inspiration from the likes of Al Qaida and Jemaah Islamiyah, but their secretive methods mean that we may not be aware of their existence until they attack.

Why are we a Target?

Australia is a target for complex reasons. But we can distil all the invective and rhetoric to a basic premise. These terrorists feel threatened by us, and by our example as a conspicuously successful modern society. We are in their way.

Transnational extremist-Muslim terrorists imagine us as part of a Zionist - Christian conspiracy aimed at bringing impiety, injustice, repression and humiliation to the Muslim world. Weakening the influence of the West would advance their political goals by helping undermine those Muslims they view as corrupt and open to Western influence. We are seen as standing in the way of their goal to transform the Muslim world into a Taliban-style society. According to their simplistic worldview, we are part of the Christian West which, to them, is un-Islamic and therefore illegitimate.

The core values we hold and which are intrinsic to our success as a liberal democratic culture are anathema to these extremists. For them, our beliefs in democratic process, racial and gender equality, religious tolerance and equality of opportunity are mere human inventions at odds with God's law. These values impede their political goals. They are confronted by the reality that it is not only people of the West who value such freedoms.

And we advance our values through an active foreign policy. We energetically support democracy, human rights and religious freedoms in our international contribution and through our participation in international forums like the United Nations. Our close alliance with the United States, our role in East Timor, our early and active engagement in the war in Afghanistan, and our involvement in the Coalition in Iraq are often cited by transnational terrorists as reasons for targeting us.

THE BALI BOMBINGS

On 12 October 2002, two bombs exploded at Kuta in Bali. The first, inside Paddy's Bar, was detonated by a suicide bomber. It was apparently intended to move people onto the street towards a second, larger device in a van outside the Sari Club. This device, also triggered by a suicide bomber, was detonated within a minute of the first explosion. Less than a minute later another device exploded, without causing casualties, near the US Consulate in nearby Denpasar.

The official death toll for the Bali attacks was 202, including 88 Australian citizens. The Bali attack was a sophisticated operation. The team that conducted it was coordinated by Jemaah Islamiyah member, Imam Samudra. It brought together logistics specialists, bomb makers, a support team, and the actual attackers - including two suicide bombers.

The attack was a Jemaah Islamiyah operation, but it is thought that Al Qaida helped with advice and training. Al Qaida and senior Jemaah Islamiyah member Hambali (arrested in Thailand in August 2003) provided funds. Jemaah Islamiyah leaders, including Hambali and Samudra, received training in Afghanistan - probably from Al Qaida.

The Australian Federal Police and the Indonesian National Police conducted a joint criminal investigation into the bombings. This led to the identification and arrest of most of those who took part in planning or executing the attack. By April 2004, 33 people had been convicted by the Indonesian courts for involvement in the attack. Three have been sentenced to death and four were given life sentences. Indonesian authorities have arrested several others who provided assistance to the Bali bombers.

Our actions are cited as evidence of the imagined conspiracy against Muslims as the terrorists attempt to draw support for their extremist views. They do this cleverly, invoking causes which resonate strongly and authentically in the broader Muslim community. But the essence of their objections is not our actions. Rather, it is our example as a people and as a society, and the values we stand for.

Australia's Global Interests

Australia's interests are global. As a fully integrated member of the international community, we have a major stake in the global campaign against terrorism. To protect our interests we need the support of other countries that share our values, just as they need ours. The terrorist threat to our global interests can only be defeated through a comprehensive and effective international response. There is no room for complacency.

Australians have a significant presence abroad. Over 3.5 million of us travel overseas each year - around one million at any one time. Some 720 000 Australians or almost 4 per cent of the population live overseas. About 120 000 of us move overseas on a long-term or permanent basis each year.

Australia has an extensive diplomatic network of 86 overseas posts as well as other official representations. About 2000 Australian Defence Force personnel are deployed on more than ten operations and training activities around the globe, including in the Middle East, Europe, Africa, South-East Asia and the Pacific. The Australian Federal Police maintains a significant overseas presence, through its International Network and with personnel currently deployed in Cyprus, East Timor and Solomon Islands. Australian non-government organisations also maintain significant overseas representation. A total of 2289 Australians worked overseas through a non-government organisation in 2003.

We have extensive global economic and business interests. Australia's trade and foreign investment is a key to our economic prosperity. Exports account for around 20 per cent of annual gross domestic product. The jobs of one in five Australians now depend directly or indirectly on the export of Australian goods and services. In 2003, Australia's two-way trade in goods and services was valued at $304 billion, including $140 billion of Australian exports. In the same year, Australia invested $152 billion abroad while international investment in Australia totalled over $233 billion. The Australian dollar is the world's seventh most traded currency.

These figures show that terrorism threatens not only the physical security of Australians travelling and living abroad. It also threatens our international economic and commercial interests. The threat of terrorism raises the cost of trade and travel and undermines investor and consumer confidence. Lower rates of economic growth are the result, particularly in an economy like Australia's, with our heavy reliance on trade and foreign investment. And the interdependence of national economies means economic disturbance is felt throughout the global marketplace.

ECONOMIC COSTS OF TERRORISM

Terrorism impacts on world economic activity in several ways. The immediate impact includes loss of life, damage to property and infrastructure and disruption to financial markets. Other short-term costs include rescue efforts and post-attack consequence management as well as the costs of remedial measures.

In the medium to long term, terrorism creates uncertainty, reduces confidence and increases risk perceptions and insurance premiums. Investors seek lower risk and shorter-term investments. These typically have weak rates of return. The cumulative effect is to reduce overall investment and slow rates of economic growth. The IMF estimates that the loss of US output resulting from terrorism-related costs could be as high as 0.75 per cent of Gross Domestic Product, or US$75 billion per year. Any decline in US real GDP compounds and prolongs the adverse impact of economic uncertainty on Asian countries and Australia.

Increased spending on counter-terrorism may provide a boost to some businesses. But there is an overall decline in economic productivity as resources are diverted to security from more productive activities. Pressure is also exerted on state budgets. Productivity losses from the threat of terrorism can be offset by improving risk perceptions. If properly managed, security measures can facilitate and secure trade and investment. New technologies introduced to strengthen trade security can increase efficiencies in trade and decrease trade costs through reduced theft, shorter delays and lower insurance costs.

Economies which fail to adopt new trade security measures or fail to cooperate in multilateral counter-terrorist measures run the risk of marginalising themselves from many international transactions.

Source: Combating terrorism in the transport sector, Economic Analytical Unit, DFAT, June 2004

Terrorism also places Australia's international relations under stress. Well established international practices, relationships and conventions are challenged by the threat of terrorism. The need for a robust response to terrorism challenges long-standing international patterns of behaviour. Australia's relationships with other countries can come under pressure because of the need to respond to situations which, while internal to a particular country, can affect our security. Overall, the international system becomes less predictable and less easy to manage.

THE NATURE OF THE TERRORIST THREAT TO AUSTRALIAN INTERESTS

Overseas

The threat to Australian interests is higher overseas than at home. Australian interests overseas are often less well protected and within easier reach, making them an easier target. Our interests are at particular threat in South-East Asia, South Asia and the Middle East. The extent and complexity of the overseas threat is recognised in the travel advisory system developed by the Department of Foreign Affairs and Trade. The volatile international security environment has resulted in raised threat levels for Australia's interests overseas in recent times.

Australian interests are at threat from terrorists wherever Western interests are targeted. A more dangerous international environment also means Australians may accidentally get caught up in attacks directed primarily at others. Terrorist attacks against Western interests in Europe or the United States could involve Australian casualties - as in the 2001 World Trade Center attack.

Australian interests can be targeted directly. This was the case in December 2001 when a Jemaah Islamiyah plot to bomb the Australian, British and United States diplomatic missions in Singapore was foiled by the Singapore authorities. Similarly, in June 2003 the Thai police uncovered a plan by Jemaah Islamiyah to bomb the Australian Embassy in Bangkok together with the embassies of the United States and United Kingdom. Australia has also been named as the primary target for terrorists in Indonesia by an Al Qaida manual titled Targeting the cities.

Australian counter-terrorism activities abroad may also be targeted. Also, peace-keeping, military, law enforcement and development cooperation projects, and the people who carry them out, can challenge the capacity of terrorists to operate freely. Threatened by this, terrorists may target these activities in an attempt to break Australian resolve. Australian interests can also be attacked if they present a 'soft' target. Should a non- Australian higher-profile target be too difficult to attack, Australian interests could be targeted instead. In these circumstances, our interests may be seen as an easier option for the terrorists.

South-East Asia

Australia has significant engagement with the countries of South-East Asia and we have a major stake in the region's security.

Despite the Bali tragedy and ongoing terrorism concerns, the region remains a popular destination for Australians. Four of the top ten destinations for Australian travellers are in South-East Asia. Around 45 000 Australians live in the region and many Australians have family there.

Australia has substantial commercial and diplomatic interests in South-East Asia as well as an overall interest in the region's security. Trade between South-East Asia and Australia now exceeds $40 billion a year - Singapore, Indonesia, Thailand and Malaysia feature in the top 15 destinations for Australian exports. The region encompasses important communication links, air routes and sea lanes vital for our trade.

Terrorists in South-East Asia have demonstrated an interest in targeting Australia and our overseas interests. As well as the threat from Jemaah Islamiyah and other known groups, there is a more diffuse threat from tomorrow's terrorists - militant groups that may commit terrorist acts in the future.

Since September 11, information indicating terrorist plans to attack Australian embassies in South-East Asia has come to light. The symbolic value of bombing diplomatic missions will ensure that they remain a likely terrorist target.

Key economic and commercial interests, including airports, airlines, shipping and transport infrastructure, have also been identified as targets. In April 2002, regional authorities disrupted a Jemaah Islamiyah plot to hijack a plane and crash it into Singapore airport. The magnitude of the terrorist threat to Australia's interests in South-East Asia depends on the effectiveness of action by countries in the region to counter that threat. Jemaah Islamiyah and other terrorist groups in the region will look for and exploit any weaknesses in the region's counter-terrorism response. The precise nature and location of the threat to our interests is likely to vary.

Pacific Islands

There is no current evidence of terrorist activity in the Pacific island countries but they remain vulnerable to exploitation by terrorist networks and even terrorist attacks. Apart from its direct consequences, a terrorist attack in the Pacific would also have a major impact on the region's important tourism sector, along with possible longer-term economic and social damage. Pacific island countries recognise their vulnerability and are working with Australia and other countries to rectify them.

At Home

The terrorist threat extends to Australia's shores and a terrorist attack on our soil is possible. This reality underpins Australia's National Counter-Terrorism Plan - to prepare for, prevent and respond to acts of terrorism and their consequences within Australia.

In the past, Australia was geographically insulated from areas that were a focus of terrorism, including the Middle East, North Africa and parts of Europe. This helped protect it from the terrorist threat. But globalisation means we are within easier reach. Today geography is no defence. The protection once afforded by the so-called 'Sea-Air Gap' no longer exists.

Terrorists do not necessarily need to enter Australia in order to launch an attack against our territory or our interests. This means that Australia's security environment has become less predictable since September 11 and the Bali bombings.

Extremists with links to transnational extremist-Muslim terrorist groups have shown interest in undertaking terrorist attacks in Australia. Al Qaida explored possible targets in Australia in 2000 and an associated group has recently been active. This suggests a serious intent to undertake terrorist attacks here.

In May 2004, Australian citizen Jack Roche pleaded guilty to charges of conspiracy to commit offences against the Crimes (Internationally Protected Persons) Act 1976. Roche was sentenced to nine years' imprisonment. Roche associated with Jemaah Islamiyah in Australia, trained in Afghanistan, and met with and took direction from Hambali and other extremist identities, including Khalid Sheikh Mohammed. Roche videotaped the Israeli embassy in Canberra and the Israeli consulate in Sydney in June 2000 as a preliminary measure to support a possible future terrorist attack in Australia.

Following the listing of Jemaah Islamiyah as a terrorist organisation by the government, the residences of individuals with suspected links to Jemaah Islamiyah were searched in October 2002.

Although no evidence of operational planning in Australia was found, these searches confirmed links between Jemaah Islamiyah members in Australia and senior Jemaah Islamiyah figures in South-East Asia.

References made by Al Qaida and affiliated groups, targeting Western countries in general and Australia in particular, highlight the enduring terrorist threat to Australian domestic interests.

Some transnational terrorist groups have small numbers of supporters in Australia. A small number of Australians have trained in terrorist camps in Afghanistan and Pakistan. The prospect of Australia being a source of funds for overseas terrorist activities is also of concern.

Strong border control measures are essential in securing Australia against external terror threats. But the terrorist threat to Australia does not only come from external sources. It can also come from people living and working in Australia.

Although we have much greater control of our security at home than abroad, the threat of the unknown remains. We have identified and successfully disrupted the activities of some groups but we must remain alert and adaptable to deal with new threats should they emerge.

The threat from chemical, biological, radiological or nuclear terrorism

The acquisition of chemical, biological, radiological or nuclear weapons by transnational terrorist groups would add a new dimension to the terrorist threat to Australia. It would seriously compromise the physical security of the Australian community. Although the range of damage that can be inflicted by this form of terrorism varies enormously, even a small incident would cause significant alarm.

We know Al Qaida has shown interest in both acquiring and developing expertise in chemical, biological, radiological and nuclear terrorism. The growing black market in the technology to support these weapons underscores the need for quick international action against proliferation threats.

The Threat to Australian Values

Muslim extremist terrorists threaten Australia's core values as much as our security. The views they espouse challenge our way of life as a tolerant, open and diverse society. Terrorists attack democratic societies by using their very openness as a weapon against them. They prey on both fear and ignorance. In threatening us, they challenge us to abandon our fundamental freedoms, community tolerance and the open nature of our civil society. They present us with the risk that, in framing a counter-terrorist response, we may sacrifice, prejudice or compromise our basic values.

The Long-term Threat

The ambiguities of the longer term present us with the most difficult challenge. The transnational terrorist threat is evolving rapidly. The structure and capacity of groups such as Al Qaida is changing and new terrorist groups are emerging. Some of these new groups are acting autonomously and adopting new tactics.

The existence of highly capable transnational terrorist groups means Australian interests will continue to be at heightened threat from terrorist attack. Together with our global partners, we have had significant successes in disrupting the operations of transnational terrorist groups. But Al Qaida and terrorist groups associated with it retain the intent and capacity to carry out sophisticated attacks. Both their rhetoric and their behaviour signal that they are in for the long haul.

Intelligence is one of our best defences. It provides us with an understanding of our security environment, allowing us to work effectively with like-minded countries to disrupt and defeat terrorist attacks before they occur. It gives us early warning of threats as they develop but it will never be able to provide the complete picture. The further we look into the future, the more difficult this becomes. No defences are foolproof.

And as we become more accustomed to living under the shadow of transnational terror, we also face the threat of our own complacency. We cannot allow further tragedy to be our wake-up call.

11

Terrorism and Infrastructural Threats

The term Critical Infrastructure came into use during the mid-90's. The United States had the strongest military and the largest economy; these two factors were both reinforcing and dependent on each other. The meteoric increase in cyber communications linked the infrastructures that were vital to the defense and economy of the United States.

In 1996, President Clinton formed a commission to study the vulnerabilities of the infrastructures critical to the United States. The commission was formed with representatives from within the government as well as several from outside the government, as many infrastructures are owned and operated by the private sector.

The critical infrastructures reviewed included telecommunications, electrical power systems, gas and oil storage and transportation, banking and finance, transportation, water supply, emergency services. The threats were broken into two categories, physical threat (damage to the tangible property) and threat to the electronic/computer-based systems (cyber attack). While the committee researched the vulnerabilities to the United States' infrastructures, the Infrastructure Protection Task Force (IPTF) was formed within the Department of Justice, chaired by the FBI. The initial charter of the IPTF was to:

1. Provide expert guidance to critical infrastructures to detect, prevent, halt or confine an attack and to restore service
2. Issue threat and warning notices

3. Provide training and education on methods of reducing vulnerabilities and responding to attacks
4. Coordinate with law enforcement during/after an attack to facilitate any investigation

The commission found that one of the biggest challenges facing the United States government in the coming decade was the effective protection of the country's critical infrastructures. Computers and the connectivity they brought to our lives, and businesses, while increasing productivity and creativity also increased our vulnerability to attacks by criminals, and terrorists. The commission's work was hailed as a success for starting the process of education and information sharing between the private sector and the government, a linkage critical to any improvement in protection. The commission looked at a wide range of threats; naturally occurring events such as earthquakes, fires and weather related incidents; physical attacks such as the World Trade Center bombing (the VBIED attack in February of 1993) and the bombing of the Oklahoma Federal Building. The commission also addressed the potential use of cyber axis's to attack U.S. national assets. A year later the commission's findings resulted in a White Paper, (The Clinton Administration's Policy on Critical Infrastructure Protection: Presidential Decision Directive 63).

The White Paper tasked organizations within the government to establish systems to protect their infrastructures, and train their personnel to protect their systems. The paper addressed the idea that our military strength would deter future enemies, whether nations, groups or individuals, from launching a direct attack, but most likely would result in a non-traditional attack against our infrastructures.

The White Paper authorized the FBI to expand the current organization of the IPTF to the National Infrastructure Protection Center (NIPC). The Department of Defense (DoD), as a result of the taskings within PDD #63, developed the Department of Defense Critical Infrastructure Protection (CIP) Plan, dated 18 November 1998. This document described the way the DoD would organize to identify and protect DoD owned infrastructure assets, as well as coordinate with other elements of the national program to ensure protection. The document explained how the DoD would coordinate for CIP from national level through installation level. The document set milestones for progress within CIP for the next several years.

In January 2003, the DoD produced a CIP Security Classifications Guide which provided updated definitions concerning DoD CIP topics as well as setting security levels for topics related to CIP.

19 August 2005, The Department of Defense issued a Directive Number 3020.40, the subject being the Defense Critical Infrastructure Program (DCIP). This directive superseded earlier plans and programs written in the late 90's. Directive 3020.40 provided new definitions, policies, and updates on responsibilities concerning the identification, assessment, and security enhancements required for defense of critical infrastructures.

Most recently the Department of Defense issued the Defense Critical Infrastructure Program (DCIP) Interim Implementation Guidance, dated 13 July 2006. this document references DoD Directive 3020.40 and Homeland Security Presidential Directive 7 among others. This document provides additional definitions as well as DCIP Acronyms, Procedures and Assessment Standards.

On 17 April 2002 the Department of Defense announced the establishment of the U.S. Northern Command (USNORTHCOM). All existing homeland defense and civil support missions previously executed by other organizations would be consolidated under USNORTHCOM. USNORTHCOM, located at Peterson Air Force Base, Colorado Springs, Colorado, began the arduous task of planning, organizing and coordinating military support to all of the nation's homeland defense and civil support missions.

The Cyber Threat

To highlight the importance of Cyber technology to the U.S. military, in July 2003, DOD had more than 3 million individual computers on 12,000 local area networks (LANs).

These interconnected systems and LANs are part of what is known as the Global Information Grid (GIG), which is the globally interconnected set of information capabilities, processes, and personnel for collecting, processing, storing, disseminating, and managing information on demand to warfighters, policymakers, and support personnel. The GIG includes all owned and leased communications and computing systems and services, software, data, security services, and other associated services necessary to achieve information superiority.

The GIG supports all DOD, National Security, and related intelligence community missions and functions in both peace and war that span the strategic, operational, tactical, and business arenas. The GIG provides capabilities from all operating locations, including bases, facilities, mobile platforms, and deployed sites; and provides interface to coalition, allied, and non-DOD users and systems.

A portion of the GIG, the Defense Information System Network (DISN), is the global, end-to-end information transfer infrastructure of DOD. It provides long haul data, voice, video, and transport networks and services needed for national defense command, control, communication, and intelligence requirements, as well as corporate defense requirements.4 Examples of the services include video teleconferencing, the Defense Switched Network (DSN), the uNclassified IP Router NETwork (NIPRNET), and the Secret IP Router NETwork (SIPRNET).

Just as the United States has capitalized on the use of computer technology, our enemies have not overlooked the fact that they must also operate in the computer age. As briefed to Congress in July 2003 by the Commander, Joint Task Force-Computer Network Operations, U.S. Strategic Command/Vice Director, Defense Information Systems Agency, the sophisticated threat to our Global Information Grid is extensive and presents a real danger to our national security. This threat includes more than 40 nation-states that have openly declared their intent to develop cyber warfare capabilities. Additionally, it includes transnational and domestic criminal organizations, hacker groups who sympathize with our [U.S.] enemies, terrorist organizations (evidenced by forensic analysis of captured computers) and "insiders" who support our enemies.

Terrorists realize the benefits they can reap from using this technology. Equipped with a personal computer and an

Internet connection, small players can level the playing field with their larger opponents in the "cyber arena." Terrorists do not have to expend large resources on a global intelligence collection organization or match the United States weapon-for-weapon on the battlefield to execute an operation. Terrorist groups can use cyber capabilities to assist them in planning and conducting their operations, and also to create destruction and turmoil by attacking our critical infrastructures. Although many people believe terrorists only operate in the world of physical violence, many terrorist groups have well educated people and modern computer equipment to compete in cyberspace.

Objectives

The objectives of this handbook are to explain the history and background behind critical infrastructure protection, the areas designated as critical infrastructures, and provide installation and garrison military and civilian staffs a better understanding of identifying that which is critical and assessing the threats to those areas.

SECTION I: DEFINING CRITICAL INFRASTRUCTURES, THEIR COMPONENTS, AND THEIR THREATS

There are certain systems in place within the United States today that are taken for granted. Americans expect to pick up the phone and have a dial tone, turn a switch and have power, adjust their thermostat and make their home warmer or cooler, be able to move from one part of the U.S. to another, turn a faucet for drinking water and call 911 and receive aid. These infrastructures which support our everyday life are much more fragile than we think. A simple act of Mother Nature or the deliberate act of a terrorist can disrupt or destroy these systems and delay their return to normalcy.

Some infrastructures at the national level are so vital that their incapacity would have a devastating affect on the defense and economic security of our entire country. We have seen over the past decade how a single attack can adversely impact multiple areas of our lives. The term "Critical Infrastructure" came into vogue in the last decade to describe those systems that keep the nation secure.

Today the term "Critical Infrastructure" is defined as "systems and assets, whether physical or virtual, so vital to the United States that the incapacity or destruction of such systems and assets would have a debilitating impact on the security, national economic security, national health or safety, or any combination of those matters."6

The assets mentioned above are further sub-divided into three categories:

1. Physical – Physical assets may include both tangible property (e.g., facilities', components, real estate, animals, and products) and the intangible (e.g., information). Physical protection becomes an even more difficult task when one considers that 85% of the nation's critical infrastructures are not federally owned. Proper protection of physical assets requires cooperation between all levels of the government and within the private sector.
2. Human – Human assets include both the employees to be protected and the personnel who may present an insider threat (e.g., due to privileged access to control systems,

   USA Patriot Act of 2001, incorporated into 2002 Act, from Interim National Infrastructure Protection Plan, Feb 2005 operations, and sensitive area and information). Those individuals who are identified as critical require protection as well as duplication of knowledge and authority.
3. Cyber – Cyber assets include the information hardware, software, data, and the networks that serve the functioning and operation of the asset. Damage to our electronic and computer networks would cause widespread disruption and damage, including casualties. Cyber networks link the United State's energy, financial and physical securities infrastructures.

Terrorists throughout the world are already exploiting information technologies and the Internet to plan attacks, raise funds, spread propaganda, collect information, communicate securely and recruit. As terrorists gain experience and technology, cyber attacks on all infrastructures becomes an increasing threat. Since the late 1990's commissions and organizations were formed to review the vulnerabilities of U.S. critical infrastructures and determine the best courses of action to protect them. The current definition of Critical Infrastructure Protection (CIP) used by the Department of Defense is, "The actions taken to prevent, remediate, or mitigate the risks resulting from vulnerabilities of critical infrastructure assets. Depending on the risk, these actions could include changes in tactics, techniques, or procedures; adding redundancy; selection of another asset; isolation or hardening; guarding, etc." A later section will discuss how to determine which infrastructures are critical to an organization. But once determined critical, how do we protect these infrastructures? After identifying those infrastructures that are critical to our organization, we need to look at them from the threats' point of view. The threat could be a man-made or natural attack or occurrence on any of the three above mentioned areas. The Army has developed methods to view "ourselves" from the threat's perspective.

The Contemporary Operational Environment (COE) is a dynamic and adaptive process for being more aware, better prepared, and ready to counter any adversity that could negatively impact an operation or task. These variables allow U.S. planners to understand impacts and changes within a "state", country or situation. These same variables can be used to view ourselves in a form of "Red Teaming". Red teaming is "a technique that involves viewing a potential target from the perspective of an attacker to identify its hidden vulnerabilities, and to anticipate possible modes of attack.8" Red teaming deepens understanding of options available to adaptive adversaries and provides groups an insight into their vulnerabilities. The result of a good red teaming session will provide a basis for plans to mitigate risks to your critical infrastructures. To understand the complex interactions of the COE, a framework of "systems" assists in assessing and gaining situational awareness. Joint doctrine uses systems of Political, Military, Economic, Social, Infrastructure, and Information (PMESII) to shape and conduct missions. PMESII, with other variables such as physical environment and time, affect circumstances and influence operations throughout the domains of air, land, sea, and space. This broader perspective, combined with mission, enemy and belligerents, friendly forces and partners, cultural sensitivities and resolve, are critical to mission success. Defining physical environmental conditions include terrain or urban settings (super-surface, surface and subsurface features), weather, topography, and hydrology. The variable of time influences action such as planning, multi-echelon decision cycles, tempo of operations, and projected pacing of popular support for operations. Whether a real world threat or an opposing force created to simulate relevant conditions for training readiness, PMESII and other variables such as physical environment and time describe the OE.

The Threat's Viewpoint

Systems Warfare is a technique or method that identifies critical systems components and attacks them to degrade or destroy the use or importance of the overall system. The enemy targets "single points of failure" to cripple larger systems. Examples of systems that might be targeted by systems warfare are; logistics, command and control, Medical evacuation, commerce, and transportation. A tactical level example is an enemy attacking a fuel convoy so that combat vehicles such as tanks or personnel carriers cannot pursue him. The enemy cannot defeat the tanks or personnel carrier's superior armor or weapons capabilities, but he can target that which supports the tank and personnel carrier. The fuel convoy is the "weak link" in the combat system that the enemy can attack and achieve a greater success. The enemy came to this realization, and identified the weak link through analysis of our systems.

The next section will explore those critical infrastructures of the United States as they are identified by the Federal Government. Observe the federal areas and see how they compare to the infrastructures within your organization, installation, or garrison.

PMESII and Other Variables

- Political
- Military
- Economic
- Social
- Information

- Infrastructure
- Physical Environment
- Time

Critical Infrastructures at the National Level

The Federal Government identified 12 areas as Critical Infrastructures requiring protection from threats. These infrastructures provide the goods and services that contribute to the national defense and strong economy. The reliability, survivability, and resiliency of these systems allow Americans to maintain a sense of confidence in their country and themselves. These infrastructures identify the quality of life within the United States, and set a standard for how other countries view America. When something happens to any of these areas we expect a rapid restoration along with an explanation as to why there was an interruption.

The National Strategy for Homeland Security has identified these twelve areas:

Agriculture & Food The production and distribution of food within the United States is one of the most efficient systems in the world. The National Strategy for the Physical Protection of Critical Infrastructures and Key Assets defines the Agriculture and Food sector as:

- Supply Chains for feed, animals, and animal products
- Corp production and supply chains of seed, fertilizer, and other necessary related materials
- Post-harvesting components of the food supply chain, from processing, production, and packaging through storage and distribution to retail sales, institutional food services, and restaurant of home consumption.

This industry accounts for close to 20% of the U.S. Gross Domestic Product. Areas of concern include: Supply chains for feed, animals and animal products; Crop production and supply chains of seed, fertilizer and other related materials; post-harvesting components of processing, production and packaging, storage, distribution. As for geographic concentration of potential targets; approximately 27% of U.S. hog inventories are located in Iowa, and another 16% are located in the eastern counties of North Carolina.

Water

This sector is divided into two areas: fresh water supply and wastewater collection. The water sector criticality extends to both public health and the economy. The nation has over 170,000 public water systems which include reservoirs, dams, wells, aquifers, treatment facilities, pumping stations, aqueducts and transmission pipelines. Waste collection extends to 19,500 municipal sanitary sewer systems, and 800,000 miles of sewer lines.

Public Health

This area consists of state/local health departments, hospitals, health clinics, mental health facilities, laboratories, mortuaries, and pharmaceutical stockpiles. All of these would be critical after any form of attack or natural event. The personnel and facilities within this sector are trained and ready to react to emergency situations, but not as the target of a terrorist attack. Of geographical concern is the fact that 25% of all pharmaceuticals are manufactured in Puerto Rico, primarily in the San Juan metropolitan area.12

Emergency Services

This area includes fire, rescue, emergency medical service (EMS), and law enforcement organizations. These areas provide the U.S. the essential protection and services that we depend on day to day.

Unfortunately past and present, foreign and domestic, experiences indicate that emergency services response infrastructure and personnel can be the target of deliberate direct or secondary attacks. The emergency services sector differs from other infrastructures in its focus and criticality is in its personnel and equipment, rather than a facility.

Government

The government itself can be viewed as a critical infrastructure, with its ability to command and control the response to any attack, terrorist or natural to any of our infrastructures. Government facilities are also key assets; they represent our nation's heritage, traditions and values. These facilities draw large amounts of tourism, and any disruption of them would impact public confidence and the economy.

Defense Industrial Base

The private sector is critical to the Department of Defense effectively conducting core defense missions, mobilizing and deploying of our military forces abroad. Private industry within the United States manufactures and provides the majority of the equipment, materials, services, and weaponry used by our armed forces. The Department of Defense has identified its own critical assets and systems over the last decade. The DoD is addressing its dependency on the Defense Industrial Base, and is taking the issues of private industry into its critical infrastructure protection efforts. As an example of the geographical focus of the DIB, over 31% of U.S. naval shipbuilding and repair capacity is in and around Norfolk, VA.

Information and Telecommunications

The telecommunications sector is vast and dispersed, containing both cyber and physical elements. The telecommunications sector provides voice and data service to the public and private users through use of the Public Switched Telecommunications Network (PSTN), the internet, and private enterprise networks. The telecommunications sector provides robust and reliable communications, meeting the needs of business and government despite its extremely dynamic nature. The communications sector, potentially more than any other infrastructure, reaches into every other critical sector.

Energy

Energy is the infrastructure that supplies the driving force in most of American life today. Energy of some kind heats our homes, moves us for one point to another and drives our businesses and industry. The energy sector is critical to the well being of our economy, national defense and quality of life. The sector is divided into to areas, electricity and oil/natural gas. Electricity is required to operate and maintain homes, hospitals, schools, businesses and industrial plants; it is also necessary to refine oil. Disruption of electrical flow or a power grid would impact the economy and defense as well as response and recovery. Natural Gas consists of three major components: exploration and production, transmission, and distribution, with the U.S. producing 20% of the world's natural gas supply.14 Oil's infrastructure consists of five components: production, crude oil transport, refining, product transport and distribution, and control and other external support systems.15 The thousands of miles of pipelines offer an endless list of targets for terrorist attacks, and during transport there are opportunities for impacting more than one critical infrastructure. Over 43% of the total U.S. oil refining capacity is clustered along the Texas and Louisiana coasts.16 This area is subject to natural attacks as well as those of terrorists.

Transportation

The area includes aviation, rail, pipelines, highways, trucking and busing, and public mass transit. The scope of the transportation sector makes it critical to both our economy and national security. The ability to provide near unlimited mobility to the U.S. population reinforces one of our most cherished individual freedoms. Interdependencies exist between transportation and nearly every other sector of the economy. As redundant as our vast transportation network is there are geographic "choke-points", that require mentioning; nearly 32% of all U.S. waterborne container shipments pass through the ports of Long Beach and Los Angeles in southern California.17 Dangerous clusters for rail movement exist in central U.S., with over 36% of U.S. freight railcars pass through Illinois, primarily around Chicago, and nearly 25% of freight railcars pass through Missouri, primarily around St. Louis.

Banking and Finance

This sector is made up of physical structures and assets as well as personnel and cyber assets. Retail and wholesale banking institutions are located in large office buildings with large groups of people. The financial sectors infrastructure includes computer networks, storage devices and telecommunications networks. This sector is also extremely vulnerable to public perception; an impression of weakness could easily result in a damaging cascading effect. Normal operations are necessary to maintain public confidence. Geographically, the banking sector is focused with nearly 46% of all U.S. securities traded on the floors of the New York and American Stock Exchanges in lower Manhattan19 and approximately 22% of U.S. security industry employees are located in New York City.

CHEMICAL INDUSTRY AND HAZARDOUS MATERIALS

This sector impacts several other sectors; finance, agriculture, water, health care, etc. This sector is currently the U.S.'s top exporter, accounting for more than ten cents of every dollar. The Chemical industry produces fertilizer for agriculture, chlorine for water purification and polymers that create plastics from petroleum, more than $97 billion of the sectors products go to health care alone.21 The sector is also a lucrative terrorist target due environmental impact from the physical destruction of many of its sites. One geographic cluster is in danger from nature and man; with over 38% of U.S. chlorine production is located in coastal Louisiana.

Postal and Shipping

The postal system is interconnected with other infrastructure systems, especially transportation. The postal service controls thousands of points of entry as well as millions of facilities. The United States Postal Service (USPS) and private industry mailing and shipping revenues exceed $200 billion annually. Everyday, more than twothirds of a billion pieces of mail enter the U.S. postal system and are delivered by over 300,000 carriers to more than 137 million addresses nationwide.23 In the fall of 2001 anthrax attacks through the postal system caused mail stoppages across the U.S. as well as widespread anxiety resulting in significant economic impact.

DIRECT AND INDIRECT EFFECTS OF INFRASTRUCTURE ATTACKS

The direct effects of infrastructure damage would be the disruption or stoppage of the functions of critical infrastructures or key assets through direct attacks on a critical node, system or function World Trade Center, which contained critical assets, was an example of a direct attack on the Banking and Finance infrastructure.

The indirect effects of an infrastructure attack would be the disruption and problems that result from a reaction to attacks on a critical infrastructure. The drawdown in air travel and other modes of mass transportation as a result of the 9/11 attacks, resulted in financial damage to each of these forms of travel. The loss of revenue in these industries resulted in loss of business and jobs. The exploitation of an infrastructure as part of an attack would be using the capabilities of one infrastructure to damage or destroy another infrastructure. An example is the use of the aviation portion of the transportation infrastructure to attack the World Trade Center (business and finance infrastructure) and the Pentagon (Government). Osama Bin Laden has repeatedly spoken of using e-mail or the internet (Telecommunications) to launch a cyber attack on the investment sector and the stock market (Banking and Finance).

Department of Homeland Security

The Department of Homeland Security (DHS) was established on 25 November 2002, by the Homeland Security Act of 2002. DHS is designed to work in the civilian arena to protect the United States within, at, and outside its borders. Its goal is to prepare for, prevent, and respond to domestic emergencies, particularly terrorism. DHS defines Critical Infrastructure as "systems and assets, whether physical or virtual, so vital to the United States that the incapacity or destruction of such systems and assets would have a debilitating impact on security, national economic security, national public health or safety, or any combination of those matters."

The Defense Critical Infrastructure Program (DCIP)

The Department of Defense Directive 3020.40, dated 19 August 2005 established the Defense Critical Infrastructure Program (DCIP). The directive requires the Army to establish, resource and execute an organizational critical infrastructure program. The directive set responsibilities for each of the different sectors of the DCIP:

DEFENSE SECTOR LEAD AGENT

Defense Industrial Base (DIB) Director, Defense Contract Management Agency

Financial Services Director, Defense Finance & Accounting Service

Global Information Grid (GIG) Director, Defense Information Systems Agency

Health Affairs Assistant Secretary of Defense of Health Affairs

Intelligence, Surveillance, and Director, Defense Intelligence Agency Reconnaissance (ISR)

Logistics Director, Defense Logistics Agency

Personnel Director, DoD Human Resources Activity

Public Works Chief, U.S. Army Corps of Engineers

Space Commander, U.S. Strategic Command

Transportation Commander, U.S. Transportation Command

Identifying Weaknesses in a Critical Infrastructure

The definition of critical infrastructure has been given and examples of the critical infrastructures of the United States are provided, but what are our critical infrastructures within our own areas of responsibility, influence and interest? Some of these are provided to us by our higher organizations and their commands. Those higher infrastructures and parts of infrastructures located in our areas of responsibility are listed to us and we ensure their protection. These areas can be labeled Mission Essential Vulnerable Areas (MEVAs). Unfortunately a list of critical infrastructures and sites is not always provided; oftentimes staffs have to decide what are their critical infrastructures and the key assets supporting them. The staff or command will need to understand the infrastructures, how they function and which parts they need to protect. On the following two pages is a flow chart designed to assist in the understanding of what is critical and the weaknesses within those systems. The flow chart was designed by NORTHCOM's J34, Assessments Branch, to assist units and organizations in looking at themselves, their missions and to identify weaknesses and single points of failure within the infrastructures.

The process starts with identifying all of the missions the higher headquarters has directed the unit to perform as well as those functions the higher headquarters perform that are located within the unit's area of responsibility. The staff works their way through the process identifying missions and requirements at their own level, their higher's level as well as those they support, and decide if each are critical. When the staff reaches the end of the process they must conduct a Dependency Analysis in an effort to identify Single Points of

Failure (SPOF). These SPOFs are the likely targets of attack as they will result in most damage for the least expenditure.

The process on the following pages is designed to help garrisons and staffs to determine what are their critical infrastructures and where are they vulnerable. These vulnerabilities are above and beyond those single points of failure that a higher office or headquarters may already have identified as critical to their operations but the physical asset is located on the lower headquarters facility or post.

The list of critical infrastructures and their vulnerabilities, those of each level of command, must be nested together so that the individuals responsible for the security of the installation know the entire lists of assets that must be secured. Simply put, what is critical to one person or level of command might not be critical to another, but those responsible for the security where the critical asset resides must know it is critical in order to protect and secure it. The nesting of these various layers can only be insured through coordination and synchronization between all levels of command. Once a list of assets and single points of failure exists it must be updated as plans and priorities change.

Critical infrastructures are composed of physical, personal, and cyber components, and as any of those three portions change so does the list of critical assets requiring security. If a plan or mission changes the need to review a CIP list is often obvious, but a change in personnel, a piece of equipment or even software can also require a review. Periodic reviews of all CIP plans is necessary to ensure that missions are updated, information from higher and lower is incorporated and changes within organizations are included.

Five-Step Process

The national CIP program is based on a risk management framework. It is continuously influenced by the ever changing threat environment, both physical and natural. The goal is to reduce the vulnerabilities to our nation's assets from attack and natural disaster. The same methodology used at the national level can be used by garrison, installation, and command staffs as part of the ongoing process of narrowing down the list or set of assets that are critical. The five steps are explained below:

1. Identifying critical assets – The first step will be to identify the critical assets located within your area of responsibility. The process should be an ongoing with constant review of unit missions, higher headquarters missions and requirements, as well as the overall operations within your location. The information collected should be used as the base for further discussion.
2. Identifying and assessing vulnerabilities – Vulnerability assessments should be conducted on those items identified in step 1. Potential areas of weakness need to be identified as well as protective measures that need to be undertaken to mitigate those vulnerabilities. Interdependencies within and between infrastructures need to be identified to minimize cascading effects. The vulnerability assessment needs to take into account effects which might cascade into other organizations.
3. Normalizing, analyzing, and prioritizing study results – The staff or group accumulating the vulnerability assessments needs to normalize the information from each subordinate section or staff, and then prioritize against all of the assets the higher organization is responsible for. This step will identify which areas offer the greatest risk and the best benefit from protective measures.
4. Implementing protective programs – The information gathered during the process will assist in developing and executing programs to protect or minimize damage to infrastructures. The staff or organization can find assistance in developing programs from their higher headquarters or through various federal agencies such as the Department of Homeland Security (DHS).
5. Measuring performance -- Metrics need to be established for each protective measure to ensure they are being performed consistently, are sustainable and are effective. Continuous review of the metrics will result in improvements to the framework and the protection plan

DEFENSE CRITICAL INFRASTRUCTURE PROGRAM PROCEDURES

Enclosure #3 of the DCIP Interim Implementation Guidance dated July 2006 outlines the DoD DCIP risk management procedures for all critical infrastructures. The purpose of the DCIP is to ensure the availability of assets critical to all DoD missions. Once risks are assessed in all tasks and missions then possible responses can be reviewed and emplaced to ensure all missions will be accomplished no matter what actions are taken against an infrastructure. The DCIP Interim Implementation Guidance stresses that Risk management is cyclical, as changes are constantly made to systems and personnel are replaced, risks to infrastructures must be re-assessed.

PHYSICAL ATTACKS

Agriculture

In 1984, a cult group poisoned salad bars at several Oregon restaurants with *Salmonella* bacteria as the first recorded event of bioterrorism in the United States. This resulted in 750 people becoming sick.24 A review of the agriculture infrastructure results in vulnerable areas such as the high concentration of the livestock industry and the centralized nature of the food processing industry. The farm-to table chain contains various points into which an attack could be launched. The threat of attack would seriously damage consumer confidence and undermine export markets. Understanding the goal of the threat points to the area most likely attacked. If the intent was economic disruption the target would be livestock and crops, but if the intent was mass casualties the point of attack would be contamination of finished food products. Damage to livestock could be very swift, the USDA calculated that foot-and mouth disease could spread to 25 states in 5 days.25 CDC is presently tracking and developing scenarios for the arrival of Avian Flu.

Banking

Prior to the destruction of the Twin Towers, physical attacks against the banking industry, such as the destruction of facilities, were rare. Unfortunately, evidence indicates that may change, in March 2005 three British al-Qa'ida operatives were indicted by a U.S. federal court on charges of conducting detailed reconnaissance of financial targets in lower Manhattan, Newark, New Jersey, and Washington, D.C. In addition to video taping the Citigroup Center and the New York Stock Exchange in New York City, the Prudential Financial building in Newark, and the headquarters of the International Monetary Fund and the World Bank in Washington D.C., the men amassed more than 500 photographs of the sites.26 The Banking infrastructures primary weakness is along its cyber axis of attack. Through phishing and banking Trojan targeting specific financial institutions, attackers reduce confidence among consumers. Recently American Express posted an alert online, including a screenshot of a pop-up that appeared when users log in to its secure site.

The attack not only attempts to obtain personal information that can be used for various operations, but also launches a virus into the user's computer. CitiBank, and Chase Manhattan Bank have both been victim during 2005 and 2006 to phishing schemes misrepresenting their services to their clients.

Energy

Recently the oil industry occupied the headlines, and the criticality of this infrastructure is not lost on terrorists. In mid-December 2004, Arab television aired an alleged audiotape message by Usama bin Laden in which he called upon his followers to wreak havoc on the U.S. and world economy by disrupting oil supplies from the Persian Gulf to the United States.28 The U.S. uses over 20.7 million barrels a day of crude oil and products and imports 58.4% of that requirement.29 On 19 January 2006 al-Qaeda leader Osama bin Laden announced in a video release that, "The war against America and its allies will not be confined to Iraq.....", and since June of 2003 there have been 298 recorded attacks against Iraqi oil facilities.30 Terrorists conduct research as to the easiest point to damage the flow of oil or to the point where the most damage can be done. Scenarios involving the oil fields themselves, a jetliner crashing into the Ras Tanura facility in Saudi Arabia could remove 10 percent of the world's energy imports in one act.31 Maritime attacks are also option for terrorists; on October 6,

2002 a French tanker carrying 397,000 barrels of crude oil from Iran to Malaysia was rammed by an explosive laden boat off of the port of Ash Shihr, 353 miles east of Aden.

The double-hulled tanker was breached, and maritime insurers tripled the rates.32 Energy most travel often long distances from the site where it is obtained to the point where it is converted into energy for use, a catastrophic event at any of the sites or along its route can adversely impact the energy infrastructure and cause ripples in other infrastructures. The security of the pipeline in Alaska increases in importance as efforts are made to make America more independent on energy use.

Economy

The U.S. economy is the end-state target of several terrorist groups as identified in the introduction quote. The means by which terrorists and other threats attempt to impact the economic infrastructure is through it's linkage to the other infrastructures. Attacks are launched at other infrastructures, such as energy or the Defense Industrial Base in an effort to achieve a "cascading" result that impacts the economy.

Cyber attacks on Banking and Finance are another effort to indirectly impact the economy. The short term impacts of the 9/11 attacks on Lower Manhattan resulted in the loss of 30% of office space and a number of businesses simply ceased to exist. Close to 200,000 jobs were destroyed or relocated out of New York City.

The destruction of physical assets was estimated in the national accounts to amount to $14 billion for private businesses, $1.5 billion for state and local government enterprises and $0.7 billion for federal enterprises. Rescue, cleanup and related costs are estimated to at least $11 billion for a total direct cost of $27.2 billion.33 The medium and long term effects cannot be accurately estimated but demonstrate the idea of cascading effects. The five main areas affected over a longer period were Insurance, Airlines, Tourism and other Service Industries, Shipping and Security and military spending. At various times terrorist rhetoric has mentioned attacks against Wall Street proper, but the more realistic damage to the economy will come through the indirect approach of cascading effects.

Transportation

The attack on commuter trains in Madrid in March of 2004 and the London bombings in July of 2005, which together killed 243 people, clearly indicated the threat to the transportation infrastructure. Statistics provided by the Brookings Institute in Washington DC show that between 1991 and 2001 42% of worldwide terrorist attacks were directed against mass transit. Transportation is viewed by terrorists as a "soft target" and one that will impact the people of a country. Mass Service Transportation (MST) is the likely target of a terrorist attack.

- MST caters to large volumes of people, crammed into narrow confined spaces
- MST is designed to move large numbers of people quickly and efficiently, which is often counter to protective measures
- MST assets are enclosed, serving to amplify explosions
- MST attacks can result in "cascading effects" because communications and power conduits are usually collocated in proximity to their routes

The Department of Homeland Security sent a "public sector notice" in May of 2006 based on two incidents of "suspicious videotaping" of European mass-transit systems.34 The individual had several tapes besides the one in his camera, none of which showed any tourist sites. The tapes focused on the insides of subway cars, the inside and outside of several stations and exit routes from the stations. In June of 2003 the FBI arrested Iyman Faris, a 34 year old naturalized American citizen who had been in contact with Al Qaeda conducting research and reconnaissance in an effort to destroy the Brooklyn Bridge.35 Mr. Faris had traveled to Afghanistan and Pakistan in 2000, meeting with Osama bin Laden, he returned to the U.S. and began gathering information concerning the Brooklyn Bridge and communicating via coded messages with Al Qaeda leaders. An attack on the bridge would have not only damaged the transportation infrastructure, but also a known American landmark. On 24 May 2006, a Pakistani immigrant was convicted on charges of plotting to blow up one of Manhattan's busiest subway stations in retaliation for the U.S. actions at the Abu Ghraib prison.

Terrorist threats to the transportation infrastructure extend beyond land to the sea. Vice Admiral Jonathan Greenert, commander of the U.S. Seventh Fleet, said "one of my nightmares would be a maritime terrorism attack in the Strait of Malacca".37 "There is a strain of al-Qaida in Southeast Asia, called Jemaah Islamiya. They are actively pursuing a maritime terrorism capability that includes diving and mining training."38 As how this might impact on the economy, $220 billion in trade comes through the Seventh Fleet area of responsibility and 98% of the commerce is moved by sea. Just as ports can be viewed a SPOF within the maritime transport system, there are certain waterway chokepoints or heavily trafficked areas that can be viewed as a high payoff target to a terrorist or result in catastrophic damage from a natural disaster.

Local Threat

The above examples demonstrate the physical threats to infrastructures at the national level, but what are the physical threats to the infrastructures within your area of responsibility? There are guards and security checks at the gates of your installation, but what of the rail line that runs through the post? What is the cargo of the trains that pass through daily? These are the questions for staffs and command groups to consider as they conduct threat assessments and review the dangers to the critical infrastructures of their organization.

Human Attacks

The safety and security of personnel is discussed in several Force Protection manuals and handbooks. The purpose of this section is not to provide ways to protect personnel, but to explain ways to ensure infrastructures are protected from loss of personnel. The human links of a critical infrastructure are all too often the overlooked potential points of failure. The loss of an individual within a military unit rarely results in the unit failing to accomplish its mission. The military trains and prepares for losses within its personnel structure so that no matter what the cause, natural or man-made, the system continues to function with little or no interruption. Unfortunately, this often is not the case within many organizations that do not practice and train for the loss of individuals responsible for issuing instructions or experts in procedures or special equipment. The loss of the Information Management Officer (IMO) during critical computer operations, the absence of a specialized technician if the water treatment plant's or electrical grid's systems fail or a multi-situational event resulting in a shortage of health or emergency personnel. Military units train everyday for the loss of a leader, member of the chain of command or special systems operator, but this contingency planning does not always extend to everyday operations or crisis planning. Even those organizations that plan for replacement of individuals rarely train for their loss which can result in delay or lack of coordination.

As an organization's critical infrastructures are identified the weaknesses and single points of failure are identified. If personnel are identified as one of the weaknesses or single points of failure, due to training, numbers of personnel, or responsibilities, a plan must be developed and trained against to ensure their absence will not result in the breakdown of the infrastructure.

Different methods of protection against damaging critical infrastructures from absence of "key personnel":

- Designate a sequence of personnel to cover the missing key personnel, and conduct training to ensure the echelon of replacements understands the specific function of the key person to the critical infrastructure.
- Reconfigure the infrastructure to negate the single point of failure or reduce the damage to the infrastructure if key personnel are absent.
- Ensure the key personnel have redundant communications available in order to provide guidance or instructions if needed.
- Ensure the key personnel have created readily available files covering situations where their importance to the infrastructure is understood to the point other could fulfill their purpose.

Too often key personnel's input into a critical infrastructure is forgotten until the crisis is at hand. Rehearsals that include the loss of certain individuals can easily identify problems early and result in reduction of risk to the critical infrastructure.

CYBER SUPPORT TO TERRORIST OPERATIONS

Terrorists recognize the benefit of cyber operations and continue to exploit information technology in every function of their operations. Macro-functions include:

Planning

Terrorists use the cyber infrastructure to plan attacks, communicate with each other, and posture for future exploitation. Employing easy-to-use encryption programs that they can easily download from the Internet, terrorists are able to communicate in a secure environment. Using steganography, they hide instructions, plans and pictures for their attacks in pictures and posted comments in chat rooms. The images and instructions can only be opened using a "private key" or code known only to the recipients. In fact, reports that use encryption are a common tool of Muslim extremists and is being taught in their training camps.39 Additionally, these encryption programs can scramble telephone conversations when the phones are plugged into a computer.

Recruitment

Recruitment is the life-blood of a terrorist organization and they use multiple methods to entice new members. In addition to traditional methods, such as written publications, local prayer leaders, audio-video cassettes and CDs promoting their cause; terrorist groups also use their own websites to recruit new members. This is accomplished by providing their view of the history of their organization, its cause, and additional information to encourage potential members to join. Additionally, they often have hyperlinks to other material to encourage membership. They also use these sites to collect "donations" for their cause.

Research

Using the Internet, terrorists can tap into thousands of databases, libraries and newsgroups around the world to gather information on any subjects that they need to research. The information can be in the form of text, maps, satellite images, pictures or even video material. The use of search engines, such as Google, have made searching the Internet very easy and allows terrorists to obtain critical information located in the public domain using very simple resources. For example, by typing "Bombs" in the Google search engine, 2,870,000 references were found in 0.17 seconds. To narrow this list, typing "Bombs AND Homemade," resulted in 47,200 references being found in 0.08 seconds. Although most of these are harmless references that may just refer to news articles, many provide detailed information on how to manufacture bombs. One site not only provided information on bombs, but also provided additional references on subjects such as drugs, fake IDs, fraud, lock picking, and weapons.

To highlight the importance terrorists place on research over the Internet, an al Qaeda training manual recovered in Afghanistan states: "Using public sources openly and without resorting to illegal means, it is possible to gather at least 80% of information about the enemy." After finding this manual, Secretary of Defense Donald Rumsfeld disseminated a memo to the armed services stating: "One must conclude our enemies access DoD Web sites on a regular basis."41 The memo directed the military to purge their websites of information that could benefit our potential enemies.

Although the military has tightened up security on their sites, terrorists can still conduct research on military units. Using a search engine, they simply type in a specific organization and the search engine will provide the links if they exist. For example, typing in "Army AND Fort Hood" resulted in the Fort Hood home page being displayed. This site provided the entire list of units assigned to III Corps simply by opening the web page. Looking at a Fort Bragg web site, available references included a map of the installation, the schedule for the installation shuttle bus, and a copy of the official telephone directory, which provides all of the units on the installation. Other critical information is available on the military, such as every Army and Air Force airfield in the United States, and the location of military ammunition depots throughout CONUS. Terrorists can also use the Internet to research information on the critical infrastructure of the United States. In the fall of 2001, police found a pattern of surveillance by Middle East and South Asia unknown browsers against Silicon Valley computers used to manage Bay Area utilities and government offices. As the FBI became involved, the trail revealed even broader surveillance, casing sites nationwide. Routed through telecommunication switches in Saudi Arabia, Indonesia, and Pakistan, surveillance was conducted on emergency telephone systems, electrical generation and transmission facilities, water storage and distribution systems, nuclear power plants, and gas facilities.

Unfortunately, using the convenience of the Internet, terrorists can virtually research any subject, to include information on potential targets, without ever leaving the safety of their locales overseas or within the United States.

Propaganda

As Christopher Harmon states in his book, *Terrorism Today*, "Propaganda is a veritable terror group standard."43 Terrorist organizations depend on the backing of a broad base of support for both recruiting and funding. They use propaganda to discredit their enemy while making themselves look good. Earlier terrorist groups published newspapers and leaflets to spread their propaganda. Although this form of media is still widely used, terrorist groups are now using the Internet.

Most radical groups of international significance operate Internet sites. These groups post articles supporting their agendas on these sites, which make them instantly available to the worldwide cyber community. Radical Islam in particular makes use of propaganda to enlist the support of their own public for jihad and to demoralize the enemy. The statement from the Hizballah website is an example of some of their propaganda.

Cyber-Terrorism

Cyber-terrorism is a development of terrorist capabilities provided by new technologies and networked organizations, which allows terrorists to conduct their operations with little or no physical risk to themselves. Cyber-terrorism is a new and somewhat nebulous concept, with debate as to whether it is a separate phenomenon, or just a facet of information warfare practiced by terrorists. Even for those that believe cyber-terrorism is a separate phenomenon; the boundaries often become blurred between information warfare, computer crime, online social activism, and cyber-terrorism.

Cyber-terrorism differs from other improvements in terrorist technology because it involves offensive information technology capabilities, either alone or in combination with other forms of attack. Some examinations of cyber-terrorism focus on the physical destruction of information hardware and software, or physical damage to personnel or equipment using information technology as the medium. Examples of this approach would include the chaos and destruction caused by disrupting a nation's air traffic control system, crashing two trains together by overriding the railroad signal and switching system, interfering with the control systems for water or electricity, or blocking and falsifying commercial communications to cause economic disruption.

One common aspect is that organizations trying to attack using information technology will more than likely want to keep the information network up, or at least limit their destruction or disruptions to discrete portions of the network. For a true "cyber-terrorist," the network is the method of attack. It is the weapon, or at the least, the medium through which an attack is delivered. Information warfare of this sort requires that messages and computer commands are transmitted, programs and malicious software be emplaced, fraudulent transactions take place, and information be available for exploitation. Defacing websites, crashing portions of a target network, accessing enemy information, denying network access to other groups, manipulating financial confidence and causing panic exemplify this warfare. Still, they require that the target network remain more or less intact. A terrorist group could crash a network through physical destruction or technological attack, but only a group whose perceived gains would offset their loss of information, communication, and other capabilities would do this.44

Outside of computer networks, communications networks can also be targeted for destruction, disruption, or hijacking. This has a direct impact on the military and the government since a large percentage of the GIG is dependent on commercial telephone links and the Internet. Destructive and disruptive attacks upon communication networks would likely be supporting operations designed to increase the effectiveness of physical attacks. Hijacking, or taking control of a communication network might support another operation, or be attempted for it's own impact. Dissident factions have already substituted their own satellite TV signals for state controlled broadcasting.45 Terrorists could exploit such capabilities to bypass mainstream media restraint in covering particularly shocking actions, or to demonstrate their power and capability to challenge their enemies.

Other views of cyber terror stress the manipulation, modification, and destruction of nonphysical items such as data, websites, or the perceptions and attitudes this information can influence. Attacks that would destroy electronic records of financial transactions, or permit large-scale electronic theft would cause significant economic damage to a country, but not truly "exist" in the physical world. Changing the information or appearance of an enemy's official web page allows the terrorist to spread negative perceptions or false information without physical intrusion.

Currently, DOD does not have a definition of cyber-terrorism, but does define cyberspace as: "The notional environment in which digitized information is communicated over computer networks."46 In the Federal Government, the FBI describes cyber-terrorism as: "Cyber-terrorism is a criminal act perpetrated by the use of computers and telecommunications capabilities, resulting in violence, destruction and/or disruption of services to create fear by causing confusion and uncertainty within a given population, with the goal of influencing a government or population to conform to a particular political, social, or ideological agenda."47 Another definition by Kevin Coleman, a former chief strategist at Netscape who writes a Homeland Security focused column for *Directions* magazine is: "The premeditated use of disruptive activities, or the threat thereof, against computers and/or networks, with the intention to cause harm or further social, ideological, religious, political or similar objectives. Or to intimidate any person in furtherance of such objectives."

These definitions spotlight the fact that cyber-terrorism is a serious threat. In the first half of 2002, there were more than 180,000 Internet based attacks on business and these attacks are increasing at an annual rate above 60%. Additionally, it is estimated that the reported incidents may represent only 10%

of the actual total. A research study conducted by the Computer Crime Research Center in 2002 reported that 90% of respondents detected computer security breaches within the previous twelve months.

In the Department of Defense, the speed and complexity of attacks are increasing. The Defense Information Systems Agency estimated in 1996 that DOD IT systems were attacked about 250,000 times per year and the Government Auditing Office (GAO) reported in the same year that only about 1 in 500 attacks were detected and reported.50 In 2002, DOD successfully defended against 50,000 intrusion attempts to gain root access to the GIG. By June 2003, there were over 21,000 attempts.

OBJECTIVES OF CYBER ATTACK

When analyzing the objectives of a cyber attack and the ultimate outcome the attack may have, the effects of cyber attack align generally into four areas. The first three effects listed below address the impact on the actual IT systems themselves, whereas the last effect addresses the impact of using the IT system for physical destructive purposes.

- Loss of Integrity. System and data integrity refers to the requirement that information be protected from improper modification. Integrity is lost if unauthorized changes are made to the data or IT system by either intentional or accidental acts. If the loss of system or data integrity is not corrected, continued use of the contaminated system or corrupted data could result in inaccuracy, fraud, or erroneous decisions. Also, violation of integrity may be the first step in a successful attack against system availability or confidentiality. For all these reasons, loss of integrity reduces the assurance of an IT system.
- Loss of Availability. If a mission-critical IT system is attacked and rendered unavailable to its end users, the organization's mission will most likely be affected. Loss of system functionality and operational effectiveness, for example, may result in loss of productive time, thus impeding the end users' performance of their functions in supporting the organization's mission.

- Loss of Confidentiality. System and data confidentiality refers to the protection of information from unauthorized disclosure. The impact of unauthorized disclosure of confidential information can range from the jeopardizing of national security to the disclosure of Privacy Act data. Unauthorized, unanticipated, or unintentional disclosure could result in loss of public confidence, embarrassment, or legal action against the organization.
- Physical Destruction. Physical destruction refers to the ability to create actual physical harm or destruction through the use of IT systems. Much of our critical infrastructure, such as transportation, power, and water companies are operated with networks of computer-controlled devices known as supervisory control and data acquisition (SCADA) systems. These systems can be attacked and used to cause operations to malfunction, such as the release of water from a dam or switching the tracks on a railroad to create a collision. There have also been concerns that a terrorist could take control of the air traffic control system and cause aircraft to crash. Fortunately these specific scenarios have not occurred, and there are normally sufficient manual checks and overrides that help prevent this type of failure. However, the possibility of taking over a SCADA system is real. There was a case in 2001 where an individual used the Internet, a wireless radio, and stolen control software to release up to 1 million liters of sewage into the river and coastal waters of Queensland, Australia. The individual had attempted to access the system 44 times, prior to being successful in his 45th attempt, without being detected.53 This example does indicate that individuals with the proper tools and knowledge can bypass security in public utilities or other organizations using SCADA systems.

Actors

Not every individual or group who uses information technology to further their agenda or attack their opponents are necessarily cyber terrorists. However, it can often be difficult to determine if an attack is originating from terrorists or from high school students with the technical expertise to access your system. It often becomes a judgment call on what is truly cyber-terrorism and what is just hacking. There are various categories of attackers that the military may be faced with in the cyber arena.

Hackers: These are advanced computer users who spend a lot of time on or with computers and work hard to find vulnerabilities in IT systems. Some hackers, known as Whitehat Hackers, look for vulnerabilities and then work with the vendor of the affected system to fix the problem. The typical hacker, though, is often referred to as a Blackhat Hacker. They are the individuals who illegally break into other computer systems to damage the system or data, steal information, or cause disruption of networks for personal motivations, such as monetary gain or status. However, they generally lack the motivation to cause violence or severe economic or social harm. An example of the systems hackers can access was demonstrated in 1998. Two teenage hackers accessed computers at Lawrence Livermore National Laboratory, the U.S. Air Force, and other organizations. After being caught by the FBI, the teenagers pleaded guilty to illegally accessing restricted computers, using "sniffer" programs to intercept computer passwords, and reprogramming computers to allow complete access to all of their files. They also inserted "backdoor" programs in the computers to allow themselves to re-enter at will.

A concern beyond just gaining access to a system is what hackers may do with information that they steal from the military. In November 1998, the Detroit News reported that a member of Harkat-ul-Ansar, a militant Pakistani group, tried to buy military software from hackers who had stolen it from DOD computers.

"Hactivists:" These are combinations of hackers and activists. They usually have a political motive for their activities, and identify that motivation by their actions, such as defacing opponents' websites with counter-information or disinformation. Alone, these actions bear the same relation to cyber-terrorism that theft, vandalism, or graffiti do to mundane physical terrorism; they may be an unrelated activity, or a supporting piece of a terrorist campaign.

An example of this type activity occurred following the inadvertent bombing of the Chinese embassy in Belgrade during the 1999 NATO bombing campaign in Yugoslavia when pro-Beijing Chinese hackers conducted mass cyber protests against U.S. government Web sites in response to this accident. This type activity occurred again in May 2001 when Chinese protesters defaced or closed over 100 sites in the U.S., after a Chinese fighter jet collided with a U.S. reconnaissance plane off the Chinese coast.

Computer Criminals: Criminals have discovered they can exploit computer systems, primarily for financial gain. Computer extortion is a form of this type crime. An example is the case of media titan Michael Bloomberg. His corporation was hacked into by two suspects who demanded two hundred thousand dollars from Bloomberg in "consulting fees" in order for them to keep quiet on how they compromised Bloomberg's computer system.

Another example deals with gaining unauthorized access to government computers and obtaining information for financial gain. In September 2003, an individual was in a conspiracy to access military, government and private sector computers. The indictment alleged that the defendant was the president of a computer security company and he was trying to gain unauthorized access to government and military computers, copy computer files and take these files to the media in order to generate public visibility for his company. He thought this would lead to new clients and increased profits. According to the indictment, the conspirators possessed government files belonging to the National Aeronautics and Space Administration (NASA), United States Army, United States Navy, Department of Energy and National Institutes of Health.

Industrial Espionage: Industrial espionage has a long history in our industrialized society and there is no question that with today's reliance on computer systems and networks to plan, document, and store research data; industrial espionage has added the electronic medium to its list of methods of operation. These industrial spies may be government sponsored or affiliated, from commercial organizations, or private individuals. Their purpose may be to discover proprietary information on financial or contractual issues, or to acquire classified information on sensitive research and development efforts.

Although industrial espionage is normally associated with civilian corporations, it can have a direct impact on the military as well. As stated by the Defense Security Service (DSS) in a 2002 report, U.S. military critical technologies are the most sought after in the world.57 The espionage may be directed against a defense contractor; against DOD's military research, development, test, and evaluations community; or against DOD's acquisition program offices. To demonstrate the assault against military technology, DSS received reports of suspicious activities concerning defense technology from sources in 75 countries in 2001. This activity covered every militarily critical technology category, with the highest interest being information systems, sensors and lasers, armaments and energetic materials, aeronautic systems, and electronics.

Insiders: Although IT professionals do everything possible to secure their systems from outsiders; there is always the threat of an insider with authorized access to a system conducting an attack. These insiders may be disgruntled employees working alone, or they may be excellent workers in concert with other terrorists to use their access to help compromise the system.

An example occurred in July 1997, when a U.S. Coast Guard employee used her insider knowledge and another employee's password and logon identification to delete data from a U.S. Coast Guard personnel database system. It took 115 agency employees over 1800 hours to recover and reenter the lost data.

Consultants/contractors: Another concern is the practice by many organizations to use outside contractors to develop software systems. This often provides these contractors with the access required to engage in cyber-terrorism.

In March 2000, Japan's Metropolitan Police Department reported that they had procured a software system to track police vehicles that had been developed by Aum Shinryko. This is the cult that released sarin gas in the Tokyo subway in 1995. The police discovered that the cult had received classified tracking data on 115 of the vehicles. Additionally, the cult had developed software for 80 Japanese firms and 10 government agencies. One of several concerns is that they had installed a Trojan horse in the systems to launch or facilitate cyber terrorist attacks at a later date.

Terrorists: Although there have been no major cyber attacks caused by terrorist groups that have taken lives or caused severe physical destruction, some government experts believe that terrorists are at the point where they may be able to use the Internet as a direct instrument to cause casualties, either alone or in conjunction with a physical attack. In fact, the FBI's director of the National Infrastructure Protection Center stated in 2002, "The event I fear most is a physical attack in conjunction with a successful cyber-attack on the responders' 911 system or on the power grid." The Cyber Division of the FBI states that in the future, cyber-terrorism may become a viable option to traditional physical acts of violence due to:61

- Anonymity
- Diverse targets
- Low risk of detection
- Low risk of personal injury
- Low investment
- Operate from nearly any location
- Few resources are needed

The following table from the National Institute of Standards and Technology summarizes threats to IT systems, including the source, their motivation, and actions.

Tools of Cyber Attacks

There are a myriad of tools that cyber terrorists will use to accomplish their objectives. Some of these are:

Backdoor: This is used to describe a back way, hidden method, or other type of method of by passing normal security in order to obtain access to a secure area. It is also referred to as a trapdoor. Sometimes backdoors are surreptitiously planted on a network element; however, there are some cases where they are purposely installed on a system. An example of this is the craft interface. This interface is on network elements and is designed to facilitate system management, maintenance, and troubleshooting operations by technicians, called craft personnel. The craft interface allows the technician to access the equipment on site, or in many cases, access it via remote terminal. Actions they can conduct include: 63

- Initial turn–up of network elements and/or systems
- Trouble verification
- Repair verification
- Monitor network element (NE) performance
- Update NE software and hardware
- Manual control of NE
- Remote inventory

Security for these interfaces is normally via userids and passwords. Unfortunately, passwords are often the weakest link in a computer security scheme because password cracking tools continue to improve and the computers used to crack passwords are more powerful than ever. Network passwords that once took weeks to crack can now be cracked in hours.

Although the craft interface allows the service provider access to conduct maintenance on the equipment, many vendors build back doors to have access to these interfaces so they can also remotely troubleshoot equipment. Unfortunately, this means a technician from outside the organization is able to gain access to the system and could facilitate cyber terrorist activities.

Denial of Service Attacks (DOS): A DOS attack is designed to disrupt network service, typically by overwhelming the system with millions of requests every second causing the network to slow down or crash. An even more effective DOS is the distributed denial of service attack (DDOS). This involves the use of numerous computers flooding the target simultaneously. Not only does this overload the target with more requests, but having the DOS from multiple paths makes backtracking the attack extremely difficult, if not impossible. Many times worms are planted on computers to create zombies that allow the attacker to use these machines as unknowing participants in the attack. To highlight the impact of these type attacks, in February 2000, DOS attacks against Yahoo, CNN, eBay and other e-commerce sites were estimated to have caused over a billion dollars in losses.64 DOS attacks have also been directed against the military. In 1999, NATO computers were hit with DOS attacks by hactivists protesting the NATO bombing in Kosovo.

E-mail Spoofing: E-mail spoofing is a method of sending e-mail to a user that appears to have originated from one source when it actually was sent from another source. This method is often an attempt to trick the user into making a damaging statement or releasing sensitive information (such as passwords). For example, e-mail could be sent claiming to be from a person in authority requesting users to send them a copy of a password file or other sensitive information.

IP Address Spoofing: A method that creates Transmission Control Protocol/Internet Protocol (TCP/IP) packets using somebody else's IP address. Routers use the "destination IP" address to forward packets through the Internet, but ignore the "source IP" address. This method is often used in DDOS attacks in order to hide the true identity of the attacker.

Keylogger: A software program or hardware device that is used to monitor and log each of the keys a user types into a computer keyboard. The user who installed the program or hardware device can then view all keys typed in by that user. Because these programs and hardware devices monitor the actual keys being typed, a user can easily obtain passwords and other information the computer operator may not wish others to know.

Logic bomb: A program routine that destroys data by reformatting the hard disk or randomly inserting garbage into data files. It may be brought into a computer by downloading a public-domain program that has been tampered with. Once it is executed, it does its damage immediately, whereas a virus keeps on destroying.

Physical Attacks: This involves the actual physical destruction of a computer system and/or network. This includes destroying transport networks as well as the terminal equipment.

Sniffer: A program and/or device that monitors data traveling over a network. Although sniffers are used for legitimate network management functions, they also are used during cyber attacks for stealing information, including passwords, off a network. Once emplaced, they are very difficult to detect and can be inserted almost anywhere through different means.

Trojan Horse: A program or utility that falsely appears to be a useful program or utility such as a screen saver. However, once installed performs a function in the background such as allowing other users to have access to your computer or sending information from your computer to other computers.

Viruses: A software program, script, or macro that has been designed to infect, destroy, modify, or cause other problems with a computer or software program. There are different types of viruses. Some of these are:

- Boot Sector Virus: Infects the first or first few sectors of a computer hard drive or diskette drive allowing the virus to activate as the drive or diskette boots.
- Companion Virus: Stores itself in a file that is named similar to another program file that is commonly executed. When that file is executed the virus will infect the computer and/or perform malicious steps such as deleting your computer hard disk drive.
- Executable Virus: Stores itself in an executable file and infects other files each time the file is run. The majority of all computer viruses are spread when a file is executed or opened.
- Overwrite Virus: Overwrites a file with its own code, helping spread the virus to other files and computers.
- Polymorphic Virus: Has the capability of changing its own code allowing the virus to have hundreds or thousands of different variants making it much more difficult to notice and/or detect.
- Resident Virus: Stores itself within memory allowing it to infect files instantaneously and does not require the user to run the "execute a file" to infect files.
- Stealth Virus: Hides its tracks after infecting the computer. Once the computer has been infected the virus can make modifications to allow the computer to appear that it has not lost any memory and or that the file size has not changed.

Worms: A destructive software program containing code capable of gaining access to computers or networks and once within the computer or network causing that computer or network harm by deleting, modifying, distributing, or otherwise manipulating the data.

Zombie: A computer or server that has been basically hijacked using some form of malicious software to help a hacker perform a Distributed Denial Of Service attack (DDOS).

Bibliography

Allison, Graham, *Nuclear Terrorism: The Ultimate Preventable Catastrophe,* New York: Times Books, 2004.

Arend, A.: *International Law and the Use of Force,* London, Routledge, 1993.

Basrur, Rajesh M., and Hasan-Askari Rizvi: *Nuclear Terrorism and South Asia,* Albuquerque, NM: Sandia National Laboratories, February 2003.

Bukharin, Oleg: *The Threat of Nuclear Terrorism and the Physical Security of Nuclear Installations and Materials in the former Soviet Union,* Monterey, CA: Center for Russian and Eurasian Studies, Monterey Institute of International Studies, 1992.

Calvocoressi, Peter, and Guy Wint: *The Total War: the Story of World War II,* New York, Pantheon Books, 1972.

Hoffman, Bruce: *Inside Terrorism,* New York: Columbia University Press, 1998.

Laquer, Walter: *The New Terrorism: Fanaticism and the Arms of Mass Destruction,* Oxford: Oxford University Press, 1999.

Norris, James A.: *The First Afghan War 1838-1842,* Cambridge, University Press, 1967.

Rhodes, Richard: *The Making of the Atomic Bomb,* New York: Simon and Schuster, 1988.

Schroeer, Dietrich: *Science, Technology, and the Nuclear Arms Race,* Ontario: John Wiley & Sons, 1984.

Spector, Leonard S.: *Going Nuclear,* Cambridge, MA: Ballinger Publishing Company, 1987.

Index

□□□